Applied Linguistics and Language Study

General Editor: C. N. Candlin

Language and Communication

Edited by
Jack C. Richards and
Richard W. Schmidt

London and New York

Longman Group Limited
Longman House, Burnt Mill, Harlow,
Essex CM20 2JE, England
and Associated Companies throughout the world

© Longman Group Limited 1983

Published in the United States of America by
Longman Inc., New York

First published 1983
ISBN 0 582 55034 3

BRITISH LIBRARY CATALOGUING IN PUBLICATION DATA
Language and communication. – (Applied linguistics
    and language study)
    1. Communication   2. Language and languages –
    Study and teaching
    I. Richards, Jack C.   II. Schmidt, Richard W.
    III. Series
    400   P90

LIBRARY OF CONGRESS CATALOGING IN PUBLICATION DATA
Main entry under title:

Language and communication.
    (Applied linguistics and language study)
    Bibliography: p.
    Includes index.
    1. Language and languages – Study and teaching –
    Addresses, essays, lectures. 2. Communication – Study
    and teaching – Addresses, essays, lectures.   I. Richards,
    Jack C.   II. Schmidt, Richard W.   III. Series.
    P53.L34   1983   418′.007   82-24909

Set in 10/12 pt. Linotron Times N.R.
Printed in Great Britain
by Butler & Tanner Ltd,
Frome, Somerset.

Contents

The Contributors

Michael Canale
The Ontario Institute for Studies in Education

Bruce Fraser
Boston University

Janet Holmes
Victoria University of Wellington

Graham Low
Language Centre, University of Hong Kong

Donald M. Morrison
Language Centre, University of Hong Kong

Andrew Pawley
University of Auckland

Jack C. Richards
University of Hawaii, Manoa

Richard W. Schmidt
University of Hawaii, Manoa

Ron Scollon
University of Alaska, Fairbanks

Suzanne B. K. Scollon
University of Alaska, Fairbanks

Frances Hodgetts Syder
University of Auckland

Nessa Wolfson
University of Pennsylvania

Preface

It is perhaps hard to imagine when reading this collection of papers, the most recent contribution to the *Applied Linguistics and Language Study* series, that it was only some ten years ago, in Europe, that those engaged in the applications of linguistics to language teaching and learning announced a concern with the promotion and development of learners' *communicative* competence as a key concept in their new thinking. Not that the concept itself was new, of course, as a glance at the heritage of some of the papers in this collection clearly shows: Firth, Malinowski and Austin were already classics to be referred to, and Halliday's work in a socially motivated theory of language, itself much influenced by Firth, indicated the path to the integrated theory announced by Canale in the opening paper of this collection. Since that time it has become difficult to discover syllabuses and teaching materials which do not proclaim their communicativeness from their opening pages. All too often, however, even the most charitable of observers must come to admit that such syllabuses and materials fail to draw widely enough on the contributing disciplines to the study of communication, or fail to make a plausible connection between interpersonal function, ideational concept and textual form, or, even worse in a discipline so much concerned with human interaction, fail to relate statements about form and meaning to the sociocultural context within which the acts of speaking and interpretation take place. I recall raising these doubts and questions in 1976, in a paper to the Georgetown University Round Table, and since that time there has been an even greater output of teaching and learning materials which fail to demonstrate an integrated understanding of language and communication.

It is in this enthusiastic but inchoate atmosphere that there is a special need for a coherent collection of specially written papers which seeks to make sense of the communicative concept and to show how the particular situation of second language learning can both provide data for an examination of communication and allow us to test the hypotheses inherent in any attempt to relate sense to force. It is to this necessary task that Jack Richards and Dick Schmidt have directed this collection, bringing together many of the key scholars in the field. The Editors suggest that readers may choose their own order for reading the papers; what one might do, to continue my earlier complaint, is to take any current language teaching manual and follow, through these papers, notions like *communication, act of speaking, speech event, interaction, encounters, interpreting value, power and solidarity, goals and processes of conversation, style and presentation of personality*, in order to build up a rich network of concepts which characterizes the use of language form in social interaction. Such a piece of detection, using references in the index as a set of clues for exploration, is one way in which to reinforce the connections between the papers described by the Editors in their Introduction. Such a way of grasping the interwoven ideas may be a useful heuristic for the individual reader; for the teacher what will be of great value are the follow-up discussion questions provided by the authors after their papers. These questions themselves constitute a programme of study in applied linguistics, especially related to language teaching and learning, and taken with the comprehensive bibliography provide the content for further research.

I have been suggesting in the foregoing that this collection offers three important 'goods' to the reader: it offers a comprehensive account of the components of communication, it offers thereby a necessary corrective to facile interpretation and application in practical methodology, and it offers the wherewithal for further research, in pragmatics, in cross-cultural ethnography, in the relationships between form and value, and in the processes of intention and interpretation in particular contexts and activity types.

There is, however, a more important long-term contribution to the study of communication which can be discerned as a kind of 'hidden agenda' behind many of the papers, though given most prominence in the paper by Scollon and Scollon. This contribution emerges, as do all of the papers in their various ways, from the distinction fundamental to pragmatics formulated by Leech as the contrast between the verbs *mean* and *mean by*. Now pragmatics is a study which is relative to particular speakers in particular events, it is context-sensitive and must take account of the varying communicative values, more or less implicit, in what people say. It is, in short, a study which calls for principles rather than rules, at least in the categorical sense. This essential relativeness, this constraint by principle, invests pragmatics with the constant potential to be an *explanatory* rather than merely *descriptive* science. Any pragmatic account contains the possibility of explanation of how, in that society and that culture, in this or that speech event and activity type, participants value utterances in various ways and have their own utterances variously valued. In terms of a programme of research, therefore, we can record what people say and provide a linguistic or, as stressed here, a pragmatic description, or we can seek to offer an explanation of why they say what they say, why they mean X by uttering Y, by making a connection, through an explanatory pragmatics, with participant ideologies, systems of values and beliefs. Now such a view of Language and Communication, suggested in some of the papers in this collection, involves us in examining how individuals betray their ideologies through their forms of talk. This view will involve the analyst in explaining the occurrence of certain forms of talk in particular activity types in terms of the communicative strategies they realize, and, ultimately the social purposes of the interactants. Insofar as particular discoursal routines are naturalized and taken-for-granted, and, we may infer, certain inferential schemata and outcomes equally predictable in particular situations, such explanatory analysis offers powerful insights into the complex system of beliefs and actions which constitutes a society and, ultimately, a culture. This explanatory direction will, in turn, have an effect upon teaching and learning materials concerned with Language and Communication. They will increasingly come to offer pragmatic explanations of discoursal acts and through these bring learners to an awareness of their own deep-seated assumptions about the behaviours and the personalities and the belief systems of the members of the society whose language they are engaged in studying. They will come to monitor themselves (in the sense of Morrison and Low) and examine the ideological practices of the particular social institutions with which they are in contact. Accounts of language in use, whether by researchers or by textbook writers and teachers thus need an explanatory pragmatic perspective if learners are to be enabled to understand, in this ideological and critical sense, what members mean. 'Communicative' language teaching is not a matter of some additive connection between form and value, they mutually define each other in the context of interaction. It is a measure of the value of this important collection by the Editors, Jack Richards and Dick Schmidt, that they have drawn on their own considerable experience of the issues and problems I have been emphasizing to bring together a set of papers which not only provides for description but suggests explanation.

Christopher N. Candlin   *Lancaster 1982*
General Editor

Introduction

This book is intended for language teachers, teachers in training, and students of applied linguistics. The purpose of this book is to present a coherent survey of major issues in the study of language and communication, and to show how these are related to questions of practical concern in the learning and teaching of second and foreign languages. Since the goal of language teaching is to enable learners to use language in ways which are communicatively effective and appropriate, the study of the communicative functions of language has taken on an increasingly important role in recent years within applied linguistics. This has meant a movement away from a narrow linguistic perspective, which is primarily message oriented, to look at the broader implications of considering speakers and hearers as social beings, operating within a context that is at the same time personal, conceptual and interpersonal, as well as being anchored in social and cultural reality.

Each of the chapters in the book has been specially written, and surveys a different aspect of language and communication. The emphasis is interdisciplinary, since the authors discuss linguistic, sociolinguistic, psycholinguistic and cultural dimensions of linguistic communication. However, the issues discussed have been selected primarily for their relevance to applied linguistics, particularly second and foreign language teaching and learning. A unifying interest emerges in how language reflects the communicative functions it performs, as well as in the processes involved in using language for communication. Ideas which have their origins in fields as diverse as linguistics (especially linguistic pragmatics, which in turn derives much from the philosophy of language and the theory of speech acts), anthropology and the ethnography of communication (especially the concept of communicative competence) and sociology (especially ethnomethodology) are drawn upon by the different contributors in their discussions of different aspects of the process of linguistic communication.

Each chapter in the book presents an essentially self-contained survey of a central issue in the study of language and communication. The papers are prefaced by introductions by the editors, which serve to link the different perspectives, and the discussion questions which follow each paper serve as guides for follow up activities and discussion and enable the book to be more effectively used as a text in applied linguistics courses. The chapters can be read in any order, however, the order in which they are presented in the book better allows for complementary perspectives to emerge. The opening paper by Canale outlines the relationship between a model of communicative competence and communicative language use. Fraser's chapter on pragmatics then focusses more narrowly on speech acts as one aspect of a theory of linguistic communication. Wolfson discusses differences among conventions for rules of speaking across languages and how these effect second and foreign language learning. Holmes looks at teachers' language and the relationship between form and functions in teachers' directives. Richards and Schmidt illustrate the complex interplay of variables which contribute to face to face conversational interaction. Scollon and Scollon consider further aspects of rules of speaking and how these are manifested in interethnic communication. Pawley and Syder discuss the implications for linguistic theory of the study of actual communication, particularly conversation, while in the final paper in the collection Morrison and Low consider the effect of monitoring on linguistic performance in a second or foreign language. The collection as a whole thus broadens our understanding of the social meaning of language and raises many issues which have been previously neglected in research on language learning and teaching. We hope that *Language and Communication* will thus enable students, teachers and applied linguists to gain a deeper understanding of crucial issues involved in language learning and communicative language teaching.

Jack C. Richards   *Honolulu*
Richard W. Schmidt   *August 1981*

Introduction to Chapter 1

In this chapter, Michael Canale provides a broad outline of the components of communicative language use, which the other chapters in this book specify in more detail. Canale distinguishes between *communicative competence* (the underlying knowledge of the rules of communication) and *actual communication* (the use of this knowledge in real acts of communication). This parallels the distinction between linguistic competence and performance; the difference, however, is that language used for communication is not an impoverished manifestation of an idealized system of knowledge but an ongoing process of negotiation and evaluation which is a product of complex interactional processes. Canale outlines four major components of communicative competence: grammatical competence, including knowledge of vocabulary, rules of word and sentence formation, linguistic semantics, pronunciation and spelling; sociolinguistic competence, including rules of appropriateness of both meanings (allowable messages) and grammatical forms in different sociolinguistic contexts; discourse competence, the knowledge required to combine forms and meanings to achieve unified spoken or written texts; and strategic competence, knowledge of verbal and non-verbal communication strategies that may be called upon to compensate for limitations in one or more of the other areas of communicative competence. The notion of *linguistic competence* is more fully discussed in this book in the chapters by Fraser, and Pawley and Syder; *sociolinguistic competence* in the chapters by Wolfson and Holmes; and *discourse competence* in the chapter by Richards and Schmidt. These dimensions of communication, Canale argues, are essential both for a theoretical understanding of communication and as a basis for practical application to language pedagogy. They suggest dimensions which must be included at the level of *syllabus* (the choice of linguistic content in language teaching) and procedures and techniques which are appropriate teaching strategies.

1 From communicative competence to communicative language pedagogy[1]

Michael Canale

Introduction

Since its introduction by Hymes in the mid-1960s, the term 'communicative competence' has enjoyed increasing popularity among teachers, researchers and others interested in language. In the field of second (and foreign) language pedagogy, this general interest in language for communication is viewed as a promising departure from the narrower and still popular focus on language as grammar. However, there is reason for concern about the less healthy status Hymes' term has acquired as a buzzword within applied linguistics and especially about the sometimes fashionable exchange of opinions on this topic that Groot (1975, p. 57) has accurately noted.

The reasons for concern are not only that there remains much disagreement and little careful research on the applications of communicative competence in second language pedagogy. Rather within applied linguistics one also finds both confusion and lack of consideration of many of the basic concepts involved in this notion. The view here is that the current disarray in conceptualization, research and application in the area of communicative language pedagogy results in large part from failure to consider and develop an adequate theoretical framework.

In a recent report (Canale and Swain 1980), the above concerns were addressed in the form of a theoretical position paper. Our purposes there were: (a) to examine carefully the assumptions, content, empirical status and pedagogical implications of current theories of communicative competence; (b) to provide a theoretical framework for this notion that is explicit, adequate and justifiable; and (c) to explore the implications of this theoretical framework for further research and for teaching and testing in general second language programmes at the initial stages of second language study.

This chapter re-examines this earlier position on communicative competence. It is based on work carried out at the Ontario Institute for Studies in Education (OISE) over the past two years on the design and implementation of a communicative testing programme for students in general French as a second language programmes in elementary and secondary schools in Ontario, Canada. It first presents a slightly revised theoretical framework for communicative competence (Section 1) and then addresses the relevance of this framework for teaching and testing purposes (Section 2, Appendix A and the questions following this chapter). Throughout, an effort is made to relate the views and work reported here to other current research on communicative competence and to point out important problems remaining in theory and practice. The chapter ends with a few summary comments and concluding remarks on research directions.

1 Theoretical framework

The essential aspects of the theoretical framework presented here concern the nature of communication, the distinction between communicative competence and actual communication, and the main components of communicative competence.

1.1 *The nature of communication*

Following Breen and Candlin (1980), Morrow (1977) and Widdowson (1978), communication is understood here to have the following characteristics: it

(a) is a form of social interaction, and is therefore normally acquired and used in social interaction;
(b) involves a high degree of unpredictability and creativity in form and message;
(c) takes place in discourse and sociocultural contexts which provide constraints on appropriate language use and also clues as to correct interpretations of utterances;
(d) is carried out under limiting psychological and other conditions such as memory constraints, fatigue and distractions;
(e) always has a purpose (for example, to establish social relations, to persuade, or to promise);

(f) involves authentic, as opposed to textbook-contrived language; and

(g) is judged as successful or not on the basis of actual outcomes. (For example, communication could be judged successful in the case of a non-native English speaker who was trying to find the train station in Toronto, uttered 'How to go train' to a passer-by, and was given directions to the train station.)

In addition, communication is understood in the present chapter as the exchange and negotiation of information between at least two individuals through the use of verbal and non-verbal symbols, oral and written/visual modes, and production and comprehension processes. Information is assumed to consist of conceptual, socio-cultural, affective and other content as discussed in Bateson and Ruesch (1951), Haley (1963), Hymes (1972b) and elsewhere. Furthermore, as pointed out by Haley (1963) and others, such information is never permanently worked out nor fixed but is constantly changing and qualified by such factors as further information, context of communication, choice of language forms, and non-verbal behaviour. In this sense communication involves the continuous evaluation and negotiation of meaning on the part of the participants, as described by Candlin (1980), Wells (1981) and others. Finally, it is assumed with Palmer (1978) that authentic communication involves a 'reduction of uncertainty' on behalf of the participants; for example, a speaker asking a (non-rhetorical) question will be uncertain as to the answer but this uncertainty will be reduced when an answer is provided. Note that although such uncertainty can be reduced at a given level of information, it does not seem likely that uncertainty can be eliminated at all levels in any authentic communication. One may speculate that ease of communication increases to the extent that uncertainty is reduced at all levels of information.

Of course this characterization of the nature of communication is not exhaustive: it reflects an interest in second language pedagogy and is intended as the *minimal* characterization adequate for the research programme at OISE on evaluating the communicative performance of (beginning) students in general second language programmes in Ontario. More comprehensive characterizations of communication may be found in Hinofotis (1981a), Wallat (1981), Wiemann and Backlund (1980) and references cited in these works, for example. It is important to signal that although communication is the focus of the work reported on in the present chapter, I in no way regard communication as the essential purpose of language nor the only purpose relevant for second language pedagogy; for further comment see Canale (1981b), Canale and Swain (1980), Chomsky (1975), Halliday (1978), and Jakobson (1960).

1.2 *Communicative competence and actual communication*

The distinction between communicative competence and actual communication remains poorly understood and, somewhat surprisingly, or marginal interest in the second language field. Canale and Swain (1980, pp. 3–8) discuss this topic in detail. Here the purpose is to clarify these notions further; in section 2.1 their relevance for communicative language pedagogy is re-emphasized.

In Canale and Swain (1980) *communicative competence* was understood as the underlying systems of knowledge and skill required for communication (e.g. knowledge of vocabulary and skill in using the sociolinguistic conventions for a given language). Furthermore, a distinction was drawn between communicative competence and what is here labelled *actual communication* – the realization of such knowledge and skill under limiting psychological and environmental conditions such as memory and perceptual constraints, fatigue, nervousness, distractions and interfering background noises. The term 'actual communication' is preferred here since the earlier term 'performance' (or 'communicative performance') used by Canale and Swain (1980) and others has been a source of much confusion in applied linguistics since Chomsky (1965, p. 4) introduced the strong and weak senses of the terms 'competence' and 'performance' into modern linguistics. Regardless of the terminological shift, the view in Canale and Swain (1980), rephrased here, is that communicative competence is an essential part of actual communication but is reflected only indirectly, and sometimes imperfectly (e.g. in random and inadvertent slips of the tongue, mixing of registers) due to general limiting conditions such as those mentioned above.

It is important to stress again (see Canale and Swain 1980, p. 34) that communicative competence refers to both knowledge and skill in using this knowledge when interacting in actual communication. Knowledge refers here to what one knows (consciously and unconsciously) about the language and about other aspects of communicative language use; skill refers to how well one can perform this knowledge in actual communication. Although the general distinction between knowledge and skill is easily drawn and largely accepted (cf. Chomsky 1980; Olson 1973; Ryle 1949), precise definitions of knowledge and skill remain elusive and controversial. The relation of this distinction to the one between communicative competence and actual communication is also a source of disagreement and possible confusion. For example, there is a tendency (e.g. Kempson 1977, pp. 54–55) to treat skill in communicating as part of a theory of actual communication (in her terms, a theory of performance) and not as part of a theory of competence. In contrast Wiemann and Backlund (1980) seek to incorporate this notion of skill into a theory of communicative competence but choose a perplexing route: 'Thus, unlike the linguistic view of competence and performance, the communication view considers performance as part of competence – not as a separate concept' (p. 188).

Again, the view here is that both knowledge and skill underlie actual communication in a systematic and necessary way, and are thus included in communicative competence. Furthermore, this view is not only consistent with the distinction between communicative competence and actual communication but depends crucially on it; in particular, this notion of skill – how well one can perform knowledge in actual situations – requires a distinction between underlying capacities (competence) and their manifestation in concrete situations (actual communication).

1.3 *Components of communicative competence*

The theoretical framework for communicative competence proposed here minimally includes four areas of knowledge and skill: grammatical competence, sociolinguistic competence, discourse competence and strategic competence. It is assumed that this theory of communicative competence interacts in as yet unspecified ways with other systems of knowledge and skill (e.g. world knowledge) as well as with a theory of human action (dealing with such factors as volition and personality). Furthermore, it is assumed that certain competencies described here are involved in uses of language other than communication (cf. Canale 1981b). This proposed framework is based on the research reported in Canale and Swain (1980) and other current work in this area. The purpose of this section is to sketch briefly the contents and boundaries of each of these four areas of competence and to discuss this theory in the light of other recently proposed theories of communicative competence.

Grammatical competence. This type of competence remains concerned with mastery of the language code (verbal or non-verbal) itself. Thus included here are features and rules of the language such as vocabulary, word formation, sentence formation, pronunciation, spelling and linguistic semantics. Such competence focusses directly on the knowledge and skill required to understand and express accurately the literal meaning of utterances; as such, grammatical competence will be an important concern for any second language programme. Note that it is still not clear that any current theory of grammar can be selected over others to characterize this competence nor in what ways a theory of grammar is directly relevant for second language pedagogy (though see the excellent discussions in Allen and Widdowson 1975 and Rutherford 1980 on this last point).

Sociolinguistic competence. In Canale and Swain (1980) this component included both sociocultural rules of use and rules of discourse; here only the former set of rules is referred to. Sociolinguistic competence thus addresses the extent to which utterances are produced and understood *appropriately* in different sociolinguistic contexts depending on contextual factors such as status of participants, purposes of the interaction, and norms or conventions of interaction (on these factors see, for example, Hymes 1967). Appropriateness of utterances refers to both appropriateness of meaning and appropriateness of form. Appropriateness of meaning concerns the extent to which particular communicative functions (e.g. commanding, complaining and inviting), attitudes (including politeness and formality) and ideas are judged to be proper in a given situation. For example, it would generally be inappropriate for a waiter in a restaurant to command a customer to order a certain menu item regardless of how the utterance and communicative function (a command) were expressed grammatically. Appropriateness of form concerns the extent to which a given meaning (including communicative functions, attitudes and propositions/ideas) is represented in a verbal and/or non-verbal form that is proper in a given sociolinguistic context. For example, a waiter trying to take an order politely in a tasteful restaurant would be using inappropriate grammatical form (here register) if he were to ask, 'OK, chump, what are you and this broad gonna eat?'. This notion of appropriateness of form thus includes what Richards (1981) and others have called 'interactional competence', which addresses appropriateness of kinesics and proxemics. It is clear that the notion of naturalness or probability of occurrence (cf. Hymes 1972a, b, p. 281) can also play an important role in determining the appropriateness of meaning and form; however, this notion may be of limited value given the unpredictable and creative aspect of communication noted in Section 1.1 above. On this last point see Blum-Kulka (1980) and Canale and Swain (1980, p. 38, footnote 2).

There is a tendency in many second language programmes to treat sociolinguistic competence as less important than grammatical competence. This tendency seems odd for two reasons. First, it gives the impression that grammatical correctness of utterances is more important than appropriateness of utterances in actual communication, an impression that is challenged by data from first language use (cf. Terrell 1980, p. 330, footnote 2) and second language use (cf. Jones 1978, p. 92). Second, this tendency ignores the fact that sociolinguistic competence is *crucial* in interpreting utterances for their 'social meaning' for example, communicative function and attitude – when this is not clear from the literal meaning of utterances or from non-verbal cues (e.g. sociocultural context and gestures). There are no doubt universal aspects of appropriate language use that need not be relearned to communicate appropriately in a second language (cf. Brown and Levinson 1978; Canale and Swain 1980; Goffman 1976; Schmidt and Richards 1980). But there are language and culture-specific aspects, too. Valuable work on this last point has been carried out by Blum-Kulka (1980), Brown and Levinson (1978), Cazden (1972), Clyne (1975), Cook-Gumperz and Gumperz (1980), Richards (1981), Scollon and Scollon (1979) and Tannen (1980), among others. For example, Blum-Kulka (1980) distinguishes three types of rules that interact in determining how effectively a given communicative function is conveyed and interpreted: pragmatic rules, social-appropriateness rules and linguistic-realization rules. Pragmatic rules refer to the situational preconditions that must be satisfied to carry out a given communicative function (e.g. to give a command, one must have the right to do so). Social-appropriateness rules deal with whether or not a given function would normally be conveyed at all and, if so, with how much directness (e.g. asking a stranger how much he or she earns). Linguistic-realization rules involve a number of considerations, such as the frequency with which a given grammatical form is used to convey a given function, the number and structural range of forms associated with each function, the generality of forms across functions and situations, and the means of modulating the attitudinal tone of a given function. Her preliminary findings are that universality of socio-linguistic appropriateness decreases as one goes from pragmatic rules to social-appropriateness rules to linguistic-realization rules. Clyne (1975) reports similar findings. Blum-Kulka's own concluding statement expresses very well the importance of sociolinguistic competence for second language pedagogy: 'It is quite clear that as long as we do not know more about the ways in which communicative functions are being achieved in different languages, [second language] learners will often fail to achieve their communicative ends in the target language, and neither they nor their teachers will really understand why.' (p. 40)

Discourse competence. This type of competence concerns mastery of how to combine grammatical forms and meanings to achieve a unified spoken or written text in different genres.[2] By genre is meant the type of text: for example, oral and written narrative, an argumentative essay, a scientific report, a business letter, and a set of instructions each represent a different genre. Unity of a text is achieved through *cohesion* in form and *coherence* in meaning. Cohesion deals with how utterances are linked structurally and facilitates interpretation of a text. For example, the use of cohesion devices such as pronouns, synonyms, ellipsis, conjunctions and parallel structures serves to relate individual utterances and to indicate how a group of utterances is to be understood (e.g. logically or chronologically) as a text. Coherence refers to the relationships among the different meanings in a text, where these meanings may be literal meanings, communicative functions, and attitudes. For example, consider the following three utterances (from Widdowson 1978, p. 29):

SPEAKER A: That's the telephone.
SPEAKER B: I'm in the bath.
SPEAKER A: OK.

Although there is no overt signal of cohesion among these utterances, Widdowson points out that they do form coherent discourse to the extent that A's first utterance functions as a request, that B's reply functions as an excuse for not complying with A's request, and that A's final remark is an acceptance of B's excuse. Very insightful discussion of coherence is provided by Charolles (1978, p. 11f.), who distinguishes four types of 'meta-rules' for achieving and judging coherence of a text. These are: repetition of meaning, to signal continuity; progression of meaning, to indicate development and direction; non-contradiction, to signal consistency; and relevance of meaning, to mark congruity. It is also clear from Charolles' work that the role of cohesion devices is to serve such meta-rules of coherence. The important work of Freedle, Fine and Fellbaum (1981) and Halliday and Hasan (1976) seeks to identify the types of cohesion devices that serve different aspects of coherence and thus contribute to the quality and unity of a text.

It is reasonably clear that this notion of discourse knowledge and skill can be distinguished from grammatical competence and sociolinguistic competence. For example, consider the following conversation (Widdowson 1978, p. 25):

SPEAKER A: What did the rain do?
SPEAKER B: The crops were destroyed by the rain.

B's reply is grammatical and sociolinguistically appropriate within our framework but does not tie in well with A's question. The violation in this example seems to be at the level of discourse and to involve the normal organization of sentences (and texts) in English in which topic (shared information) precedes comment (new information), as Widdowson points out. Note that this principle of discourse restricts the grammatical form of utterances that can co-occur with A's question, filtering out compatible forms from incompatible ones regardless of their grammaticality and sociolinguistic appropriateness. This interaction of grammatical, sociolinguistic and discourse rules is suggestive of the complexity of communicative competence and is consistent with the distinction that is proposed here among these three areas of competence. However, it is not clear that all discourse rules must be distinguished from grammatical rules (as concerns cohesion) and sociolinguistic rules (as concerns coherence); see Morgan (1981) and Williams (1977) for discussion of the formal distinction between rules of grammar and rules of discourse.

Strategic competence. This component is composed of mastery of verbal and non-verbal communication strategies that may be called into action for two main reasons: (a) to compensate for breakdowns in communication due to limiting conditions in actual communication (e.g. momentary inability to recall an idea or grammatical form) or to insufficient competence in one or more of the other areas of communicative competence; and (b) to enhance the effectiveness of communication (e.g. deliberately slow and soft speech for rhetorical effect). For example, when one does not remember a given grammatical form, one compensatory strategy that can be used is paraphrase. Thus if a learner did not know the English term 'train station', he or she might try a paraphrase such as 'the place where trains go' or 'the place for trains'. Of course such strategies need not be limited to resolving grammatical problems: actual communication will also require learners to handle problems of a sociolinguistic nature (e.g. how to address strangers when unsure of their social status) and of a discourse nature (e.g. how to achieve coherence in a text when unsure of cohesion devices). Interesting discussion and examples of communication strategies may be found in Bialystok, Fröhlich and Howard (1979), Palmer (1977), Stern (1978), Swain (1977), Tarone (1977, 1980) and Terrell (1977). Furthermore, Hinofotis (1981a), Lepicq (1980), Wiemann and Backlund (1980) and Wong-Fillmore (1979) draw attention to the role of affective variables in contributing to effective communication. For instance, Lepicq (1980) reports that in the view of native-speaker judges, learners' confidence in themselves and willingness to communicate can compensate for their difficulties in grammatical accuracy.

Terrell (1977, p. 334) argues strongly that communication strategies are crucial at the beginning stages of second language learning. Two possible objections to actually teaching such strategies in the second language classroom are that they are universal and are picked up in mastering the first language. However, in Swain and Canale (1979) it is pointed out that although a general strategy such as paraphrase is indeed universal and used in first language communication, learners must be shown how such a strategy can be implemented in the second language (e.g. what the equivalent forms are for 'power vocabulary' items such as English 'place', 'person', and 'thing'). Furthermore, learners must be encouraged to use such strategies (rather than remain silent if they cannot produce grammatically accurate forms, for example) and must be given the opportunity to use them. See especially Stern (1978) on this latter point.

The potential value of such strategies to the second language learner can perhaps be highlighted more if we think of the teacher of the second language as a learner of the first language. For example, consider a teacher of French as a second language who speaks only French to a group of anglophone learners. From the students' point of view, the teacher (speaking only French) can be viewed as a learner (of English as a second language) who knows almost no English and yet is trying to communicate effectively. To the extent that the teacher is understood by relying on communication strategies, then these strategies are crucial for communication to take place at all. This particular example is not as bizarre as it may seem on the surface; for instance, there is a striking resemblance between teachers' speech to second language learners (cf. Hatch 1979; also Terrell 1980, p. 9) and the learners' own second language output. The point is this: if teachers are trained in the use of techniques to make themselves understood in the second language by learners, then why should learners not also be instructed in such techniques?

Two general comments should be made about the status of the above components of communicative competence. First, the four areas of competence distinguished here serve only to illustrate *what* communicative competence (minimally) includes: they are levels of analysis that can (and in my view must) be distinguished as part of the theoretical framework. The question of *how* these components interact with one another (or with other factors involved in actual communication) has been largely ignored here; that is, this theoretical framework is not a model of communicative competence, where model implies some specification of the manner and order in which the components interact and in which the various competencies are normally acquired. Halliday's (1973) theory of language qualifies better as a model in this sense (cf. also Munby 1978 for application of a similar model to communication in a second language). Ultimately, it is a model of communicative competence that must be articulated for second language pedagogy since a model has more direct applications for pedagogy than does a framework. However, description of a theoretical framework is a necessary step in constructing a model since the specification of how various sets of knowledge and skills interact and develop (a model) can only be as strong as the specification of these various competencies (a framework).

The second comment concerns the nature of this theoretical framework. In contrast to the view of communicative competence as a single, global factor (as argued by Oller 1978, for example), the view expressed here is a modular, or compartmentalized one. That is, in the present framework communicative competence is analysed as composed of several separate factors (areas of competence) that interact. In adopting and maintaining such a view, I have tried to respond to two key questions: first, why adopt a modular view at all?; and second, why distinguish these particular areas of competence?

In response to the first question, there is compelling empirical evidence for a modular view and against a global one. For example, Cummins (1980, 1981a, 1981b) reviews a variety of evidence that supports a distinction between the language proficiency required within school and that required outside it in both first and second languages. Bachman and Palmer (in press) and Palmer and Bachman (1981) report that confirmatory factor analysis of their second language testing data supports a divisible language competence model (a modular model) over a unitary language competence model (a global model).

With respect to the second question, there is still relatively little empirical evidence for distinguishing the four areas of competence proposed here. Some tentative evidence comes from current work at OISE on assessing knowledge and skills in these areas. An analysis of results on 37 French speaking tasks was carried out, where each task was administered to 174 students of French as a second language in Grade 6 and Grade 10 in Ontario. The correlations among the scoring criteria Information, Grammaticality, Pronunciation, (Sociolinguistic) Appropriateness, and Discourse were small, positive and non-significant ($r \leq .20$). These scoring criteria are discussed in Canale (1980b, 1981a). Furthermore, students achieved better results on tasks dealing with grammar than on ones dealing with sociolinguistic points. Such results are consistent with the distinctions among competence areas and the above theoretical framework thus gains in plausibility. Additional screenings of assessment instruments based on this theoretical framework are now underway in Ontario. Bachman and Palmer (1981), Clifford (1980, 1981) and Hinofotis (1981b) are also involved in empirical studies designed to address similar distinctions. Of particular interest are Bachman and Palmer's (1981) findings that their second language testing data is best accounted for by a model of communicative competence that distinguishes grammatical competence (word formation and sentence formation), pragmatic competence (vocabulary and discourse rules), sociolinguistic competence (appropriateness, naturalness and cultural references), and a general factor (unidentified but most associated with the oral interview method used by Bachman and Palmer).

In spite of the still small amount of evidence for the theoretical framework proposed here, there are reasons for assuming it as a working hypothesis. For instance, it has been developed on the basis of a careful analysis of empirical and theoretical studies bearing on communicative competence (see Canale and Swain 1980). Also it is similar in many respects to other current frameworks that represent the work of prominent researchers in the fields of language and second language pedagogy (e.g. Allen 1980; Chomsky 1980; Halliday 1973; Hymes 1972b; and Stern 1978). Finally, these distinctions are reasonable and traditional ones that figured importantly in the Cartesian view of language, for example (cf. Chomsky 1968, pp. 10–11).

2 Applications for second language teaching and testing

From the perspective of second language pedagogy, concerns about the correctness of this theoretical framework are, at least initially, less pressing than concerns about its relevance and potential applications. The present section deals with these latter concerns. It focusses on two points of general relevance to both second language teaching and testing: the distinction between knowledge and skill in performing this knowledge; and guiding principles for a communicative approach. In addition, Appendix A offers a sample outline of objectives in a communicative approach. With the exception of the guiding principles for a communicative approach, the presentation here is intended to complement but not replace nor repeat the applications of the framework discussed in Canale and Swain (1980, Sections 3.3 and 3.4).

2.1 *Knowledge-oriented and skill-oriented teaching and testing*

In Section 1.2 it was proposed that communicative competence be distinguished from actual communication and that within communicative competence a further distinction be adopted between knowledge and skill in performing this knowledge. These notions of knowledge and skill in using this knowledge are of crucial relevance to second language pedagogy. The reason is this. In practice (if not in theory) second language pedagogy has often proceeded on the assumption that knowledge about the second language (and more recently, about communication in the second language) is sufficient for effective use of the second language in actual communication situations (cf. Morrow 1977, pp. 1–11 and Terrell 1977, pp. 326–330). Such an approach may be called *knowledge-oriented*. Perhaps knowledge-oriented approaches, with their emphasis on controlled drills and explanation of rules, are practical for dealing with problems such as large groups of learners, short class periods, lack of teachers who are communicatively competent in the second language, and classroom discipline. But such approaches do not seem to be sufficient for preparing learners to use the second language well in authentic situations: they fail to provide learners with the opportunities and experience in handling authentic communication situations in the second language, and thus fail to help learners to master the necessary skills in using knowledge. The value of these latter *skill-oriented* activities is supported by a growing body of empirical data (e.g. Bialystok 1980b; Harley and Swain 1978; Savignon 1972; and Upshur and Palmer 1974) and theoretical studies (e.g. Allen 1980; Bialystok 1980a; Breen and Candlin 1980; Krashen 1979c; Rivers 1975; Stern 1978; and Terrell 1977, 1980). As stated by Savignon (1972, p. 9), 'the most significant findings of this study point to the value of training in communicative skills from the very beginning of the foreign language program'. And Rivers (1980, p. 51) draws attention to 'the fact (frequently observed and experienced) that one is constantly repeating the same error and then immediately correcting oneself, often with a sense of mortification and exasperation at one's inability to perform according to foreign-language rules one has studied and feels one "knows".'

Note that to make the claim that knowledge-oriented activities are insufficient is not to dismiss them as unnecessary for the development of effective performance skills. The importance of both knowledge-oriented and skill-oriented activities for adolescent and adult learners is signalled by Bialystok (1980a), Rivers (1975), Swain (1980), Swain and Canale (1979) and Terrell (1977), among others. For example, Terrell (1977), in reference to grammar exercises, claims: 'Explanation and practice with form is essential if we expect any improvement in the output of the students' developing grammars . . .' (p. 330)[3]

As stated above, it is somewhat surprising that second language pedagogy has put skill-oriented activities into practice only infrequently and sporadically. Concerns of a practical nature are certainly important; but it is an exercise in futility and frustration to employ essentially knowledge-oriented techniques that are insufficient for attaining programme goals concerned with actual language use. Consider such a state of affairs in other domains: for example, a driver training programme. Suppose that such a programme focussed on knowledge of traffic laws, recognition of road signs, and how to operate an automobile – perhaps including simulated or actual driving on a specially designed and controlled course – but provided no opportunity to drive in actual traffic. Suppose further that for the students in such a programme this was their only exposure to driving, i.e. that they were otherwise unfamiliar with automobiles and traffic. How well would graduates of this programme fare in the real situation? To what extent would they have gained sufficient confidence even to try to make use of training when placed in actual traffic?

It may be useful to pursue this example further to clarify the necessity and usefulness of knowledge-oriented and skill-oriented activities in second language pedagogy. Consider the procedure followed in many countries for obtaining a driving permit. There is a training stage and a testing stage, both of which have a knowledge-oriented component and a skill-oriented one. For example, at the training stage there are knowledge-oriented activities such as sensitization to the meaning of various road and traffic signs, presentation and explanation of rules of the road, tips on safety and accident prevention, information about automobiles and their operation, and feedback on students' problems and questions. Skill-oriented activities at this stage may include simulated driving or driving on a special course as well as actual on-road experience with an instructor. At the testing stage there is a knowledge-oriented pencil-and-paper test (usually in a multiple-choice format) and a skill-oriented on-road driving test. Can any of these activities and tests be justifiably ignored? Presumably not at the teaching stage, as pointed out above. Nor does it seem justifiable to drop either component at the testing stage. By ignoring the skill-oriented test one would have little direct evidence as to the student drivers' skill in handling actual traffic and would risk giving them the impression that only knowledge about driving is worth testing – and hence worth learning (cf. Clark 1972 and Jones 1981). By ignoring the knowledge-oriented test one would lose useful diagnostic information. For example, suppose that a student drove past a stop sign without stopping, during an on-road driving test. How could one specify the student's problem? Perhaps he or she did not know what a stop sign means, or knew but was unable to execute this knowledge because of preoccupation with other aspects of driving. A knowledge-oriented test (which addressed the meaning of a stop sign) could serve as a back-up instrument to help diagnose the precise problem and to suggest the type and amount of teaching further required (cf. Lado 1978 on the value of diagnostic instruments). Of course it might also be the case that different learners prefer and profit from different dosages of knowledge-oriented and skill-oriented teaching and testing methods (as suggested by Rivers 1980, pp. 49–50; and Naiman, Fröhlich, Stern and Todesco 1975, among others). Such learner differences are no doubt important, especially as concerns motivation, and must therefore be handled by a theory of second language learning. But the argument for different dosages of knowledge-oriented and skill-oriented methods for certain learners is by no means an argument against the necessity of both methods for the majority of learners.

Two final points relate to the notions of knowledge and skill and are important for second language pedagogy. One is that learners must receive as much comprehensible input in the second language as possible. According to researchers such as Krashen (1978) and Terrell (1977, 1980), such maximum comprehensible exposure to the second language is crucial for acquisition of basic knowledge and skills required for effective second language use. On the view here such exposure to the second language is thus both a (comprehension) skill-oriented activity and a knowledge-oriented one while exposure to the first language in the second language classroom is (at best) only a knowledge-oriented activity designed to teach about communication. The other point is that there seems to be a comprehension stage which must precede a production stage in second language learning; that is, production of the second language must not be *forced* during this initial stage (cf. Krashen 1978; Swain 1980; and Terrell 1980). The significance of this claim in the present discussion is that at the initial stages of second language learning, knowledge- and skill-oriented activities for listening and reading should perhaps be emphasized before ones devoted to speaking and writing, other things being equal.

2.2 *Guiding principles for a communicative approach*

This theoretical framework is intended to be applied to second language teaching and testing according to the five guiding principles presented below. Such a communicative approach is thus an integrative one in which the main goal is to prepare and encourage learners to exploit in an optimal way their limited communicative competence in the second language in order to participate in actual communication situations. It seems reasonable to assume that quality of communication at initial stages of second language learning will depend heavily on learners' communicative competence in their dominant language (cf. Cummins 1980), teachers' and learners' motivation and attitudes (cf. Wong-Fillmore 1979) and the effective use of communication strategies by both the learner and other participant(s) in communication situations.

The five guiding principles are as follows (cf. Canale and Swain 1980: Section 3.1 for more thorough presentation).

(*a*) *Coverage of competence areas.* Communicative competence must be viewed as minimally including four areas of knowledge and skill: grammatical competence, sociolinguistic competence, discourse competence and strategic competence. There is no evidence for the view that grammatical competence is any more or less crucial to successful communication than is sociolinguistic, discourse or strategic competence. The primary goal of a communicative approach must be to facilitate the *integration* of these types of competence for the learner, an outcome that is not likely to result from over-emphasis on one area of competence over the others throughout a second language programme.

(*b*) *Communication needs.* A communicative approach must be based on and respond to the learner's (often changing) communication needs and interests. These must be specified with respect to grammatical competence (for example, the levels of grammatical accuracy required in different situations), sociolinguistic competence (for example, the settings, topics and communicative functions to be handled most frequently), discourse competence (for example, the types of text to be dealt with) and strategic competence (for example, verbal compensatory strategies for paraphrasing lexical items that have not been mastered sufficiently). It is particularly important to base a communicative approach at least in part on the varieties of the second language that the learner is most likely to be in contact with in genuine communicative situations, and on the minimum levels of competence that various groups of native speakers (such as age groups, occupational groups) expect of the learner in such situations and that the majority of learners may be expected to attain.

(*c*) *Meaningful and realistic interaction.* The second language learner must have the opportunity to take part in meaningful communicative interaction with highly competent speakers of the language – that is, to respond to genuine communication needs and interests in realistic second language situations. This principle is important not only with respect to classroom activities but to testing as well. For example, it has been argued that paper-and-pencil tests, tape-recorded listening and speaking tests, and the like do not allow the learner to try out his/her communication skills in a realistic communication situation and thus cannot have the same psychological and instructional impact as do testing activities that directly involve more authentic and meaningful communicative interaction (again see Clark 1972, p. 132; see also Shohamy 1980).

(*d*) *The learner's native language skills.* Particularly at the early stages of second language learning, optimal use must be made of those communication skills that the learner has developed through use of the native (or dominant) language and that are common to communication skills required in the second language. It is particularly important that the more arbitrary and less universal aspects of communication in the second language (for example, certain features of the grammatical code such as vocabulary) be presented and practised in the context of less arbitrary and more universal ones (such as the basic sociolinguistic rules involved in greeting a peer in French or English).

(*e*) *Curriculum-wide approach.* The primary objective of a communication-oriented second language programme must be to provide the learners with the information, practice and much of the experience needed to meet their communication needs in the second language. In addition, the learners should be taught about *language*, drawing as much as possible from the first language programme, and about the *second language culture*, drawing as much as possible from other subject areas. It is thought that such a curriculum-wide approach may facilitate a natural integration of knowledge of the second language, knowledge of the second language culture and knowledge of language in general (cf. Breen and Candlin 1980; Widdowson 1978).

3 Concluding remarks

In summary, this chapter has expanded on the contents and pedagogical applications of the theoretical framework for communicative competence proposed by Canale and Swain (1980). An attempt has been made to clarify further the essential aspects of this framework, namely: the nature of communication, the distinction between communicative competence and actual communication, and the components of communicative competence. Moreover, this presentation has stressed the relevance of this framework for second language pedagogy and has offered suggestions and examples as to its realization in a communicative approach. Where possible, an effort has been made to assess both the framework and approach in light of current research; it is unfortunate that so much of this discussion remains more of an exchange of opinion than of fact.

Nonetheless, there are important research contributions of both a theoretical and applied nature that can serve to guide further work on communicative competence and communicative approaches to second language pedagogy. As concerns a theoretical framework, the research programmes of Bachman and Palmer (1981), Blum-Kulka (1980), Candlin (1980) and Larsen-Freeman (1981) seem especially valuable for identifying the nature and interaction of different components of communicative competence. The theories of second language learning espoused by Bialystok (1980a), Cummins (1981a, b), Krashen (1979c) and Terrell (1980) provide interesting and instructive accounts of the relationships among various types of second language teaching, acquisition environments, mastery levels and use. Also, exemplary classroom techniques and activities are found in the work of Allen *et al.* (1980), Johnson and Morrow (1979), Krashen and Terrell (forthcoming), Paulston and Bruder (1976) and Sampson (1979). Breen and Candlin (1980) and Clifford (1981) contain insightful discussion of communicative syllabus design. Finally, excellent surveys and examples of communicative testing techniques are offered by Bachman and Palmer (1981), Carroll (1980), Farhady (1980), Fillmore (1981), Jones (1977), Low (1981), Lowe (1981), Morrow (1977), Oller (1979) and Savignon (1972, 1981).

In closing, it is worth pointing out that both subjective and objective feedback can play important roles in research on a theory of communicative competence and its applications. In work here at OISE on a communicative testing programme, subjective feedback from teachers and students has been invaluable in dealing with questions of scoring reliability, content validity, practicality and acceptability of assessment instruments. Furthermore, such involvement has served to provide some teacher training in the essential yet frequently ignored (in teacher training programmes) area of communicative testing. In these ways, then, it has been possible to assure that the theoretical framework we have adopted is relevant for second language pedagogy. However, such subjective feedback cannot replace more objective feedback if questions of the correctness of a theory are to be addressed: correctness, or construct validity must be determined in as rigorous an empirical manner as possible. As pointed out several times above, it is not clear how well the theoretical framework suggested here (and others) will bear the weight of hard empirical data. But the present chapter may help to clarify the types of empirical questions that must be asked and why they are worthwhile.

Notes

1. I would like to express my gratitude to the Ontario Ministry of Education for its financial support of the research reported here (under the contract 'The Ontario Assessment Instrument Pool, French as a Second Language'). I am indebted to my colleagues on that project at OISE, especially Ellen Bialystok and Merrill Swain, and to the students in my seminar on communicative competence at York University for helpful discussion of many of the ideas and views expressed in this chapter. Thanks also goes to Chris Candlin, Jim Cummins, Hossein Farhady, Adrian Palmer, Jack Richards and Merrill Swain for comments on an earlier draft of this work.
2. I ignore here the important differences that exist between oral and written texts; see Bennett and Slaughter (1981), Bereiter and Scardamalia (1981) and Wetzel and Ladd (1979) for discussion of such differences.
3. As Terrell (personal communication) has pointed out, the use of 'any' in this quote is perhaps too strong.

Appendix A

Sample outline of communication objectives

The following outline of communication objectives was prepared for the Ontario Ministry of Education as a concise statement of objectives for general French as a second language programmes at the elementary and secondary school levels (cf. Canale 1980b; Canale and Swain 1979). This outline is based on the above theoretical framework and reflects the work of Munby (1978, Chapter 7). It is a tentative and evolving outline whose inclusion here is intended to illustrate more clearly the content of a communicative approach. The outline is organized in terms of both the competence areas that teaching and testing must address and the modes – (L)istening comprehension, (S)peaking, (R)eading comprehension and (W)riting – in which each competence objective is rele-

vant. Both competence objectives and modes may be combined
to provide more integrative activities for learners. For example,
the same activity might address both vocabulary usage and sentence formation, and modes may be combined to address areas
such as conversation (Listening and Speaking) and note-taking
(Listening and Writing).

Competence area	Mode
1 **GRAMMATICAL COMPETENCE**	
1.1 **Phonology:**	
1.1.1 Pronunciation of lexical items in connected speech	L, S
1.1.2 Liaison (e.g. *Je suis⌣arrivé.*)	L, S
1.1.3 Word stress in connected speech:	
1.1.3.1 Normal word stress	L, S
1.1.3.2 Emphatic or contrastive word stress (e.g. *Marie est compétente mais Paul est <u>in</u>compétent.*)	L, S
1.1.4 Intonation patterns in connected speech:	
1.1.4.1 Normal intonation for different clause types (e.g. imperative, declarative, interrogative)	L, S
1.1.4.2 Emphatic or contrastive intonation patterns for different clause types (e.g. *Il est venu?* with rising intonation to signal an interrogative)	L, S
1.2 **Orthography:**	
1.2.1 Graphemes	R, W
1.2.2 Spelling conventions (including accents) for:	
1.2.2.1 Individual lexical items	R, W
1.2.2.2 Compounds (e.g. use of hyphens as in *un tire-bouchon*)	R, W
1.2.2.3 Other (e.g. *Parle-t-il?*)	R, W
1.2.3 Punctuation conventions	R, W
1.3 **Vocabulary:**	
1.3.1 Common vocabulary related to topics selected according to analysis of learners' communicative needs and interests:	
1.3.1.1 Basic meaning of content vocabulary items in context	L, S, R, W
1.3.1.2 Gender of nouns and pronouns	L, S, R, W
1.3.2 Meaning of idioms in context	L, S, R, W
1.3.3 Basic meaning of other vocabulary items in	

	context (that is, grammatical function words such as prepositions and articles)	L, S, R, W
1.4	**Word formation:**	
1.4.1	Inflection, in context, of:	
1.4.1.1	Nouns for number (singular/plural)	L, S, R, W
1.4.1.2	Adjectives for number and gender	L, S, R, W
1.4.1.3	Verbs for person, number, tense	L, S, R, W
1.4.2	Agreement, in context, of:	
1.4.2.1	Pronouns with nouns (number and gender)	L, S, R, W
1.4.2.2	Adjectives with nouns/pronouns (number and gender)	L, S, R, W
1.4.2.3	Nouns/pronouns with verbs (person and number for verbs, case for pronouns)	L, S, R, W
1.4.3	Derivation of new words (e.g. *refaire* from *faire*, *lentement* from *lent/e*)	L, S, R, W
1.4.4	Variation at word boundaries in context (e.g. *à + le = au*)	L, S, R, W
1.5	**Sentence formation:**	
1.5.1	Common sentence and subsentence structures selected according to analysis of learners' communicative needs and interests:	
1.5.1.1	Form of a given structure in context	L, S, R, W
1.5.1.2	Literal meaning of a sentence having a given structure (with vocabulary) in context	L, S, R, W
2	**SOCIOLINGUISTIC COMPETENCE**	
2.1	**Expression and understanding of appropriate social meanings (that is, communicative functions, attitudes and topics) in different sociolinguistic contexts**	L, S, R, W
2.2	**Expression and understanding of appropriate grammatical forms for different communicative functions in different sociolinguistic contexts (where functions and contexts are selected according to analysis of learners' communicative needs and interests)**	L, S, R, W
3	**DISCOURSE COMPETENCE**	
3.1	**Common oral and written genres selected according to analysis of learners' communication needs and interests:**	
3.1.1	*Cohesion in different genres:*	
3.1.1.1	Lexical cohesion devices in context (e.g. repetition of lexical items, use of synonyms)	L, S, R, W

24 *Michael Canale*

3.1.1.2	Grammatical cohesion devices in context (e.g. co-reference of nouns with pronouns, ellipsis, logical connectors, parallel structures)	L, S, R, W
3.1.2	*Coherence in different genres:*	
3.1.2.1	Oral discourse patterns, e.g. the normal progression of meanings (particularly literal meanings and communicative functions) in a casual conversation	L, S, R
3.1.2.2	Written discourse patterns, e.g. the normal progression of meanings in a business letter	R, W

4   STRATEGIC COMPETENCE

4.1   For grammatical difficulties:

4.1.1	Use of reference sources (e.g. dictionary, grammar book)	R, W
4.1.2	Grammatical and lexical paraphrase (e.g. use of *devoir* + infinitive or *falloir* + infinitive instead of *il faut que* + subjunctive; or use of general vocabulary items such as *la chose, l'affaire, le truc, la personne, l'endroit, le temps*, etc. followed by a description to serve as a paraphrase for an unmastered vocabulary item)	S, W
4.1.3	Requests for repetition, clarification, or slower speech	S, L
4.1.4	Use of non-verbal symbols (e.g. gestures, drawings)	W, W

4.2   For sociolinguistic difficulties:

4.2.1	Use of a single grammatical form for different communicative functions (e.g. a declarative such as *On sert le dîner à 17 heures*, which may be used as a statement, a question (with rising intonation), a promise, an order, an invitation, or a threat depending on sociolinguistic context)	L, S, R, W
4.2.2	Use of the most sociolinguistically neutral grammatical form when uncertain about appropriateness of other forms in a given communicative situation (e.g. use of the form *Comment ça va?* instead of *Comment allez-vous?* or *Comment vas-tu?* in greeting a stranger)	S, W
4.2.3	Use of first language knowledge about appropriateness of grammatical forms or communicative functions in the second language	L, S, R, W

4.3   For discourse difficulties:

4.3.1	Use of non-verbal symbols or emphatic stress and intonation to indicate cohesion

	and coherence (e.g. use of drawings to indicate sequencing of actions and ideas)	S, W
4.3.2	Use of first language knowledge about oral or written discourse patterns when uncertain about such aspects of second language discourse	L, S, R, W

4.4   For performance factors:

4.4.1	Coping with background noise, interruptions, and other distractions	S, L
4.4.2	Use of pause fillers (e.g. *eh bien, enfin, alors*) to maintain conversation while searching for ideas or grammatical forms	S, L

Questions for discussion, study and further research

1. How directly do the components of communicative competence (Section 1.3) and the guiding principles for a communicative approach (Section 2.2) address each of the seven features of communication proposed by Morrow (Section 1.1)? For those features that do not seem to be handled adequately, discuss how teaching and testing activities could serve to address them.

2. It is often assumed that a communicative approach is not suitable for learners at the beginning stages of second language study. On what grounds would you accept or question this assumption?

3. Second language syllabuses are organized on different bases: for example, some are organized mainly on grammatical principles, others on notions and communicative functions, and still others on situations and topics. As long as each of these syllabuses was implemented in line with the communicative approach suggested in this chapter, would you expect the syllabus differences to figure crucially in learner's communicative competence? Explain your answer.

4. On the basis of interviews, questionnaires or several classroom visits, prepare a communication profile of a second language class. Obtain and analyse data on teaching and testing activities with respect to the following categories: (a) grammatical, sociolinguistic, discourse and strategic competencies; (b) knowledge-oriented and skill-oriented; (c) variety of grammatical forms, communicative functions, sociocultural contents, discourse contexts, and communicatively competent second language speakers that learners are exposed to; and (d) amount of comprehensible second language input for the learner and output from the learner. Prepare

recommendations for making the approach under study more communication-oriented and discuss them with the educators involved.

5. Prepare a description of five or so communication situations that differ according to sociocultural variables such as role and age of participants, purpose of communication, topic and location. Note the language forms that native speakers would use most frequently (or naturally) to address the given purpose and topic in each situation. What sociocultural variables seem most important in determining the appropriate forms in each situation? Use this information to help organize sociolinguistic activities that are knowledge-oriented or skill-oriented.

6. In Canale and Swain (1980, p. 21 ff.), the following criteria were presented to help in the specification and sequencing of grammatical forms in a second language programme: (a) grammatical complexity; (b) semantic transparency of a form with respect to its communicative function (e.g. *I suggest you try the fish* is a more transparent grammatical encoding of the function of suggesting than is the form *The fish is nice*); (c) generalizability to other communicative functions and sociocultural contexts; (d) role in facilitating mastery of other grammatical forms; (e) conceptual and perceptual complexity; and (f) markedness in terms of dialect and style. To what extent is each of these criteria satisfied in the choice and presentation of grammatical forms in the programme with which you are most familiar?

7. Consider the following skill-oriented classroom activity. Students are shown a map of a section of a city with which they are familiar. Only major streets and major social and cultural landmarks (e.g. major stores, parks and historical sites) appear on the map. Activities might involve having students identify where certain conversations might be heard, where certain people might live or work, how to get from one place to another, or what route a city tour might follow and why. Plan, discuss and try out these and other tasks relating to such a map. What use do such tasks serve? What is the reception of students and teachers to their use?

8. Consider the following skill-oriented test items for assessing sociolinguistic skill in the speaking mode (from the Ontario Assessment Instrument Pool for French as a Second Language, Research and Evaluation Branch, Ontario Ministry of Education, Toronto):

(a) Imagine you and your parents are visiting some of their friends, Mr and Mrs Duval. Their son Paul has gone to play with his friends. It's the first time you have gone to visit the family and you want to know if it would be all right to ride Paul's bicycle. Pretend that I'm Mr or Mrs Duval and I'm busy, talking with your parents. What should you say in French to interrupt me politely and ask to ride Paul's bicycle?

(b) Imagine that I'm one of your school friends and that you want to invite me to the movies for Saturday night. What should you say to me?

(c) Provide other examples of items that could be used to assess sociolinguistic skill in the speaking mode. What scoring criteria would be relevant? On what basis would you decide to present the item in the students' first/dominant language or in the second language?

Introduction to Chapter 2

This chapter is an account of the relationship between what is *said* in communication (i.e. the concepts and meanings that are communicated by the speaker's choice of particular words and constructions) and what is *done* in communication (i.e. the effects the speaker's utterance has on the hearer, such as to convince, inform, amuse, etc.). This focus on speaker-meaning and hearer-effects and how the two are related is defined by Fraser as *pragmatics*, and his theory of linguistic communication (which relates to what Canale refers to as grammatical competence, but has implications for sociolinguistic competence as well) encompasses the use of linguistic items for the coding of meaning, as a communicative system. It is a two-way system of interaction. It is speaker-based in that it is concerned with meanings the speaker selects, the construction of propositions from concepts, and the speaker's attitudes towards these propositions. It is also hearer-based in that the propositions have perlocutionary effects on hearers. It is hence essentially a theory of speech acts.

The concept of speech acts, which, following Austin (1962), is concerned with the acts that we perform through speaking, has been studied extensively in recent years, and has constituted a topical focus for scholars from a great number of disciplines (see Schmidt and Richards 1980). Speech act theory has been central to the work of researchers in conversational analysis, discourse analysis and semantics, and is referred to elsewhere in this book in the chapters by Wolfson, Holmes, and Richards and Schmidt. Fraser's focus is on how propositions are interpreted as different types of speech acts, and he discusses this in terms of the assumptions about the world, about communication, and about linguistic meaning which speakers and hearers share and which they appear to make use of in interpreting utterances and assigning them appropriate meanings. Fraser formulates a model which is illustrated from discussion of a wide variety of different types of speech acts.

2 The domain of pragmatics[1]

Bruce Fraser

> The essence of language is human activity – activity on the part of one individual to make himself understood by another, and activity on the part of that other to understand what was in the mind of the first. These two individuals, the producer and the recipient of language, or as we may more conveniently call them, the speaker and the hearer, and their relations to one another, should never be lost sight of if we want to understand the nature of language and of that part of language which is dealt with in grammar.
>
> Jesperson: *The Philosophy of Grammar*, p. 17

Introduction

Consider the following facts about the use of English:

'How are you?' counts as a greeting, not a farewell.

'Can you pass the salt?' is frequently used as a request, while 'Are you able to pass the salt?' is not.

'John is married to his work' involves a metaphor.

'I will be there' is used as a promise, a warning, a threat or a prediction, but not as a criticism or a request.

'Well' at the beginning of an utterance may signal a sense of contemplation, annoyance, or surprise.

'Your breath smells so bad it would knock a buzzard off a manure wagon' will be heard as an insult.

Each of these facts goes beyond what we would want to ascribe as knowledge a native speaker has about the grammar of English. Knowing a grammar, at least as the term is used in contemporary linguistics, is to know the rules for characterizing language form. Knowing facts of the sort presented above, however, involves knowing rules for language use as well.

When we use language, we characteristically do three things: (1) we say something; (2) we indicate how we intend the hearer to take what we have said; and (3) we have definite effects on the hearer as a result.[2] Usually we expect to do all three things at once. For example, if I tell you, 'The police stopped drinking by midnight', I might intend to *say* that the police enforced a midnight curfew (rather than to say that they, themselves, ceased imbibing). In so speaking, I might intend to *communicate* to you that what I have said is to be taken as a claim on my part (rather than, say, an admission). And because I have made this claim about the police, I might intend to *affect* you in a certain way, for example, to relieve you rather than anger or surprise you, perhaps because I know you were worrying about how late your children were out.

Although we communicate in many different modes, linguistic communication occurs only in those cases in which we *intend* in using language to convey certain attitudes to our hearer (for example, that we want our utterance to have the force of a request) and the hearer *recognizes* what these attitudes are, based upon what we have said. Such communication is based on but certainly not exhausted by what we say when we speak. On the other hand, such communication does not extend to how we have affected the hearer because we have said something and have communicated our intended force (attitude). Any effects beyond the successful recognition of the speaker's intentions, such as convincing, annoying, or confusing the hearer, are not part of communication but the result of communication, or perhaps the result of failure to communicate

Pragmatics is the theory of linguistic communication. My purpose in this paper is to present an overview of what is involved in linguistic communication: what can be communicated; how the speaker goes about accomplishing the intended communication; and why certain strategies are selected under particular circumstances to bring about the communication. It is my hope that upon finishing the paper, the reader will have a basic understanding of the issues involved in constructing an adequate theory of pragmatics – a theory of linguistic communication – as well as an appreciation for the nascent stage it currently enjoys.[3]

Before embarking on this overview, I want to make several clarifying comments. First, when talking about linguistic communication, I am referring to the case in which the speaker is attempting to communicate to the hearer by relying at least in part on the semantic interpretation of the linguistic form uttered. For example, to shout, 'The ice is thin', may linguistically communicate a warning; to comment, 'That was certainly a dumb thing for me to do', may be taken as an apology, depending on the situation in which I spoke, and my manner of speaking. What does not fall within this notion of linguistic communication, however, would be my announcing to you that I have arrived home by beginning to recite the Pledge of Allegiance to the flag upon entering the house. I have successfully announced my arrival, but not linguistically.

Second, linguistic communication succeeds only when the speaker has an attitude which he *intends* to convey to the hearer in using language, and the hearer recognizes this attitude. If, for example, I am terribly embarrassed by a past action and comment on my thoughtlessness, you might take me as issuing an apology. But only if I intend to apologize have I communicated an apology to you. You may have correctly understood my feelings, but not by way of linguistic communication. Similarly, if I say, 'I will take you skiing for your birthday', intending it to be a promise, but you hear it as a threat since you abhor skiing, I will have failed to communicate either a threat or a promise: I did not intend the former, you did not recognize my intent of the latter.

Finally, there is an area that is specifically excluded from the theory, namely, the theory of conversation. Schegloff (1972), among others, has studied the organization of conversations and suggested that normal conversation may include elements such as openings, closings, repairs, responses, discussions, explanations, clarifications, and a variety of other conversational acts. Consider the utterance, 'Good morning. How are you?' This counts as a greeting. just as the utterance of 'Excuse me. Could I talk to you for a moment?' may count as an apology followed by a request. But the fact that either of these utterances can count as a conversational opening is not an aspect of linguistic communication, even if the hearer recognizes the speaker's purpose in uttering them. At best, they communicate a proposal to engage in conversation. Utterances intended to count as conversational openings, for example, do not count as such simply in virtue of the speaker's intending it and the hearer's recognizing this intention, as do apologies or requests. A conversational opening comes about because the speaker says something which is (usually) indirectly interpreted as a proposal to open the conversation, and only after the proposal is accepted can the initial utterance count as the opening. Such acts are constructed within the theory of conversational interaction, not within the more restricted theory of linguistic communication. I do not see them as a part of a theory of pragmatics, although certainly within any theory of communicative competence.

Saying something

To ask what a speaker has said is to ask the question: what is the operational meaning of the speaker's utterance: what did he mean? As a first approximation, we might conclude that the speaker has said whatever is understood to be the semantic interpretation of the sentence uttered.

A consideration of the issues involved indicates, however, that there are at least three factors which play a role in determining the answer to this question for a given utterance: (1) the sense (s) of the sentence uttered; (2) the identity of the objects in the real world referred to by the speaker; and (3) whether or not the speaker was speaking literally or figuratively. We will discuss these factors in order, making the assumption in discussing the first two factors that the speaker is speaking literally.

The issue of what sense the speaker intends for an utterance involves the potential ambiguity of the sentence used. On the assumption that in uttering a sentence the speaker always means one and only one sense to be understood, the task of the hearer is to determine which one.[4] A sentence such as, 'Smoking children can be a nuisance', might appear to be unambiguous at first glance, but in addition to the interpretation that children who smoke annoy us, we have a variety of other interpretations; for example, treating children as cigarettes, considering the nuisance value of children on fire, and the trouble entailed in curing children, much as one would cure ham. Part of determining what the speaker has said involves determining which of the possible semantic interpretations of the sentence was the intended one.[5]

The second factor in determining operational meaning is what we can call the referential problem: what objects in the real world do the referring terms refer to? For example, if I say to you, 'We shall overcome', is the 'we' referring to just me and my compatriots, or does it include you as well? Or, if someone tells me, 'The crayon is over there', where is the 'there'? Or, if I hear that 'The President was not in Washington then', when was the 'then'? Without the answers to these questions in each case, the hearer cannot determine what the speaker intends to be the meaning of the utterance, although he might be able to determine which of several senses (ambiguities) was intended. To compound these relatively straightforward problems for the hearer of determining the intended sense and reference of what the speaker literally said, we find a number of potential additional problems. For example, what has the speaker said when she intended to say, 'The milkman is erratic', but uttered instead, 'The milkman is erotic'? What has been said when someone utters, 'Look at that huge fish', when pointing to a whale swimming by? Or, if the speaker Spoonerizes and says, 'You have tasted the whole worm', rather than the intended 'You have wasted the whole term', what has been said? What if the speaker is mistaken about the meaning of a word, (for example, the frequent misuse of *imply* for *infer*) but the hearer is aware of the mistake and interprets the use of *imply* as if *infer* had been used? Or perhaps, less likely, what if both are mistaken about the meaning of a word, for example, *ingenuous*, where both speaker and hearer believe it to mean 'insincere' and interpret it as such? These issues are of more than philosophical interest, since no theory of linguistic communication can begin to reach the level of descriptive adequacy until such thorny issues are resolved.

The third factor in determining what has been said is the issue of literal versus figurative use of language. If the speaker is speaking literally, then the operational meaning of the utterance involves one of semantic interpretation of the linguistic expression uttered. In fact, it would seem worthwhile to posit, as a working assumption of language use, an assumption of literalness which dictates that unless there is evidence to the contrary, the hearer should operate under the assumption that the speaker is speaking literally. Following this assumption, the hearer would forgo processing the utterance for its literal operational meaning only if there were reason to.

What would this evidence look like? There are a variety of ways in which the speaker, should he be so inclined, can notify his listener that the present utterance should be interpreted figuratively: that is, what the speaker *says* is not one of the semantic interpretations of the sentence uttered. One way to notify the hearer is to actually announce your intention. Beginning your utterance with, 'Speaking metaphorically . . .', 'At the risk of exaggerating . . .', 'Figuratively speaking . . .', 'If I may engage in hyperbole . . .', or 'In a manner of speaking . . .', serves to put the hearer on notice. There are, however, other less explicit ways. For example, the utterance of a clearly semantically anomalous sentence such as 'Colourless green ideas sleep furiously' demands a non-literal (figurative) interpretation. (Several people have suggested that the quoted sentence could be interpreted to mean, 'Uninteresting, untried ideas often smoulder just beneath the surface of expression', this reading itself demanding a figurative interpretation.) Sentences such as, 'The future is now', or 'We do it all for you', which are clearly false, might be naive and unsuccessful attempts by the speaker to lie, but might be more fairly taken as attempts at the figurative use of language. Similarly, a sentence which is obviously true, for example, 'No man is an island' or 'I wasn't born yesterday', again might reflect carelessness or stupidity on the part of the speaker; or, more reasonably, it might signal that the speaker is requesting a figurative interpretation.

Various types of figurative language exist, and I will mention only some of them here, with no detailed discussion.[6] Sarcasm (e.g., 'I just love people who turn in front of me without signalling') arises when the speaker appears to say one thing but means something close to the opposite and, moreover, intends the comment to be derisive. In metaphor, (e.g., 'John is married to his work') the speaker is using the predicate in a non-literal way, and an analogy must be constructed in order to interpret the intended operational meaning. Synecdoche and metonymy are closely related; in both, a referring expression is used non-literally, (e.g. '*All hands* are to report to the Captain'; The *Fords* won at LeMans.) Hyperbole (exaggeration) and meiosis (understatement) are at opposite ends of a continuum, but unlike the other tropes just mentioned, they vary in the degree to which they deviate from strict literalness. We talk of 'slightly exaggerated' and 'greatly exaggerated' but never the somewhat synecdochic use of language. Similes are figurative, much like metaphors, already mentioned. To say that 'He is wise like a fox' or 'He is as big as a house' is to announce to the hearer not only that the speaker intends to be heard as speaking figuratively, but to indicate as well the type of figurative device being utilized.

Idioms do not constitute a figurative use of language. An idiom, as the term is usually construed, consists of two or more words which receive a consistent semantic interpretation, but whose meaning cannot be determined from the component parts. The idiomatic meaning of 'to kick the bucket' as 'to die' simply cannot be computed from the meanings of 'kick' and 'bucket', although historically this was possible. It would be safe to say that all idioms today were originally examples of figurative use of language where one of the possible figurative interpretations became fixed and where, depending on the history and the recency of the coinage, the present language users may be totally unaware of the original meaning. Thus, to say, 'He kicked the bucket', and mean 'He died' is to speak literally, although the meaning of the phrase 'kick the bucket' is not computed compositionally as it would be if the intended meaning were that he struck the bucket with his foot.

To summarize, the hearer operates on the assumption that the speaker is using the language seriously and attempting to communicate with his hearers. He initially assumes that the speaker is speaking literally and, therefore, attempts to determine what the speaker is literally saying – the literal operational meaning of the utterance. If this fails, either because no reasonable literal interpretation can be made or there are clues that the utterance is intended to be taken figuratively, then the hearer must consider both the potential semantic interpretations of the sentence as well as his theory of figurative language interpretation to then determine the operational meaning of the utterance, but in this case, what the speaker has figuratively said. In either the literal or the figurative case – the speaker is never doing both at the same time with the same utterance – the hearer has, at this point in understanding the speaker, arrived at the operational meaning of the utterance.

Illocutionary acts

If all we did in using language was to say something, the theory of pragmatics would have to deal only with the issues just raised: notions of literal/figurative intention, specifying of indexicals, and resolving which leg of an ambiguity was meant. However, we do much more, as even a casual consideration of the matter will show. We intend what we say to have a specific force. We make requests, give authorizations, make promises, make offers, concede another's position, and make apologies, to name but several of the hundreds of different speech acts we can perform when we use language. It is in performing these speech acts, named by Austin (1962) as *illocutionary acts*, that we are linguistically communicating. We want to consider first what acts of communication are available to a speaker and then, second, what means are available for effecting this communication.

The best way to view linguistic communication is in terms of what the speaker is trying to accomplish in using language beyond the simple issuing of statements. To begin, every sentence is 'about' something, independent of its syntactic form or intended use. The sentence, 'I will be home by noon', is about the speaker's anticipated presence at his home at midday. So are the sentences, 'Will I be home by noon?', 'I will be home by noon?' and 'By noon I will be home'. The term 'propositional content' will be used to refer to this notion of what a sentence is about. As we will discuss later, part of sentence meaning, and hence what the speaker says, often goes beyond the propositional content of the sentence. The utterance of 'I will be home at noon', for example, can be intended as a promise and when intended as such commits the speaker to a much different attitude towards the future action of home-coming than when the very same sentence is uttered and intended to be a threat, a warning, or simply a prediction. The most useful way to distinguish between these and other examples of using language is in terms of the attitude that the speaker holds *towards* the propositional content of what he says. In promising, the speaker intends his utterance to commit him to carrying out the action specified, while for a warning, the attitude is that the speaker believes that the facts represented by the proposition pose an unfavourable consequence to the hearer. Similarly, if the speaker says, 'You are to leave at once', and intends it as an order, then his attitude is one of desiring that the hearer carry out the action of leaving at once in virtue of the speaker's authority over the hearer. The same sentence used as a report carries the attitude of belief that the hearer is supposed to leave immediately.

Although there are several hundred speech acts such as promising, requesting, and reporting, there appear to be four major attitudes which can be expressed by the speaker and which partition these acts into types:[7]

A   *Belief*: Speaker expresses belief that proposition is true

B   *Desire*: Speaker expresses a desire concerning the action specified in the proposition

C   *Commitment*: Speaker expresses an intention to undertake a commitment associated with the action specified in the proposition

D   *Evaluation*: Speaker expresses a personal evaluation towards some past action

We succeed in linguistically communicating when we get the hearer to recognize what we have said and what attitude we hold toward the propositional content of our utterance. The communicative effect on the hearer is not a new belief but rather, a recognition of what attitude I hold towards the proposition I have expressed. For example, if I make a request of you, my intention is to express my desire that you carry out the action specified in the utterance; I have successfully communicated if you recognize this attitude on my part. Whether or not you do in fact carry out the action after you recognize my intention to request is a different issue, not part of requesting, and not part of linguistic communication.

There are two important points here. First, some, but not all, modifications of a basic attitude presented above have labels associated with them. One that does, for example, is the speaker's desire that the hearer carry out some action and do so in virtue of the speaker's wanting this done: this is a request. Slightly different is an order, in which the same desire is there, but the action is expected to be carried out because of the speaker's authority over the hearer. Yet a third is the act of pleading, a request with the added condition that the speaker who is pleading is unable to carry out the action effectively himself. However, there is no label, in English at least, for the act of expressing your desire that the hearer act in virtue of the fact that you have asked him twice previously, or that she is your sister-in-law, or that he has the moral obligation to do so. In fact, there isn't a label for the basic expressing of your desire that the hearer act – what would be conveyed by, 'I want you to do that'.

Second, although we have indicated (and will discuss in more detail below) that there are four speaker attitudes which characterize the intentions underlying linguistic communication, these four certainly do not exhaust the possible attitudes a speaker might hold towards what he has said. What distinguishes each of these four attitudes is that once one is recognized as being the attitude intended by the speaker, the speaker has successfully communicated to the hearer. Thus, if you recognize that I intend my utterance to count as a request, an apology, or a statement, I have succeeded in making a request, an apology, or a statement at the very moment you recognize that this was my intention. Such is the nature of linguistic communication. However, if I intend my attitude towards what I say to count as a boast or an eloquent testimony to your abilities, I have neither boasted nor eloquently testified about your abilities just because you have recognized my intentions. You might not hear me boasting by what I have said, and you might find my prose quite ineloquent. Such intentions on the part of the speaker are not accomplished simply by being recognized as intended, and go beyond the notion of linguistic communication, hence beyond pragmatics. They fall under what Austin called 'perlocutionary effects'.

Before examining how the speaker signals to the hearer his illocutionary intents, we shall investigate briefly the set of illocutionary acts available to the speaker of English.

The first genus of illocutionary acts is that in which the speaker expresses his belief that the propositional content of the utterance is true. These are known as *Representatives*. Acts of asserting, predicting, describing, advising, certifying, admitting and agreeing are all instances of the speaker's expressing his attitude of belief. However, as we might expect, within this genus of Representatives, there are a number of species and sub-species involving conditions surrounding the cause and basis of belief on the part of the speaker. We present a general outline below.[8]

Representatives: Speaker expresses belief that the propositional content is true and:

A   Indicates the belief is his own opinion

   1   without time restrictions
     (affirm, allege, assert, aver, claim, declare, maintain, say, state)

   2   with future time restriction
     (forecast, predict, prophesy)

   3   with past time restriction
     (report, recount)

B   Indicates the belief rests with some verifiable knowledge
   (advise, announce, apprise, disclose, inform, insist, notify, point out, report, reveal, tell, testify)

C   Indicates the belief rests with some truth-seeking procedure
   (appraise, assess, certify, conclude, confirm, corroborate, diagnose, find, judge, substantiate, validate, verify)

D   Indicates the belief is contrary to the previous belief

(acknowledge, admit, agree, allow, assent, concede, concur, confer, grant)

E   Indicates the belief is no longer held by him
    (correct, disavow, disclaim, renounce, retract, deny)

F   Indicates the belief is that of another person
    (accept, agree, assent, concur)

G   Indicates the belief is not that of another person
    (differ, disagree, dissent, reject)

H   Indicates the belief is tentative
    (conjecture, guess, hypothesize, speculate, suggest)

I   Indicates the belief is worth consideration
    (assume, hypothesize, postulate, stipulate, suppose, theorize)

J   Indicates the belief is not shared by all
    (demur, dispute, object, protest, question)

K   Indicates the belief accurately characterizes some object
    (appraise, assess, call, categorize, characterize, classify,
    date, describe, diagnose, evaluate, grade, identify, rank)

The second genus, *Directives*, includes those acts in which the speaker expresses an attitude towards a prospective action by the hearer. Acts such as pleading, requesting, ordering, forbidding, and suggesting all fall within this genus of which, again, there are a number of species.

Directives: Speaker expresses a desire regarding the action specified in the propositional content, namely:

A   The hearer is to carry out the action

   1   indicating that the hearer do so in virtue of the speaker's
     desire
     (ask, beg, beseech, implore, invite, petition, plead,
     request, solicit, summon, urge, inquire, question)

   2   indicating that the hearer do so in virtue of the speaker's
     authority over the hearer
     (bid, charge, command, dictate, direct, enjoin, instruct,
     order, proscribe, require)

B   The hearer not carry out the action indicating that the

hearer *not* do so in virtue of the authority of the speaker over the hearer
(enjoin, forbid, prohibit, proscribe, restrict)

C 'The hearer is to believe the hearer is now entitled to carry out the action in virtue of the speaker's authority over the hearer
(agree to, allow, authorize, bless, consent to dismiss, excuse, exempt, forgive, grant, license, pardon, release, sanction)

D The hearer is to consider the merits of taking the action in virtue of the speaker's belief that there is sufficient reason for the hearer to act
(admonish, advise, caution, counsel, propose, recommend, suggest, urge, warn)

The third genus of illocutionary acts, *Commissives*, are acts in which the speaker expresses his intentions concerning some future action. There are two main species.

Commissives: Speaker intends that his utterance obligates him to carry out the action specified in the propositional content:

A Without any further preconditions
(promise, swear, guarantee, vow)

B Subject to a favourable response by the hearer
(offer, propose, bet, volunteer, bid)

The fourth group of acts, *Evaluatives*, are those acts in which the speaker expresses his attitude towards some earlier action. The following species are typical.

Evaluatives: Speaker expresses:

A Regret for a prior action for the hearer; feels responsible
(apologize)

B Sympathy for the hearer's having suffered
(condole, commiserate)

C Gladness for the hearer's having performed some action
(compliment, congratulate)

D Pleasure at having encountered the hearer
(greet)

E   Gratitude for the hearer's participation in some prior action
    (thank)

Not surprisingly, there are some hybrid acts which seem to fall
into at least two of the genera just discussed. One of these is the
act of inviting, wherein the speaker is both suggesting the hearer
consider the merits of some action and, at the same time, promising that the speaker will approve of the action should the hearer
perform it. Another is the act of surrendering, in which the
speaker both admits defeat (a Representative) and, simultaneously, promises to cease fighting. There are surely more of these,
but we will not discuss them here.

Conditions on illocutionary acts

Austin (1962) introduced three categories of conditions which are
associated with the successful and non-defective performance of
an illocutionary act. Although these conditions are often treated
as equally relevant for the performance of a given act, it is worthwhile to make a distinction between Success Conditions, those
which are necessary and sufficient for the act to have been performed at all, and Felicity Conditions, those conditions in addition
which are required for there to be no defect in the performance.
In the discussion above, the defining conditions on a particular act
constitute its Success Conditions. For requesting, for example,
these require both that the speaker express his desire that the
hearer carry out the act specified in the propositional content of
the utterance and indicate that the hearer do so in virtue of the
speaker's desire.

Felicity conditions, on the other hand, are not required for the
successful performance of the act, but their failure to be met gives
rise to more-or-less serious defects. A first generalization is that
felicity conditions can be inferred from the success conditions by
applying certain general rules of rational behaviour. Considering
the act of requesting, again, we might fairly expect the following:
(1) that the speaker is sincere in his expression of desire that the
hearer act, that is, the speaker really wants the hearer to act; (2)
that a requester believes that the hearer can, in fact, perform the
action; and finally, (3) that the speaker does not believe that the
act is going to be performed in the absence of a request. Of course,
I can successfully request my young son to go upstairs to fetch the
stapler, not really want the stapler but only want him out of the

room, and know that he cannot fulfil the request since the stapler is sitting on the table behind me. Or, again, somewhat defectively, I can ask someone to tell me the time even though I have just heard him tell another that he is about to announce it publicly.

Insincerity is ordinarily not made obvious by the speaker; it is, nevertheless, sometimes obvious. Consider the situation in which someone tells you that he is stone-cold sober while holding a half-empty bottle of Sauterne, reeking of alcohol, and swaying to and fro with glassy eyes. In claiming that he is sober, he expresses the belief that he is sober; certainly by uttering, 'I am sober', he has done this. The speaker has, thus, made a bona fide claim, although a claim that neither the hearer nor probably the speaker himself believes. But the act performed is a claim, nevertheless, since it was the intention of the speaker that his utterance count as such. The obvious insincerity of the speaker does not preclude him from performing the illocutionary act of expressing attitudes he doesn't have; rather, the obvious insincerity prevents the hearer from believing that this belief in sobriety is held by the speaker (if the speaker, at that time, believes anything).

Having presented some idea of the nature of the speech acts we perform as speakers of a language in the process of communicating linguistically, we will now turn to a second, very difficult question: how do we signal our illocutionary intentions?

Performing illocutionary acts

Recall that in characterizing an illocutionary act we defined it in terms of the attitude the speaker intends to express about some proposition. As a shorthand, we will refer to a particular illocutionary act with the notation, $F(P)$, where the F characterizes the attitude to be expressed in performing the act, and the P characterizes the proposition about which the attitude is held.

A more careful consideration of these defining attitudes (not provided here, but see Bach and Harnish (1979), Fraser (1981) reveals that they place restrictions on the proposition about which the attitude is held. For example, an apology involves the speaker's expressing regret for a past act for which the speaker believes he was (at least partly) responsible. Thus, one can normally apologize for stepping on your toe but not for being about to step on your toe, nor for the fact that Harry over there stepped on your toe. Indeed, I can appear to apologize for having to miss your recital tomorrow or appear to apologize for my son's breaking your window, but in the former case my apology addresses my past poor planning, while in the latter I am assuming responsibility for my son's actions although I did not actually participate. The upshot of these observations is that each attitude places some restrictions on the proposition about which the attitude is held.

Returning to the initial question, how the speaker signals his illocutionary intent, it is clear that the utterance meaning – what the speaker says – provides the initial basis on which the hearer operates. But the utterance meaning provides information *beyond* the intended propositional content: it also provides clues to the intended force of the utterance.

When the speaker utters a declarative sentence, for example, 'The cat is on the mat', he is saying that it is the case that the cat is on the mat, and hence he is expressing the belief that the cat is on the mat. The declarative syntactic form entails that the speaker is expressing the attitude of belief toward the propositional content. To utter an imperative sentence is to say that the hearer is to make it the case that the action specified in the propositional content is carried out, hence, the speaker expresses the desire that the hearer carry out the action. To utter a yes/no interrogative sentence, the speaker is expressing his desire that the hearer tell whether or not it is the case that the proposition is true. If a *Wh* question such as, 'Who was there?', is posed, the speaker is expressing his desire that the hearer fill in the missing referential term referred to by the *Wh*-word in the sentence. Syntactic form *does* contribute to sentence meaning and therefore to what the speaker says in uttering a particular sentence. Of course, the use of a simple declarative may only make it clear that the intention of the speaker is to express the attitude of the belief but leave quite open the question of which particular representative act is specifically intended. Sentence meaning does not determine intended force, but it certainly does limit it.

Nevertheless, on the basis of what the speaker says, the hearer can assign an *illocutionary act potential* to the utterance. A sentence has the potential of some particular illocutionary act just in case its propositional content does not violate the propositional constraints on the act (for example, it conforms to the tense, mood, and other constraints), and if the force-indicating aspects of the sentence are consistent with the attitude defining the act. For example, 'I was there', has the potential of a claim but not a prediction, due to the tense of the propositional content, and the potential of a claim but not an order due to its force-indicating properties: the speaker is expressing belief, not desire. A given sentence may have many potential forces, and the problem of which one is intended on a particular occasion can only be resolved by considering the context and the manner of speaking. Certainly a most visible force-indicating property – is the so-called performative verb. Verbs such as *request* and *promise*, when used in sentences such as, 'I request that you sit down' and 'I promise that I will arrive on time', are said to be used performatively because they 'announce' to the hearer the intention of the speaker. In the first sentence, for example, the 'I request' has the force-indicating property of expressing the speaker's intention of having the utterance count as a request, while the 'you sit down' captures the propositional content about which the attitude of requesting is held. One might argue that the speaker in uttering the sentence, 'I request that . . .', is not necessarily saying that he is requesting with that utterance but, rather, that he is reporting on what he characteristically does, for example, when dinner guests are assembled around the table: 'What do I do then? Why, I request that you sit down!' However, this difference turns on the ambiguity of the verb *request* – either it was intended with the habitual interpretation or with the announcing interpretation, the same interpretation intended in the use of the sentence, 'I requested three things in that letter', which is not performative, because of the past tense.

The speaker ordinarily intends the hearer to recognize which particular attitude he holds towards the expressed proposition, either because he has made his intentions explicit or provided clues which enable the hearer to decide. Under such conditions of speaking, we say that the speaker has *directly* performed an illocutionary act; if the intended act is recognized as such by the hearer, then the speaker has directly communicated. Note that the speaker can directly perform a particular illocutionary act either literally or figuratively. If I utter, 'This room is a pigsty', and speak literally, saying that this particular room is a home for pigs, then I have directly claimed that this room is a home for pigs. If I utter the same sentence but intend it to be taken figuratively, thereby saying that this room is a frightful mess, I have directly claimed that this room is a frightful mess. Whether or not I speak literally or figuratively, in both cases I am saying something (part propositional content, part force-indicating properties, as we have now seen), and what it is that I have said is evaluated for its illocutionary force potential. If one of the potential acts is intended, and subsequently recognized, I have directly performed that act.

Of course, the problem of how a hearer determines the specific intended force is not solved. A particular utterance can be analysed to have certain illocutionary force potential, more or less explicitly determined by the utterance meaning; but the hearer must choose among the competing possibilities. Clearly, a model for interpreting intended direct illocutionary force must go beyond determining the illocutionary force potential and provide a theory for how the potential is narrowed down to a single intended force. For example, if I hear someone say, 'I will be there', how do I determine if the person is directly issuing a threat, a warning, a promise or a prediction?

In addition, an adequate theory of pragmatics must account for the fact that some communication is not explicit, but only implied, that is, not direct but indirect. To consider this aspect, we will introduce a notion that we have tacitly assumed in the discussion so far, what we call Mutually Shared Beliefs (MSBs). We will say that a belief is mutually shared just in case that (1) both the speaker and the hearer believe it, (2) each believes the other believes it, and (3) each assumes the other will rely on this belief in their interaction. There is no requirement that what they mutually believe need be true or even sensible. Nor is there any limit in principle on what sorts of things might be mutually believed. For example, two speakers might mutually believe that Rev. Moon has mystical powers, that sentences over nine words signify senility, that people ordinarily lie when talking about sexual abilities, or that pot-smoking causes warts. However, there appear to be certain mutually shared beliefs which aid in using language effectively.[9]

This is nicely illustrated by Grice (1975), who argues that ordinary conversations are governed by a certain set of conversational rules, what he referred to as 'maxims'. However, as Grice points out, although we take these rules to be mutually shared beliefs about how the speakers behave in a conversation, any or all of them may be violated at a given point in a conversation, necessitating the conclusion on the part of the hearer that the speaker has spoken contextually inappropriately, or that some other explanation to account for the violation must be found. The maxims Grice proposes may be summarized as the following:

Quantity: Say no more or no less than is necessary.
Quality: Say what you believe to be true.
Relevance: Be to the point.
Manner: Be clear and brief.

One of the most difficult parts of working with Grice's proposal is the fact that each of the maxims is delightfully vague. What, for example, does it mean to be relevant? In terms of the notions we are working with, we might refine relevance slightly to require that whatever the force of an utterance it follows appropriately within the structure of the conversation, and whatever the content of the illocutionary act, that it abides by the maxims of *Quantity* and *Quality* presented above. Thus, *Relevance* would seem to incorporate the first two of Grice's maxims, although in doing so we haven't solved any important problems.

In addition to Relevance (however one is to eventually characterize this notion), we should mention several other conversational presumptions that a speaker can be expected to be meeting. First, *Sincerity*: that the speaker actually has the attitude that he expresses. For a Representative, that the speaker believes what he says; for a Commissive, that the speaker intends to undertake the commitment, and so forth. Second, *Style*: that the speaker uses a vocabulary and syntax consistent with the speech situation. Third, *Politeness*: that the speaker exercises those rights and fulfils those expectations that the relationship with the other speaker requires; and finally, *Responsibility*: that the speaker's actions are consistent with the ethics of the situation in which he is speaking. Without question, these expectations are vague, surely as vague as Grice's original four, and we offer them only as additional points that a theory of conversational behaviour will eventually have to incorporate in some form or another. At the present moment, it is fair to conclude that if such conversational maxims are not met in a given case, this may be an indication of one of several things: that the speaker intends no particular sentence semantic interpretation; that the speaker is asking the hearer to interpret the utterance figuratively; or that there is a meaning of the utterance intended by the speaker beyond that which is apparent from what the speaker has said. It is this last point we now turn to.

The issue here is what is usually referred to as the performance of *indirect speech acts* – those illocutionary acts which are not *directly* performed in the sense in which we have used the term, but which are intended to be *inferred* by the speaker on the basis of what has been said, the way in which it was said, and the context of speaking.

To begin, we return for a moment to Grice and focus on his notion of *conversational implicature*. Under the assumption that the speaker is cooperating in the conversation, that he is trying to make the required conversational contribution when appropriate and in an appropriate way, then whenever there is a failure to observe a maxim, the hearer must determine what the speaker is intending to convey: what he is intending to *implicate to* the hearer but not say.

For example, suppose I ask you for your opinion of Jones, your student, who is applying for a position, and you reply, 'Mr Jones dresses very carefully and comes to class on time.' Now, if I assume you are still cooperating, I must conclude you have a reason for your failure to provide relevant information. I might conclude that you are attempting to 'tell' me that Jones does not have your recommendation, perhaps 'Jones isn't the right person'. Grice would argue that the second sentence has been implicated. He characterizes conversational implication as follows: In saying S_1, the speaker is implicating S_2 if the speaker is presumed to be acting cooperatively, and if S_2 is required in order for the saying of S_1 to be consistent with behaving cooperatively.

Grice talks about what the speaker says and what the speaker implicates, but does not mention illocutionary force. However, determining what the speaker says is a preliminary step to determining what *direct* illocutionary act has been intended. Analogously, what is *implicated*, in Grice's terms, is what is indirectly said. And it is quite reasonable to move beyond Grice's discussion to talk of what the speaker says and the corresponding direct illocutionary force (whether performed by speaking literally or figuratively) to what the speaker *implicates* and its associated *indirect* illocutionary force.

Placed in this light, Grice's major contribution is to point out how our understanding of what constitutes a normal view of conversational behaviour can, when violated, lead us to work on what might be indirectly intended by the speaker. Native speakers are aware that a hostess speaking on the phone following her party saying, 'I found the most beautiful plant in my living room this morning', is directly reporting her behaviour but indirectly asking, 'Did you give me this plant?' By indirectly requesting the information, she need not commit herself to ignorance of the donor. Courting behaviour is fraught with such indirect communication: few believe that the claim, 'It sure is hot in here', has no indirect intention. And the mother who speaks figuratively to her child saying, 'Your room smells like a barn', is figuratively directly making the claim that the room smells foul, but indirectly ordering that it be cleaned up without delay. Examples abound, as anyone who is familiar with the speech act literature can testify.

That much of what we communicate is done through the performance of indirect speech acts is surely without contest; what is less clear is why certain utterances are construed as reflecting the intention on the part of the speaker to communicate indirectly while others are not. To use an oft-quoted example, if my desire is for you to pass the salt at the dinner table, I can be direct and say, 'Please pass the salt to me', or indirect and say, 'Can you pass the salt?', 'Could I have the salt?', or perhaps, 'Is there any salt on the table?' What I cannot do is utter, 'The price of salt has risen 3¢ per pound over the last year', or 'Who cooked this meal?', or 'I am not suffering from goitre', and, without some special preparation or coding arrangements, expect my listeners to interpret my utterance as an indirect request for the salt.

A variety of efforts have been offered by researchers in pursuit of how the performance of a given illocutionary act relates to those utterances that can, without special considerations, be interpreted as indirectly performing that act. The most common approach has been to first set out (much as we have done above) the definition of the act and then show how particular utterances relate to one or more of the conditions. For example, one felicity condition on requesting is that the speaker believe that the hearer is able to perform the act requested. Hence, asking of the hearer, 'Can you do . . .?', is questioning this presumed speaker belief, and it is argued that an utterance following this principle indirectly performs a request. (It directly 'asks' a yes/no question.) However, like most simple solutions to complicated problems, this approach fails. For the particular case given, it is only necessary to note (as several researchers have done) that semantic variations of the 'can', such as 'Are you able to . . .?' or 'Is it within your ability to . . .?' are clearly not requests of the same sort, if requests at all. Moreover, there are many strategies for requesting indirectly (for example, 'I think the food needs salt' or 'May I ask you to pass the salt?') which do not relate in any obvious way to any of the conditions which characterize the act of requesting.

Leaving aside any necessary relationships between a strategy for performing an illocutionary act indirectly and the defining conditions on the act, a second effort is the approach taken notably by Sadock (1974), who argues that many, although not all, indirect strategies are in reality cases of ambiguity: for example, he argues that 'Can you . . .?' is two ways ambiguous, the first reading counting as a direct request for information, the other counting as a direct (albeit idiomatic) request for action. To support his argument, he marshals evidence that such cases on their 'idiomatic' reading actually behave as imperatives (for example, take *please*) but do not behave as interrogatives (for example, the example above has a variation, 'Do that, can you?', which is not available on the interrogative reading). We will not discuss further the merits of this 'ambiguity' analysis other than to comment that it raises some important distributional questions not as yet answered by any research on the topic. In any event, even if he is correct on some of the cases, there are many which still remain unidiomatic and require explanation in some other way.

Searle (1975) provides a detailed account of how the hearer might proceed logically (although certainly not necessarily in practice) from what the speaker has said to what he indirectly intended.[10] Considering a variety of examples, all of which are used standardly to make an indirect request, for example, 'Can you pass the salt?', he makes the following assumptions: that the sentence meaning does not involve the imperative force; that they are not force-ambiguous (as Sadock would have it) and do have a bona fide literal direct interpretation; that when uttered to make a request, the sentences maintain their literal meaning and are uttered with that meaning intended directly. He suggests that a recontruction of the steps for the hearer to derive the request interpretation to pass the salt from the question about the hearer's ability might run roughly as follows:

1. Speaker requested information about my abilities.
2. I assume he is abiding by the cooperative principle.
3. Context does not indicate any speaker interest in my actual salt-passing ability.
4. Speaker probably already knows the answer to the question.
5. There must, therefore, be some other reason for asking.
6. One condition on a request is the ability of the hearer to perform the act.
7. Thus, the speaker has asked me a question whose affirmative answer would entail that the preparatory condition for requesting me to pass the salt is satisfied.
8. Context is at dinner where passing the salt is appropriate.

9. Speaker has alluded to satisfaction of a preparation condition for a request whose fulfilment is quite reasonable.
10. In the absence of any other plausible illocutionary point, speaker is probably asking me to pass the salt.

Whether or not the logic reflected in the abbreviated account above bears the test of further examination, it does seem clear that for those non-idiomatic cases of indirect performance, there must be some systematic way by which the hearer reaches the intended indirect illocutionary act. In some cases, the path between the direct act (e.g., a claim as in, 'I must apologize for doing that') and the indirect act, an apology, will seem to be quite straightforward; in other cases such as 'That was dumb of me' which is a very different claim, an apology may also be intended. Without going into any detail, we can safely assume that not only will an account take into consideration the conditions defining the intended indirect act, what the speaker has directly done, the manner of speaking, and the context of speaking, but also a set of mutually shared beliefs.

As I have been indicating, although there must be a systematic route between the direct and indirect illocutionary acts, it seems quite clear that the hearer does not and cannot be expected to traverse this route in most instances. Whereas the claim that 'The toast is burned' might require a certain amount of processing to infer that the speaker is indirectly asking you to take the toaster out for repairs, no such processing is required for our 'Can you pass the salt?' It would be possible to reach the requesting interpretation by a sequence of interpretation steps along the lines Searle suggested, but our intuitions are that the move to the indirect request is much more immediate. If we reject the hypothesis that such strategies reflect a sentential ambiguity, we can explain the immediacy with what Bach and Harnish (1979) called the Standardization Thesis: a strategy is standardly used to perform an illocutionary act if and only if it is mutually shared as a belief that generally when someone utters the strategy his illocutionary intent is to indirectly perform the illocutionary act; and when the utterance of this strategy is in a context where its literal direct interpretation would run counter to one's conversational expectations, the speaker generally intends to perform this illocutionary act. Thus, when a strategy is uttered, our mutually shared beliefs about the standard use of this strategy are activated

and thereby permit us as hearers to avoid any complicated inferential processing. It is, of course, the obvious insincerity associated with many of the strategies for indirectly acting that cue the
hearer that the speaker is, in fact, moving directly from the literal
direct interpretation to the standardized indirect one. One need
only consider, 'Can you change $5?' when asked of one's four-
year-old son, or of the cashier selling tickets, or of someone on
the street to recognize how the sense of obvious insincerity varies
with context.

Pragmatic formatives

Let us go back now to the point at which we talked about sentence
meaning, where we stated that a sentence contains both propositional content (perhaps ambiguous) as well as certain illocutionary force-indicating devices. What the speaker says requires the
hearer to choose which of the legs of the sentential ambiguity is
intended or, if figuratively spoken, the intended figurative interpretation, and to then fill in the indexicals (referents of time, place
and person). To determine what direct illocutionary act has been
intended requires the hearer to determine the illocutionary act
potential for what the speaker has said and to decide which of the
potential acts has been intended.

I now wish to suggest that a sentence often, although not always,
contains a third type of meaningful element which is not part of
the propositional content nor of the force-indicating devices. This
element has no semantic content but signals by itself certain types
of Representative Illocutionary Acts. I will call these elements
pragmatic formatives.

Consider the sentence, 'You can damn well leave', which has the
form of a declarative sentence and the propositional content that
you can leave. What, then, is the work being done – if any – by
the *damn well*? I would argue that this lexical formative serves to
convey an illocutionary intent of the speaker, an assertion that the
speaker is angry. We cannot tell why the speaker is angry, since
the focus of the anger is not obvious from the utterance; it may
be that the hearer has not yet left, that the hearer has violated
some social rule, or for any number of other reasons. All we can
tell from *damn well*, on our analysis, is that in addition to claiming
directly that the speaker is able to leave (and perhaps ordering
indirectly that he leave), the speaker is asserting (or claiming, if
you wish) that he is angry. Note that a dictionary definition of

damn well – if the entry is even present – will likely fail to capture the illocutionary intent of this expression. I am not suggesting that such a lexical pragmatic formative can occur willy-nilly in a sentence; far from it. They have very definite and highly restricted privileges of co-occurrence, much as do lexical items with semantic content. But, given that they do occur, I am arguing that they are extra-propositional (or para-propositional) and permit the speaker to *directly* convey more than one illocutionary intent with the same utterance.

Another such pragmatic formative is the familiar *well* which is found in sentence-initial position with a vast number of interpretations:

Well, I would like you to stop now.
Well, it isn't obvious.
Well, what do we have here?
Well, who's going to begin?
Well (now), let me see.
Well, George, how'd we do today?
Well! (à la Jack Benny)

However we are to account for the interpretation of these *wells*, it seems to be dependent on the illocutionary force of the sentence that follows. Important here as well is the fact that the *well* seems to demand different phonological renderings for a given following force. Manner of speaking interacts with lexical material here.

If we have lexical pragmatic formatives, we certainly could expect to find phonological pragmatic formatives. And we do, although they would not properly be part of the sentence but part of the utterance. The speaker who says, 'I will go there tomorrow', intending it as a claim, may say it with clenched teeth, conveying the assertion that he is angry, or a wavering voice, conveying the assertion that he is anxious, and so forth. What I am suggesting here is unsubstantiated by empirical results, but their formatives appear to function as part of linguistic communication. Each of these pragmatic formatives ought to be viewed as pragmatic idioms, much like 'How about V-ing?' is an idiom, where its pragmatic interpretation – 'I suggest that you V' – cannot be systematically derived from its component parts.

Representing emotional states of the speaker is not the only function of lexical or phonological pragmatic formatives. The lexical item, *please*, is another such formative which does not function as part of the proposition with which it may be associated in a sentence. But *please*, rather than conveying an emotional state of the speaker, communicates an aspect of the speaker's belief about the relationship between himself and the hearer. In using *please*, the speaker is intending to communicate some aspect of the relationship between himself and the hearer, and this communication takes the form of a representative, an assertion. The utterance, 'Please sit down', is literally and directly a directive (probably a request but perhaps a polite order) but also, literally and directly, the assertion that the speaker owes the hearer some signal of deference. This belief need not rest on the assumption that the speaker is of lower status than the hearer, for people in authority often hold this position towards subordinates, except in the military or in paramilitary organizations.

Moreover, there are numerous other ways in which the speaker can indirectly make an assertion about deference.[11] To request the salt with, 'Would you mind passing the salt?' is far more deferential than 'I would like the salt,' and this interpretation derives from the fact that the first example makes an indirect claim that the speaker owes the hearer deference; while the second makes just the opposite claim. Note, that these claims are associated with the particular strategy selected to indirectly communicate the request. Only after the hearer has determined that either of the above-mentioned utterances was used to indirectly issue a directive (while directly used to ask a question or make a statement of desire, respectively) can he then infer from the strategy used to convey the directive the accompanying claim of speaker deference.[12]

Perlocutionary acts

Let us now turn to the third aspect of using language, namely, intending to have some effect(s) on the hearer because of what was said and because of the force of the utterance. Austin (1962) coined the term 'perlocutionary acts' (or effects), arguing that

> Saying something will often, or even normally, produce
> certain consequential effects upon the feelings, thoughts, or
> actions of the audience, or of the speaker, or of other
> persons . . . we shall call the performance of an act of this
> kind the performance of a perlocutionary act or
> perlocution . . . (perlocutionary acts) are not conventional,
> although conventional acts may be made use of in order to

> bring off the perlocutionary act . . . It is characteristic of
> perlocutionary acts that the response achieved or the sequel
> can be achieved by additional or entirely by non-locutionary
> means: thus, intimidation may be achieved by waving a
> stick or pointing a gun. (p. 119)

Thus, the effect of an utterance may be to convince you, surprise
you, bore you, annoy you, intimidate you, please you, cause you
to find the speaker pompous, or insult you. And the effect (or
effects) of a particular utterance may or may not have been
intended by the speaker. In uttering, 'Sit right down here, dam-
mit', I may very well intend my utterance to intimidate you. On
the other hand, my utterance of 'How nice of you to invite me'
may totally surprise and confuse you if you believe you never
invited me to the party.

In contrast to illocutionary acts, if a perlocutionary effect is
intended, there is no conventional way for the speaker to guarantee that it will be brought about. Indeed, if I say to you that
fifteen studies have shown that cigarette-smokers develop lung
cancer three times more often than non-smokers, and intend this
to convince you that cigarette-smoking is dangerous to your
health, I might feel confident that I will convince you. But there
is no way to guarantee success in convincing you even if you recognize my purpose in speaking was to do so. Perlocutionary effects
come about not as a *part* of linguistic communication, but because
of linguistic communication and how it relates to some more general area of human interaction. Perlocutionary effects are not part
of pragmatics.

This means, then, that perlocutionary effects cannot be systematically related to illocutionary acts. But it does not mean that
intended perlocutionary effects are not standardly associated with
given illocutionary acts. We use the term 'standard' here, as earlier, to refer to what is usually anticipated to be the case, but need
not be.

There appear to be two types of association. The first involves
the association of the intended effect with the particular act itself.
Recall that in making an apology the speaker intends to express
his regret for some prior act for which he believes he bears some
responsibility. Standardly associated with an apology is the
intended perlocutionary effect to put right the currently out-of-
joint social relationship. Similarly, associated with the act of
requesting is the intention of the speaker to convince the hearer

to actually carry out the request; associated with the act of claiming is the intention to convince the hearer to believe the propositional content of the claim; and associated with the act of promising is the speaker's intention to please the hearer as a result of the promise.

But, although we can argue that there is some small set of speaker intentions such as these standardly associated with a particular illocutionary act, these intentions are *not* part of the definition of the act, nor are they necessarily true of the speaker's intentions when he performs the act. I can issue an apology because I believe it will get you off my back, not because I want to reinstate our former cordial relationship; I can request you to do something but not really want you to carry it out; I can claim something and not intend you to believe it, merely wanting to impress on you the strength of my own beliefs and I can promise because I feel I ought to, not because I wish to please you in any way.

What should be apparent from these examples is that each of them violates in some way what Austin dubbed the 'felicity conditions' on the illocutionary act: those conditions which when violated give rise to minor defects in the performance of the act. What I am suggesting here is that most, if not all, of Austin's felicity conditions are correctly analysed as indicating perlocutionary intentions of the speaker which are standardly associated with the performance of the act. But just like his own felicity conditions, their violation surprises one but doesn't vitiate the act itself.

The second type of standard association of intended perlocutionary effect is not with the type of illocutionary act performed, as above, but rather with the content of the act itself. The best example I know of is the area of insults.[13] Many insults are carried off in the guise of a simple Representation, more specifically, a claim. However, the content of the claim embodies some characteristic that is devalued in that society. This might be done, for example, by literally telling someone, 'You are the dumbest person I've ever met', given that the property of lacking intelligence is devalued; or it may be done figuratively, for example, by saying to someone, 'Your breath is so bad it would knock a buzzard off a manure wagon', and letting the listener figure out just how badly he has been insulted. Relevant to our discussion is the fact that certain intended perlocutionary effects are standardly associated with specific propositional content.

Conclusion

'Pragmatics' has enjoyed a wide range of interpretations, thereby contributing more confusion to an area of language already suffering from a paucity of clear theoretical proposals. In the preceding, I have attempted to present one view of what ought to be embodied in a pragmatic theory and argued that it should be seen as a theory of linguistic communication. Such a theory depends upon linguistic theory to provide an account of sentence meaning, and must, if it is to become an adequate account, provide a model for how the hearer determines what the speaker is saying and recognizes both the intended direct and indirect illocutionary force(s). In contrast to many statements about pragmatics, my account does not entail notions of conversational structure, conversational interaction, discourse analysis, text analysis, or communicative competence. These areas go well beyond the domain of pragmatics, although it is clear a theory of any one of these would include a pragmatic theory, much as a pragmatic theory includes a theory of grammar.

The paper contains a number of suggestions, indicates some research insights, and poses some problem areas. It is, however, only an overview to the area, and certainly not intended to present a theory. There is no theory of pragmatics at present, of whatever the domain, but it is my hope that by limiting the area of investigation, a beginning will be made.

Notes

1. I wish to thank Robert M. Harnish, Steven Horst, and Jean Fraser for many critical and insightful comments during the development of this paper. None of them agrees with all herein, for which I cannot blame them.
2. These three types of acts correspond to Austin's (1962) taxonomy of Locutionary, Illocutionary, and Perlocutionary Acts. I will use this terminology later on.
3. The reader is referred to Bach and Harnish (1979) for a detailed and controversial account of a theory of linguistic communication.
4. Much humour relies on the hearer failing to recognize the potential ambiguity of a sentence until it is 'too late'. We will assume humourless conversation for purposes of discussion.
5. Obviously, any adequate pragmatic theory would have to explain just how such disambiguation is brought about. For our purposes, however, identifying the problem as one of those encompassed by the theory is sufficient.
6. A useful reference for figurative language in general and metaphor in particular is Ortony (1979).

7. A more detailed analysis can be found in Bach and Harnish (1979). The present discussion does not include what we call 'Ceremonial Acts', for example, doubling at bridge, baptizing, christening, adjourning a meeting, which are analysed in Fraser (1981) as special cases of the following analysis.

8. It is important to distinguish between the names of verbs and the names of illocutionary acts. In general, each act is named by a single verb, but this is not always the case; for example, *avow* and *aver* appear to refer to the same act, at least on one reading. We will use verb names for convenience without worrying about this distinction.

9. This term is borrowed from Bach and Harnish (1979). One special type of MSB is what we call conventions, a mutually recognized means for doing something, counting as such only because it is mutually recognized, perhaps by having been agreed upon or learned as such. We say that X is a convention for doing A just in the case that it is a mutually shared belief that to X is to do A and that X counts as doing A only because it is mutually believed to be the case. All donotative word meaning is conventional; for example, that the word 'table' refers to the sort of objects that my typewriter is sitting on and saying 'table' counts as referring to this sort of object only because we, as speakers of English, believe it to count as this. Similarly, the raised hand with two fingers in the 'v' position is a signal of victory (or 'peace'), but a convention only in certain societies. Note that although we might mutually believe that putting on a coat is an effective way to get warm, putting on a coat does not reach the status of a convention unless and un'il it counts as a way to get warm because it is mutually believed to ι e the case. It is, of course, an interesting question if many mutually shared beliefs reach the level of a convention without some underlying basis for practical belief.

10. See also Bach and Harnish (1979), and Fraser (1981), for alternative analysis of such examples.

11. See Fraser and Nolen (1980), for analysis of deference and its relationship to the concept of politeness.

12. See Fraser (1981b) for a discussion of insults in general and some cross-cultural differences in particular. In the preceding discussion, I suggested that part of the linguistic communication and hence part of pragmatics are certain perlocutionary intentions standardly associated with a given illocutionary act or its content. In these cases, the fact that the speaker intends to cause the particular perlocutionary effect was overt; in these cases, the likelihood of success is enhanced to the extent that the hearer is aware of the speaker's intentions. However, not all intended perlocutionary effects enjoy such openness; in fact, there appears to be a continuum.

Kidding, for example, is, roughly, to say something about someone but not really mean it – or not mean it if challenged. In general, you can't kid someone you don't know, and the better you know the hearer the more liberal and potentially damaging you can make your kidding. The utterance of 'Nice going!' to a friend who has just fallen on the ski slopes would be acceptable kidding, while the same statement to Jean-Claude Killy would be taken in a very different vein. We sometimes intend to kid another without his immediately or even ultimately being aware of our intention. (Of course, if there is no appreciative audience, it would seem futile to covertly kid someone.)

13. Deception, on the other hand, lies at an extreme end of the overtness continuum, since one can be successful in deceiving another only if this purpose is not recognized. It is obvious, then, why we wouldn't expect to find any perlocutionary intentions of deceiving being standardly associated with an illocutionary act. It is interesting that while deception can be brought about by various misrepresenting tactics such as stating or implicating something you know to be false, or using a sentence with a presupposition that you know to be false, only the first case, stating something false, has a name – *lying*.

Questions for discussion, study and further research

1. When we use language we characteristically intend to do three things: (1) we say something; (2) we indicate how we intend the hearer to take what we have said; and (3) we have definite effects on the hearer as a result. Collect ten examples of utterances you have observed and discuss them according to the three dimensions identified in the quotation.

2. In English, the body is used as the source of a great deal of figurative language. Consider, for example, expressions such as: to stick one's neck out, to take it on the chin, to carry a burden on one's shoulders, to give someone a cold shoulder, etc. Collect as many additional examples as possible. Do these seem to you to be metaphors or idioms, as these are defined in this chapter?

3. Classify the following examples, labelling each utterance according to illocutionary act type. Which are representatives, directives, etc? Which utterances are ambiguous or indirect? Discuss the relationships between syntactic form and direct or indirect illocutionary point in these examples and others you may run across.

Dinner is served.
This is one game I'm going to win, no matter what.
Unfortunately, I'll be out of town when you arrive.
Wow, this is a great apartment.
I'd like everybody to be on time for Monday's meeting.

It is my unpleasant duty to inform you that your services are no longer required.

Thank you for not smoking. (sign posted in public place)

4. Examine a paragraph of written discourse and discuss the relationships you find in it between direct and indirect illocutionary point.

5. Tape-record a dinner table conversation at home, after getting permission from everyone present, and analyse it according to pragmatic theory. What kinds of illocutionary acts occur most frequently? What kinds of deference markers can you identify? Can you find examples of pragmatic formatives? How do illocutionary act realizations vary depending on who is speaking to whom or what is being talked about?

6. Collect at least twenty directives (requests, etc.) from real life interaction and analyse them. How do speakers signal their illocutionary intents to hearers in your examples?

7. Can you identify success conditions and felicity conditions for other types of speech acts than those discussed on p. 41, e.g. for *threats*?

8. Are illocutionary act strategies universal? Choose one type of act, e.g. suggestions or apologies, and think of all the possible ways to communicate such acts in English. Then consider another language you know well, and subject it to the same kind of analysis. Compare your results. Do all of the English forms have equivalent forms (exact or close translations) in the other language? Do translational equivalents in the two languages generally convey the same act? With comparable levels of deference?

9. Can you find real examples, through observation of conversational interaction, of where speakers fail to communicate intentions to hearers? How do they correct these miscommunications?

10. The discussion in this chapter has not specifically dealt with humour, although the components of linguistic communication discussed here may all be systematically manipulated for humorous effect. Examine some humorous prose, or collect some jokes. To what extent does humour in your data derive from what is said, what is communicated, or the perlocutionary effect of what is said?

Introduction to Chapter 3

Nessa Wolfson's paper complements Bruce Fraser's account of the pragmatic dimensions of communication by broadening the perspective of what the participants in a speech event must know in order to communicate effectively, to include knowledge of what she refers to as *rules of speaking*. These include knowledge not only of the lexical and grammatical system of the language, but of the communicative system of the language, namely, how it is appropriate to talk to different types of speakers, what it is appropriate to talk about, how different sorts of speech events develop as discourse, etc. Wolfson focusses on three aspects of rules of speaking: (1) *address-systems*, which govern the terms of address which speakers use in social interaction: (2) *remedial interchanges* and interactional strategies which create a suitable atmosphere for communication and which may serve to remedy difficulty in social encounters (cf. Canale's discussion of *strategic competence*): and (3) *speech acts* such as apologies, invitations and compliments.

Wolfson draws attention to the potential difficulty in second language learning and communication created by differences between L1 and L2 conventions for rules of speaking. She surveys research that has been carried out in this area, and emphasizes the need for empirical research on rules of speaking and discusses its relevance to applied linguistics. She discusses differences between linguistic norms for the realization of particular categories of speech acts and shows how such differences can lead to misunderstanding in cross-cultural communication.

3 Rules of speaking[1]

Nessa Wolfson

From the point of view of language learning and of intercultural communication, it is important to recognize that the individual who wishes to learn a new language must, in addition to acquiring a new vocabulary and a new set of phonological and syntactic rules, learn what Hymes (1972a) calls the rules of speaking: the patterns of sociolinguistic behaviour of the target language. Applied linguistics as a discipline has broadened in recent years as scholars in the field have increasingly recognized the need to include the insights and perspectives of sociolinguistic studies. It is a well-known axiom of sociolinguistics that languages differ from one another not only in such areas as phonology, syntax and lexicon, but in the very use to which these linguistic resources are put. Patterns of interaction vary, sometimes strikingly, from one speech community to another. Indeed, if we agree with Hymes (1972a, b), it is just this which sets one speech community off from another since his very definition of a speech community implies that members share not only a language but also knowledge of the speech conduct appropriate to the various events which make up their daily existence.

It follows from this that the understanding and knowledge of appropriate speech behaviour is crucial if learners are to communicate effectively with native speakers of the language they are learning. Communicative competence thus includes not only the mastery of grammar and lexicon, but also the rules of speaking; for example, knowing when it is appropriate to open a conversation and how, what topics are appropriate to particular speech events, which forms of address are to be used to whom and in which situations, and how such speech acts as greetings, compliments, apologies, invitations and complaints are to be given, interpreted and responded to.

Since how people speak is part of what they say, language learners may be unable to interpret the meaning of an utterance even though they 'know all the words'. Worse, they may interpret what they hear according to the rules of speaking of their native language, thus frequently misunderstanding the speaker's intention and perhaps perceiving insincerity or offence where none was meant. As will be seen in the discussion which follows, such seemingly simple interactions as those involving conversational openings, invitations and compliments are all open to serious misinterpretation on the part of the language learner, misinterpretation which may lead to shock, disappointment and even grievous insult. In addition to the problem of misunderstanding the meaning or function of what is said, language learners face the equally serious problem of having their own speech behaviour misunderstood by native speakers with whom they interact. A form of address or a personal question which may be perfectly appropriate or even mandatory in the learner's native language might, when translated into the new language and its setting, seem absurd or even insulting. The sort of miscommunication which occurs when people transfer the rules of their own native speech communities to what seems to them to be a corresponding situation in a new speech community may be termed, as Hymes (personal communication) suggests, *communicative interference*.

What needs to be understood here is that rules of speaking, or more generally, norms of interaction are both culture specific and largely unconscious. This means that speakers, although perfectly competent in the uses and interpretation of patterns of speech behaviour which prevail in their own communities, are, with the exception of a few overtly taught formulas, quite unconscious of the patterned nature of their own speech behaviour and generally unaware that quite different norms and patterns are likely to prevail in other societies. In interacting with foreigners, native speakers tend to be rather tolerant of errors in pronunciation or syntax. In contrast, violations of rules of speaking are often interpreted as bad manners since the naive native speaker is unlikely to be aware of sociolinguistic relativity. For these reasons, it has been stressed again and again (e.g. Paulston 1974, Wolfson and Taylor 1978) that language instruction must not be limited to the teaching of the traditional written and oral skills but rather that the aim of such instruction must be what has come to be known as communicative competence (cf. Hymes 1972b).

The inclusion of sociolinguistic interests within language teaching and the recognition of the necessity to make communicative competence the goal of the second language curriculum is a major step both for the theory and the practice of language teaching. Nevertheless, it is necessary for us to be aware of an important problem which arises from this alliance of applied linguistics with sociolinguistics. It is not enough simply to be willing to teach sociolinguistic rules. What must be understood and what has, unfortunately, not been recognized, is that in order to make such material an intrinsic part of classroom second or foreign language instruction, teachers and writers of textbooks need specific information as to what the rules of speaking *are*. Too often the assumption has been made that persons who are themselves native speakers of English are already in possession of the conscious knowledge necessary to impart these rules to others. This assumption is, unfortunately, unwarranted. While it is true that the intuitions of the native speaker may be a useful tool in the recognition and analysis of sociolinguistic rules, it is, nevertheless, of extreme importance to realize that the rules themselves are generally well below the level of conscious awareness. It is only through training in sociolinguistic analysis and through careful research that it is possible to discover the underlying patterns which make up the rules of speaking of any language, including one's own. That this is true should come as no surprise to anyone who has ever attempted to teach the phonological or grammatical rules of his own language without first having been trained to do so. The fact is that untrained native speakers, although they obviously 'know' the rules of their language, are generally unaware of their structures and the extent to which such usage is patterned. The untrained native speaker would be hard put to explain to a learner why, for example, it is correct to say 'who went?' but not 'why he went?' The analogy is clear enough. It must not be assumed that teachers, simply because they follow a set of sociolinguistic rules in their daily lives, have conscious access to these rules or can be objective enough to teach them without specific training.

In contrast, native speakers have little difficulty in recognizing when a sociolinguistic rule has been broken and, depending on how complex the rule is, will usually be able to say what they think *should* have been done. That is, native speakers are usually able to express the *norms* of their own speech communities. The problem here is that norms express ideals and may be very far from actual behaviour (Blom and Gumperz 1972). If learners are to be able to interpret and conform to the rules, they will need instruction based on how people *actually* speak in their everyday interactions, not about how they *think* they speak.

What is needed, then is systematic empirical analysis of the everyday speech behaviour of native speakers so that patterns may be uncovered, described and taught. A great deal of work remains to be done, for while there has been much valuable research on the rules of speaking in a wide variety of societies (Hymes 1964a, Fishman 1968, Gumperz and Hymes 1972, Bauman and Sherzer 1974) it is still the case that no one is yet in a position to describe the rules for even one speech community.

When we look specifically for analyses of sociolinguistic usage in American English, we find that although much remains to be done, a good start has been made. In the remainder of this paper, I will review some of the findings which have been reported and discuss work currently in progress.

One of the earliest studies of sociolinguistic behaviour in American English focussed on terms of address. In an article first published in 1961, Roger Brown and Marguerite Ford set forth a model of the reciprocal and non-reciprocal patterns which govern the way middle class Americans address one another. Brown and Ford took their data from plays, from naturalistic observation and from self-reports in the form of questionnaires, a method which enabled them not only to discover a pattern but to cross-check it. They found that most dyads in this society follow a reciprocal pattern, addressing each other by mutual first name (FN) or by mutual title plus last name (TLN) but that of these, the vast majority used mutual FN. According to their data, mutual TLN is usually found between newly acquainted adults, when TLN occurs at all. In addition to the reciprocal patterns of address, Brown and Ford also found a non-reciprocal pattern in which one member of the dyad gives FN but receives TLN, by virtue of greater occupational status or age. Where age and status do not coincide, status will prevail over age such that if the younger member of the dyad has higher occupational status, s/he will receive TLN while using FN to address the interlocutor. Neither usage is, of course, static, and a change or perceived change in the relationship (including simply further acquaintance) may result in a switch from TLN, whether mutual or non-reciprocal, to FN. What is of particular interest, however, is that in either case, the initiative to switch from the more to the less formal term of address must always come from the person of higher status or greater age.

What is particularly useful about Brown and Ford's model is that it provides a concrete way of looking at address systems, and makes it possible for native speakers to expand and elaborate on these rules, using little more than casual observation to see how the rules of their own speech communities coincide with those described by Brown and Ford. Thus, building upon this earlier work, Ervin-Tripp (1969) gives a much fuller description of the rules of address for American English. From the point of view of the second language teacher, Ervin-Tripp's discussion is extremely valuable since she includes not only the rules for using FN or TLN, but goes into a detailed description of occupational titles. It is important for the learner of American English to know for example that:

> A priest, physician, dentist, or judge may be addressed by title alone, but a plain citizen or an academic person may not. In the latter cases, if the name is unknown, there is no address form (or zero, ø) available and we simply no-name the addressee. The parentheses below refer to optional elements, the bracketed elements to social selectional categories.
>
> | [Cardinal]: | Your excellency |
> |---|---|
> | [US President]: | Mr President |
> | [Priest]: | Father (+ LN) |
> | [Nun]: | Sister (+ religious name) |
> | [Physician]: | Doctor (+ LN) |
> | [Ph.D., Ed.D.], etc.: | (Doctor + LN) |
> | [Professor]: | (Professor + LN) |
> | [Adult], etc.: | (Mister + LN) |
> | | (Mrs + LN) |
> | | (Miss + LN) |
>
> Whenever the parenthetical items cannot be fully realized, as when the last name (LN) is unknown, and there is no lone title, the addressee is no-named by a set of rules of the form as follows: Father + ø → Father, Professor + ø → ø, Mister + ø → ø, etc. An older male addressee may be called 'sir', if deference is intended, as an optional extra marking.
>
> (Ervin-Tripp 1969, pp. 20–21)

As Ervin-Tripp points out, language learners may deviate from the system by making either sociolinguistic or linguistic errors. A linguistic error would involve using a form of address which is outside the system altogether, such as 'Thank you, Mrs' and although it will be judged as strange or foreign by native speakers, it is very unlikely to be interpreted as insulting. A sociolinguistic error, on the other hand, would involve the use of a linguistically correct form to the 'wrong' person (e.g., the use of TLN to a classmate or of FN to someone of much higher status) and is very likely to be interpreted as offensively cold or overfamiliar as the case may be. Obviously, it is important for the learner to know that the form *Mrs*, unlike the parallel forms *Miss* or *Mr*, is not a free form in modern American English and cannot be used without the addition of the addressee's last name. However, it is impossible to state too strongly that of the two kinds of errors, linguistic and sociolinguistic, it is the sociolinguistic error which is the more significant as it will cause the learner to be judged more harshly.

It should be noted that sociolinguistic rules are subject to considerable variation with respect to region and social class. Thus, Wolfson and Manes (1979) report that the address form 'ma'am' has different meanings in the south of the United States than it has in the northeast and that it occurs in rather different sociolinguistic contexts. In the south, the single term *ma'am* functions as the equivalent of *I beg your pardon?* or *Pardon?* to indicate that the speaker would like the addressee to repeat what was said. In addition, it was found that the phrase *yes, ma'am* functions as an alternant to *you're welcome* and thus frequently occurs in response to an expression *thank you*. With respect to context, it was found that the term *ma'am* occurs not only between strangers as it does in the northeast, but was also used to acquaintances and even intimates who had the same or lower status:

> For example, when a graduate student at the University of Virginia brought one of her professors a cup of coffee, the professor responded with 'Thank you, ma'am'. Similarly a male colleague of one of the researchers, who is a good deal older than she is and who generally addresses her by first name or a diminutive, responds to direct questions from her with 'yes, ma'am' or 'no, ma'am'. Even more striking to a transplanted northerner, is the young man from South Carolina who, when his wife says something which he does not hear, questions her with 'ma'am'.
>
> (Wolfson and Manes 1979)

With respect to social class differences in the use of terms of address, Ervin-Tripp (1969) remarks that members of lower-status occupational groups often use titles such as *Doctor* without last name as address forms and this author has frequently been so addressed by maintenance men, for example, though never by students. Because Brown and Ford's model is rather general, it allows for such sociolinguistic variation, and once aware of the general principles, teachers should have little difficulty in describing the specifics for the particular speech community in question.

Another dimension along which sociolinguistic rules are likely to vary is that of time. With respect to rules of address, it is clear that considerable changes have occurred over the last twenty years, a fact which must obviously be taken into consideration when writing and revising textbook materials. Twenty years ago it was common for university instructors to exchange mutual TLN with their students while it is now not uncommon to hear mutual FN in the same circumstances, although in many places the student receives non-reciprocal FN, addressing the instructor as TLN. Since these rules are subject to change over time in general and also over the span of a particular relationship, it is important to point out, as Brown and Ford are careful to do, that where speakers are uncertain of the appropriate form of address, they may choose to use no form at all. It is, in fact, quite useful for learners to know that the practice of using the zero form, or no-naming, is not at all uncommon in American English, and will be far less noticeable than the erroneous choice of a sociolinguistically inappropriate form.

Another aspect of address rules has to do with the way Americans address strangers in public situations, and specifically in service encounters (e.g., address by waiters, sales clerks, gas station attendants). In this regard it is of interest to point out that women in American society are often addressed with a good deal less deference than are men. In an ethnographic study of the forms of address used to women in service encounters (Wolfson and Manes 1979) approximately 1,000 naturally occurring interactions were observed and recorded in which women of various ages, occupations and ethnic backgrounds were addressed by men and women of equally varying backgrounds. Although it is generally assumed (and often stated in ESL textbooks) that where names are unknown, the respect forms *ma'am* and *sir* will be used, this was not found to be altogether the case. In actual fact, a woman whose name is unknown may be addressed as *ma'am*, as zero (no address form at all) or by a so-called term of endearment such as *hon* or *dear*. Two of these three major address types occurring in service encounters are used in quite parallel fashion to men and women. That is, both sexes may be addressed with the appropriate respect form, *ma'am* or *sir*, or both may be addressed by the zero form, no address term at all. The third address type, terms of endearment, are used infrequently to males in service encounters and apparently never by other males. Women, on the other hand, quite frequently receive terms of endearment both from men and from other women. Thus, it is quite common for the same speaker to address a series of male and female customers regularly using *sir* to the males and *dear* or *hon* to the females. There are no instances of the reverse occurring. What is particularly interesting about this usage is that it is non-reciprocal and therefore carries with it the implication that the addressee is in some sense subordinate to the speaker. Thus, the fact that females of all ages and occupations are addressed publicly in this way may be seen as a sign that females as a group are taken less seriously in American society than are males. Since individual speakers who use these terms of endearment to women are merely following a general pattern of speech usage, the learner of American English should be warned not to take offence when she is addressed in this way. On the other hand, it must be pointed out that since many American women *are* irritated by being addressed in this way and since the usage clearly has sexist overtones, it would be much better for learners to avoid using these forms.

The concept behind the use of appropriate forms of address is not difficult for language learners to grasp since all languages make use of address forms in some sense. Indeed, it has been pointed out (e.g. Ferguson 1976, Brown and Levinson 1978) that politeness may itself be universal and that it is likely that all languages make use of precoded routines or what Ferguson calls 'politeness formulas' which speakers are expected to utter under the appropriate conditions. Erving Goffman, whose work has focussed on the everyday behaviour of the American middle classes, has observed that in our society these linguistic formulas serve to create and maintain what he calls 'the public order' (Goffman 1971). An example is what Goffman calls the remedial interchange in which speakers attempt to remedy potentially difficult social situations by offering an explanation or an apology. Interested more in the overall patterns of social interaction than in the rules for the use of specific formulas, Goffman himself does not go into detail about the forms themselves or their distribution, but two scholars, Borkin and Reinhart (1978) have done a very useful analysis of two formulaic expressions associated with apologies; *excuse me* and *I'm sorry*.

According to this basically semantic analysis, the form *I'm sorry*, though commonly thought of as the expression of apology in English, is not necessarily used to apologize at all. Rather the authors find that *I'm sorry* is basically an expression of dismay or regret about a state of affairs viewed or portrayed as unfortunate. Thus it is perfectly appropriate for English speakers to say *I'm sorry* even when no injury or potential injury has been inflicted on the addressee when there is no question of a social norm being violated. The form *excuse me*, on the other hand, is found to be specifically used to 'remedy a past or immediately forthcoming breach of etiquette' on the part of the speaker. Of course the authors recognize that there is an area of overlap and that both *excuse me* and *I'm sorry* may be used as remedies. Nevertheless, they insist that the basic meanings of the forms differ and that the semantic distinction which they have isolated is related directly to the patterns of usage found:

> *Excuse me* is more appropriate in remedial exchanges when the speaker's main concern is about a rule violation on his or her part, while *I'm sorry* is used in remedial interchanges when the speaker's main concern is about a violation of another person's rights or damage to another person's feelings; in other words, the basic concern behind *excuse me* is 'I have broken or am in danger of breaking a social rule', and the basic concern behind *I'm sorry* is 'You are or you may be hurt'. Even in situations which either of the two forms might be used to perform the same remedial function, we feel that *excuse me* primarily expresses the speaker's relationship to a rule or a set of rules, while *I'm sorry* primarily expresses the speaker's relation to another person.

These generalizations are extremely interesting and useful. As Borkin and Reinhart point out, *excuse me* and *I'm sorry* are frequently used inappropriately by learners, and native speaking teachers are themselves unable to explain what the rules are:

> . . . Being native speakers of English is not enough to equip teachers with the kind of conscious knowledge of sociolinguistic rules that is necessary to help students use these formulae in routine, but important, social interactions with native speakers of English.

Borkin and Reinhart make no claim to have worked out all the sociolinguistic rules for apologizing in American English; they are interested specifically in the use of just these two forms. Unfortunately, theirs is the only detailed attempt to analyse the rules of speaking for such remedial formulas. The fact is that speakers do use expressions other than *excuse me* and *I'm sorry* and therefore, although this analysis is a useful contribution, we are still in the awkward position of not knowing where to place the other forms (e.g., *I apologize*) in this semantic set. A study which took as its focus the giving of apologies rather than certain specific semantic items might well turn up a range of other forms and routines which would make it possible to describe this speech act more fully.

One of the most tantalizing aspects of a study of apologies is that such an analysis could not help but lead to a great deal of additional information on other rules of speaking in American English. A description of appropriate usage would, after all, need to indicate when and under what circumstances such remedies are called for. The fact that some of these occasions will necessarily be related to violations of sociolinguistic rules means that such a study would automatically shed light on the norms of speaking for that group. Again, as in all rules of speaking, these norms will be culture bound in a way not always appreciated even by scholars whose business it is to study language use.

An interesting cross-cultural example of the differing rules for the occurrence of apologies is given by Godard (1977) in her analysis of telephone call beginnings in the United States and France. Although she agrees with Schegloff (1968) that the ringing of the telephone and the answerer's 'Hello' together constitute a summons-response sequence, she points out that there is a difference in the way the two societies regard the speech event of telephoning and that these different viewpoints cause speakers to follow quite different rules. While it is mandatory for a French caller to apologize for disturbing the answerer, no such apologies are required in the United States unless the call is made at a time known to be inappropriate. This is not to say that Americans never begin telephone calls by apologizing but it does mean that such behaviour is not expected and that in interpreting the behaviour of American callers, non-active speakers should not conclude that rudeness is intended. Rather, says Godard, people in the United States have a different attitude toward the telephone than do, for example, the French. Here the initiation of a telephone conversation is seen as positive social behaviour and people often call one another for no other purpose than to keep in touch and to chat. French callers are expected not only to check that they have reached the right number and to identify themselves but also to apologize for having interrupted the answerer, while callers in the United States may simply begin a conversation after the initial greetings have been exchanged. Godard found it particularly striking that callers in the United States, if they have not reached the intended addressee, frequently ask for him or her directly, behaving as though the answerer were merely a part of the instrument even when he may, in fact, be an acquaintance. No such behaviour is possible in France, where the caller is expected to chat for a time with any acquaintance who happens to answer the telephone, whether or not the answerer is the intended addressee. On the other hand, Godard found that if the intended addressee was unavailable, callers in the United States would always identify themselves to the answerer; leaving one's name appears to be obligatory even if there is no possibility that the message will be passed on (see Godard 1977).

Schegloff's (1968) analysis of the way telephone call beginnings are sequenced points out that in the United States, the ring of the telephone is heard as a summons and that the person who answers it must always be the one to say hello. It is then up to the caller to introduce the first topic of the conversation which proceeds in an a-b-a-b-a-b sequence. In discussing the forms used for self-identification, Schegloff makes the point that in telephone conversations, it is customary to frame one's name by saying 'This is _____', a form never used in face-to-face interaction except when introducing a third party. He then goes on to say that the frame, 'I am _____', which frequently occurs in face-to-face interaction is never used on the telephone while the frame, 'My name is _____' may be used in both speech situations. My own analysis of these frames is somewhat different. While I agree with Schegloff that 'This is _____' is a very common frame for self-identification on the telephone, I do not agree that the frame 'I am _____' is used for self-identification at all. Rather, 'I am _____', like 'My name is _____' functions as a means of self-introduction, and it may be used both on the telephone and in face-to-face interactions. Observational data indicate that 'I am _____', when used in telephone calls, is usually given the further frame, 'You don't know me but . . .' and serves not only to introduce the speaker but also to lead into the reason for the call.

The rules for self-identification in telephone call openings are, of course, quite variable across cultures. Schmidt (1975) in a comparison of telephone call beginnings in Cairo, examined three interactions between two Germans, two Americans and two Egyptians and found that of these, only the German answerer identifies himself without being asked to do so. The American caller verifies that he has reached his intended addressee by saying her name ('Betsey?') with rising question intonation, while the Egyptian interlocutors counter one another's greetings and demands for identification until they have successfully guessed each other's identity:

> The first thing we notice is that at the beginning of the conversation there is a series of *hellos* with no identification by either speaker. On his second turn, the caller requests identification from the answerer, but this is refused by the answerer, who counters by demanding the identity of the caller. The caller in turn leaves the question of his identity unanswered, but instead guesses the identity of the answerer. The answerer then attempts to guess the identity of the caller. After both guesses are confirmed, talk proceeds through a series of greetings and responses until finally after twelve speaking turns, the message is introduced – or at least the caller has indicated that he has a topic to introduce. A common reaction of foreigners living in Egypt is that there are no rules for telephone conversations at all.   (Schmidt 1975)

Schmidt found such repeated *hellos* and demands and counter demands for identification on the part of both caller and answerer, to be a very frequent pattern in the 215 telephone calls in his corpus. If Westerners find such telephone behaviour peculiar or offensive, this simply indicates that their own rules, which they take for granted, are rather different.

The fact that sociolinguistic rules are not usually open to conscious reflection means that speakers tend to be unaware that such rules exist at all. It is only when sociolinguistic patterns are not followed that speakers are jogged into recognizing them. Thus, Godard (1977) says:

> As a foreigner who has lived in the United States for only a few months, I have been made conscious of some differences in the speech behaviour related to telephone calls: I have sometimes been irritated and even insulted and I have sometimes been amused . . . What does this mean? Simply that I am not fully a member of the community in which I am at the moment residing. That is, although I

share the grammar to a certain extent with members of the
speech community, I do not share all the norms of
interaction, such as those for the speech event in question.
I have been made aware of some norms of telephone
behaviour in my own country – France – just because they
are not observed in the United States. I felt that they had
been broken and in this way became conscious that they
were, in fact, rules of speaking.

Telephone call openings are, of course, not the only speech
behaviour open to misunderstanding, and the shock, irritation or
amusement reported by Godard may be felt by either the native
or the non-native speaker.

Once a pattern has been shown to exist, it can of course be
analysed and the insights gained may be made available to language learners. A case in point is a study of invitations in American English (Wolfson 1979b). For years I had been struck by the
comments made by foreign learners of English to the effect that
the Americans they met were insincere. Numerous grievances
were cited but one which recurred very often had to do with the
problem of invitations. Non-native speakers were often furious at
imagined slights which occurred when Americans made promises
to invite which they never fulfilled, or repeatedly suggested social
arrangements and then never followed up. Intrigued with the situation, I began to study it in the everyday speech behaviour of
Americans and to collect data on the ways in which invitations are
given.

In the initial stages of the analysis, it appeared that there was
a simple dichotomy between genuine invitations on the one hand
and, on the other, forms which have the appearance of invitations
but which are intended to be taken as statements of good intention
in a sort of social formula. That is, there are utterances in American English which can easily be identified as genuine invitations
(e.g. 'Come over for dinner next Saturday night') and utterances
which any native speaker would place in the category of polite
formulas (e.g. at leave-takings or at the end of conversations held
during chance encounters, Americans can frequently be heard
uttering such phrases as, 'Let's have lunch together sometime').
A very straightforward example is the following which I quote
from the data:

(1) s: I have to run to class.
     a: See you later.

s: See you later.
a: Okay. We'll have to get together again.
s: Uh huh.

However, sociolinguistic rules are rarely so simple or straightforward as intuition might lead one to imagine. As the analysis proceeded, it became clear that this was only a part of the pattern.

The fact is that there are many invitation-like forms which may or may not result in an appointment being made and that the form itself is simply not enough to allow the addressee to know what the result of the interaction will be. Rather than a simple dichotomy, what we have here is a continuum. At one extreme is the invitation which is pre-planned and non-negotiable. The speaker mentions time and place, and the addressee either accepts or refuses. Thus, the following will always be heard as a true invitation:

(2)   s: I wanted to ask you – are you and Fred free on
          Saturday night?
      a: Yes, we are.
      s: Good. How would you like to go out with us?
      a: That's a good idea. I've been wanting to get together.
          Do you want to go to dinner or just a movie . . .

Or even more straightforward:

(3)   s: We're going to see 'The Boys from Brazil' with Sally
          and Sam tonight. Would you like to join us?

Clearly these two examples share some structural correlates which can provide us with an operational means for identifying their boundaries. Yes/no questions with specific agreements and mention of time and place are the most salient of these.

Examples of invitation-like forms which are *not* counted as true invitations by native speakers are the following:

(4)   s: Hi, A.
      a: Hi.
      s: When are we going to get together?
      a: We really should.
      s: You know my office number. Just give me a call.
      a: Okay.
      s: Good. So long.
      a: Bye.

Or:

(5) s: Listen, I have a lot to talk about to you. I think we
should have lunch together one day soon.
A: Okay.
s: Good. I'll call you.

The cues which allow native speakers to recognize utterances
which are not to be taken as true invitations are the absence of
yes/no questions, time expressions like *soon, one day, sometime,*
and any of the phrases beginning with 'when' (e.g. 'Let's have
lunch together when things settle down . . .'). Other cues to statements which are not to be taken literally are the very words which
language learners might easily expect to carry the most weight;
words like 'definitely', for example, as in: 'Let's definitely get
together', are dead giveaways that the invitation is not to be taken
seriously.

The forms which are difficult for the non-native speaker to learn
to interpret and respond appropriately to are those which occupy
the midsection of the continuum, since although they seem to be
nothing more than social formulas, they actually have important
functions. The fact is that these utterances are given and heard
not as invitations which are insincere, but as statements of good
intention and, more importantly, as openings which allow the participants in the conversation to negotiate for an invitation or an
actual appointment. The distinction between non-specific invitations which may be negotiated to the point of a social commitment and those which may not has to do with a constraint based on
possible imposition and the responsibility for hospitality. The rule
is that if hospitality is being offered only the potential host or hostess extends the invitation and if negotiation takes place it is initiated by the person who will take responsibility for the hospitality.
Thus, if an invitation involves hospitality and it is left unspecific,
it is inappropriate for the addressee to attempt to negotiate for a
specific date since this would come dangerously close to self-invi-
tation. Indeed, it has been found that most invitations given by a
potential host or hostess are of the specific type, unless we include
such formulaic phrases as 'Come again soon . . .' In contrast, it
seems clear that most social arrangements which involve the sharing of expenses or of any other responsibility for entertainment
and which are entered into by people of approximately equal
status are of the negotiated variety. This is crucial information for

language learners because it means that in interacting in American society, the learner, as a participant in the speech act, can change the character of an interaction so that what starts out as a statement of good intention or an opening, can become an actual commitment. Not all such pseudo-invitations have this result, of course, because it is not always what both parties in the interaction desire. That, of course, is the purpose of negotiation. In the following example, the outcome is no commitment:

(6) s: Okay, good talking to you. Let's get together some time.
     A: I'd love to.
     s: Good. I'll call you soon and we'll have lunch together.
     A: Great.

The same interaction could have had a very different outcome if A had wanted to negotiate for a true commitment. The next example, taken from a similar social situation, has a very different outcome:

(7) s: Okay, thanks for the information. Let's get together soon.
     A: I'd love to.
     s: Good, I'll give you a call and we'll make a date for lunch.
     A: If you want, we can make a date now. When are you free?
     s: Uh, okay, let's. I'm available almost any day next week. What about you?
     A: Well, Wednesday is my best day.
     s: Okay, let's make it Wednesday.
     A: Noon okay for you?
     s: Noon is fine. Shall I pick you up at your place?
     A: That would be great.
     s: I'll be there at noon on Wednesday.
     A: Great. See you then.

The important point here is that in all but the most definite kinds of invitations, those that are pre-planned and that specify time or place and require a commitment, social arrangements are negotiated by both parties. The emergent character of the interaction is an important fact since learners must become competent not only in identifying the *kind* of social formulas which do not result in invitations and are not intended to, but also the sort, the very great majority, where the boundaries between polite formula and statement of good intention are a bit vague but which can nevertheless be changed by the right responses into true social engagements.

The knowledge of how to give and respond to invitations appropriately, to recognize true invitations and to interpret utterances which are invitation-like in form only but which allow the speaker to enter into negotiations which result in desired social commitments – all this is but a small part of the sociolinguistic information which the learner will need if he is to interact successfully with speakers of the target language.

Recently attention has been focussed on the speech behaviour associated with compliments and to compliment responses (Pomerantz 1978, Manes and Wolfson 1981). Much has been learned about the specific rules for the speech act of complimenting and about underlying cultural assumptions of native speakers of American English. In their study of compliments, Manes and Wolfson (1981) showed that, in American English, compliments are so highly patterned that they may be regarded as formulas. That is, although it is not explicitly recognized by native speakers, compliments tend to have clearly definable forms just as do greetings, apologies or expressions of gratitude.

The analysis of compliments in American English is based on a corpus of 686 examples collected in a great variety of everyday speech situations. An ethnographic approach toward the collection of data makes possible a sampling of the speech behaviour of men and women of different ages and a wide range of occupational and educational backgrounds. Thus, the data include compliments given and received by jewellers, hairdressers, clergymen, doctors and sales clerks, employers and employees, landlords and tenants, professors and students, classmates, friends, co-workers and family members. The topics of the compliments collected include personal attributes and possessions, children, pets, accomplishments and changes in appearance.

Analysis of the syntax of all the compliments collected reveals a regularity not hitherto suspected. Well over 50 per cent of all the compliments in the corpus make use of a single syntactic pattern:

(1) NP $\begin{smallmatrix} \text{is} \\ \text{looks} \end{smallmatrix}$ (really) ADJ
    (e.g. 'Your blouse is beautiful.')

Two other syntactic patterns:

$$(2)\quad \text{I (really) } \begin{bmatrix} \text{like} \\ \text{love} \end{bmatrix} \text{ NP}$$

        (e.g. 'I like your car.')

and

(3) PRO is (really) (a) ADJ NP

      (e.g. 'That's a nice wall hanging.')

account for an additional 16.1 per cent and 14.3 per cent of the data respectively. As Manes and Wolfson say:

> Thus only three patterns are necessary to describe fully 85% of the data. Indeed, only nine patterns occur with any regularity and these account for 97.2% of our data. In addition to the three major patterns already described, we find the following six:
>
> (4) You v (a) (really) ADJ NP   (3.3%)
>
>   (e.g. 'You did a good job.')
>
> (5) You v (NP) (really) ADV   (2.4%)
>
>   (e.g. 'You really handled that situation well.')
>
> (6) You have (a) ADJ NP   (2.4%)
>
>   (e.g. 'You have such beautiful hair!')
>
> (7) What (a) ADJ NP   (1.6%)
>
>   (e.g. 'What a lovely baby you have!')
>
> (8) ADJ NP   (1.6%)
>
>   (e.g. 'Nice game!')
>
> (9) Isn't NP ADJ   (1.0%)
>
>   (e.g. 'Isn't your ring beautiful! Isn't it pretty!')
>
> No pattern other than those listed above occurs more than twice in our data.

Since nine patterns suffice to account for virtually all of the data and only three patterns account for 85 per cent of it, we must conclude that what we have here is a syntactic formula. When we turn to an analysis of the semantic composition of compliments, we see that in this respect as well, compliments exhibit a striking regularity. In order to see just how formulaic the choice of lexical item is, it is necessary to recognize first that compliments fall into two major categories, the adjectival and the verbal, depending on the term which carries the positive evaluation. Of these categories, it is the adjectival which predominates to such an extent that out of the 686 compliments in the corpus, there are 546 in which the positive semantic load is carried by an adjective. What is of interest here is that although the range of positive adjectives is enormous and although some 75 different adjectives occur in the data, the great majority of adjectival compliments make use of only 5 different adjectives: *nice, good, beautiful, pretty* and *great*, with all the rest occurring only once or twice. If we consider the extremely wide privileges of occurrence of these five adjectives (as opposed to such topic-specific adjectives as *curly*) it is not surprising that they should prove so frequent. Indeed, the two most commonly used adjectives, *nice* and *good* are so vague and general that they are equally appropriate when referring to such diverse subjects as hair (e.g. 'That's a good haircut.'), clothing ('That sweater looks good.'), ability ('He's a good actor.') and accomplishments ('Nice shot!' and 'Your lecture was good.').

Of compliments which make use of verbs to carry the positive semantic evaluation, the overwhelming majority have either *like* or *love*; and these two verbs can be applied to virtually any topic from kittens and ice cream to sports, clothing, jewellery, and people. Again, relatively weak semantic load favours frequency; 86 per cent of all compliments which rely on a verb for their positive evaluation make use of either *like* or *love*.

Although 96 per cent of the data consist of compliments which use semantically positive adjectives and verbs, a few do rely on an adverb, usually *well*, to express the positive evaluation and an additional few depend on a noun (e.g. 'You're just a whiz at sewing.') It is clear, however, that in American English, there is an overwhelming tendency for speakers to choose from one of only five adjectives and two verbs to express their positive evaluations. As Manes and Wolfson (1981) point out:

> The combination of a restricted semantic set and an even more restricted set of syntactic structures makes it clear that what we are dealing with here is not simply a matter of frequency. Rather, we are forced to recognize that *compliments are formulas*, as much so as thanks and greetings. The speech act of complimenting is, in fact, characterized by the formulaic nature of its syntactic and semantic composition. Compliments are not merely

sentences which remark on a particularly attractive item or attribute; they are highly structured formulas which can be adapted with minimal effort to a wide variety of situations in which a favorable comment is required or desired. By substituting the correct noun phrase, 'I really like NP' or 'NP looks nice' can be appropriately applied to haircuts, homemade bread, shirts, new cars or a job well done.

For language learners, teachers, and materials writers, there should be little difficulty in applying the findings described above. The formulaic nature of compliments should, indeed, make this topic particularly amendable to explicit presentation. It should also be pointed out that because compliments are expressions of approval, they necessarily contain valuable information concerning the underlying cultural assumptions of speakers. The occurrence of large numbers of compliments with the same referents allows us to see what is valued by the speech community. Although analysis of this aspect of the compliment data is as yet incomplete, learners should be encouraged to take notice of what it is that forms the topics of the compliments they hear.

In her study of compliment responses, Pomerantz (1978) takes note of a different sort of cultural value at work in the compliment/response interaction. Thus, although the preferred behaviour (social norm) is for the recipient of a compliment to accept it with what Pomerantz calls an appreciation (thanks), this conflicts with another norm or what she calls 'the self-praise avoidance' constraint. For this reason, it frequently happens that speakers will downgrade the compliment by praising the same referent in weaker terms or by shifting the credit away from themselves. This shift or credit is an important technique, occurring rather frequently in the Manes and Wolfson corpus as well. Thus Pomerantz gives the example:

F: This is beautiful.
K: 'N that nice.
R: Yah. It really is.
K: It wove itself. Once it was set up.

and from the Manes and Wolfson corpus we have:

S: This is beautiful. I've been admiring it since I came in.
A: It's from Israel.

and

    s: Boy, that's nice work. I don't know how you do it.
    a: It's easy when you have good tools.

Another very frequent response is to return the compliment and Pomerantz points out that this is most frequent 'in openings and closings of interactions', for example in an opening:

    s: Yr lookin good.
    a: Great, So'r you.

On the other hand, Pomerantz also points out that thanks, or what she calls appreciations, are usually used to respond to compliments 'when the parties are asymmetrically related to the referents of the compliments'. That is, when compliments cannot be exchanged because the referent is a belonging, attribute or accomplishment of the addressee and the speaker has no equivalent object on which a compliment can be focussed.

From the point of view of the language learner, it is important to know that simple appreciations are virtually always appropriate as compliment responses but that what Pomerantz calls 'the self-praise avoidance' constraint will often lead the addressee of a compliment to downgrade it or to shift credit or even to disagree with the speaker though this last is much less frequent and usually restricted to relationships between intimates.

It is also important for the learner to understand that the status and the relationship between speaker and addressee has a crucial bearing on both the compliment and the response-type. Although analysis of this aspect of complimenting behaviour is still incomplete, it seems clear to me that the self-praise avoidance solutions discussed by Pomerantz are used primarily with intimates or good acquaintances where the relationship between speaker and addressee is symmetrical.

In discussing both the giving and responding to compliments, it is important to stress that the findings presented relate specifically to American English. The patterns described here, like all other sociolinguistic patterns, must be expected to vary across speech communities in a variety of ways. What counts as a compliment will differ from society to society, making interpretation of speaker intentions extremely difficult at times. Even where societies have rather similar value systems, differences will occur and it is often here that the most misunderstandings are found. Thus, some of the comments that speakers of American English regularly accept as compliments could seem very insulting to someone who understood the words but not the rules for interpreting them. For example, we have compliments in which the speaker, in saying that the addressee looks unusually well, implies that the reverse is usually the case. Thus, two men meet at an elevator and one says to the other:

A: Hey, what's the occasion? You look really nice today.

or two friends meet and one greets the other by exclaiming:

A: WOW! Linda! What did you do to your hair? I almost didn't recognize you. It looks great.

Indeed, this sort of compliment, immediately recognizable to any native speaker of American English by its intonational contour, has more than once been perceived as a serious insult by a non-native speaker who was unfamiliar with the meaning of the intonation and who could only interpret the words by their literal meaning.

The frequency and distribution of compliments in American English are also open to misinterpretation. In this society, compliments occur in a very wide variety of situations and are quite frequent even among strangers. It is not uncommon to hear non-native speakers remark on what is perceived as excessive use of compliments or comment on their seeming insincerity, especially when they express approval of something not held in particular esteem by their own native speech communities.

Like compliments, expressions of disapproval are heavily value-laden and must be expected to vary cross-culturally both in form and in content. Reisner (forthcoming) in her analysis of adult to adult scolding in American English focusses mainly on the linguistic form which these expressions take. Using an ethnographic approach, Reisner tape-recorded everyday conversations to discover where and how adults in our society reprimand one another. In analysing her data, she found that these expressions could be either 'dressed' or 'undressed', the undressed variant taking the form of imperatives while the dressed has the surface structure of interrogatives or declaratives. Thus, any surface form can express disapproval, but the undressed forms are more direct. Dressed disapproval may take the form of interrogatives and here we have two categories, the RQ, or rhetorical question, and the REQ, or response-expected question. RQs typically begin with the word *what* but no answer is expected:

'What are you, some kind of nut?'

whereas REQs, which Reisner finds to be more common among intimates, may begin with a variety of other question words:

'Why did you eat that cheese?' or 'What are you doing with my water?'

Declaratives may also be used to express disapproval:

'These things have been ready for two weeks.'

and Reisner finds that although the most dressed disapprovals take this form, the message can nonetheless be conveyed with severity.

Of the various forms which expressions of disapproval may take, it is perhaps the RQ which will present the most difficulties for the learner of English. This study, which uncovers the structure of these utterances, should prove invaluable to teachers and developers of materials in their efforts to present an extremely complicated subject.

Obviously, the findings presented above are only a small part of what needs to be known about the rules of speaking in American English, but it is a beginning. With respect to the validity of the analyses reported here, two important methodological problems must be pointed out. First, although I have spoken throughout of speech patterns in American English, this is, in reality, a great oversimplification, since the data upon which each of the studies were based were, of necessity, gathered in specific places and within specific speech communities. Thus, the study of complimenting behaviour (Manes and Wolfson 1981) was carried out primarily in Charlottesville, Virginia and in Philadelphia, Pennsylvania. Although data gathered in a number of other areas indicates that the patterns and regularities uncovered are rather widespread, it is still important to recognize that a strong claim for the validity of the analysis can only be made for the two speech communities in which compliments were studied, and not for the language as a whole or even for all of American English. It must be left to other researchers to replicate the study elsewhere and to confirm the findings or to find differences for other speech communities in order to add to the stock of knowledge about rules of speaking in the United States. Unfortunately, not all analysts give information as to where or under what circumstances their data was collected. Thus, I can, for example, state without hesitation, that the study of invitations (Wolfson 1979b) is based on data gathered among middle class speakers in and around Philadelphia, and that the study of forms of address to women in service encounters (Wolfson and Manes 1979) was conducted in Charlottesville, Virginia and in Philadelphia, Pennsylvania, with additional data collected in other areas of the northeast, the midwest and the west coast. I can also state that Reisner's data on expressions of disapproval was gathered in Hartford, Connecticut and in Philadelphia, Pennsylvania, while Ervin-Tripp bases her analysis of forms of address on the observation of speech behaviour in a large western university. Borkin and Reinehart (1978), in their analysis of apologies, indicate that their examples of appropriate and inappropriate uses of *excuse me* and *I'm sorry* were observed in the speech behaviour of native and non-native speakers of English at the University of Michigan. In contrast, Pomerantz (1978), in her study of compliment responses, gives no information at all regarding the source of her data and this makes it difficult indeed to appraise critically the extent to which the rules given may be applicable.

Lack of information as to the nature of the data upon which sociolinguistic analyses are based leads to the second methodological problem involved in this sort of work. This is that sociolinguistics vary considerably with regard to the methods they use to collect data and the amount of data they consider sufficient as a basis upon which to generalize. In far too many cases, little or no indication is given as to the amount of data collected, the method used (questionnaire, interview, observation) or the range of speech situations sampled. In other cases such as Schegloff's work on telephone call openings, the data is restricted to examples gathered in a single setting. While such work is certainly valuable, the findings do not represent the range of situations and participants necessary to give us a picture of how this speech event is patterned in everyday interactions.

What, then, can be done to collect data which is broad enough in scope to give us information on how a particular speech act occurs among different groups of people in speaking of different topics over a broad range of situations? The answer is clear: only ethnographic observation of naturally occurring speech behaviour can be used to collect the range and breadth of data which we must have to study rules of speaking adequately.

In my own work on conversational narrative (Wolfson 1976b, 1978, 1979a), as well as in the work on forms of address (Wolfson and Manes 1979), on invitations (Wolfson 1979b) and on compliments (Manes and Wolfson 1981), the data were gathered in everyday interactions which the researchers observed or in which they participated. Every effort was made to sample as large a variety of speech situations as possible. In the study of complimenting behaviour, for example, the speakers and addressees were men and women of all ages and from a range of occupational and educational backgrounds. In addition to collecting the compliments and the responses to them, the observers were careful to take note of the sex, approximate age and occupation of both speaker and addressee, as well as their relationship to one another, wherever such information was available. In addition to collecting as broad and varied a sample as possible, detailed observation of specific individuals and social situations was carried out. The nature and topic of each interaction were noted and all compliments were recorded exactly. The corpus thus included nearly seven hundred compliments along with a great deal of information concerning the speech setting, the participants and their relationship to one another. Thus, in exploring the structure and function of compliments, we attempted to provide an empirical basis for the analysis of one type of sociolinguistic behaviour.

The important thing to recognize, then, is that sociolinguistic research is a necessary complement to language teaching and that this research must, if it is to be valid, base itself on specific speech communities and on language in use. If communicative competence is our aim for language learners, then we must begin by finding out how people make use of their linguistic resources, how they vary their use of language according to the speech situation, and how they both express and create relationships with one another by their choice of linguistic features. Language use must be recognized as being conditioned by factors outside the purely linguistic structure such that there is always a cross-relationship between internal meaning and extra-linguistic factors. And in order for us to know what forms are actually used by native speakers and how these are patterned with respect to rules of speaking, we must have access to data taken from real speech samples across a range of speech situations. If the current interest in sociolinguistics is not to be just another short-lived fad in ESL teaching, we need concrete information on what exactly constitute the rules of speaking for American English.

In conclusion, it should be pointed out that the theoretical importance of the study of rules of speaking goes well beyond the analysis of norms and usage pertinent to specific speech acts, as interesting and useful as this information is. The true significance of the study of such rules in American English is that taken together these analyses reveal the underlying cultural assumptions of our society.

Note

1. I am indebted to Dell Hymes for introducing this term and the theoretical framework which has made such work as mine possible. My gratitude to Richard Laprade, Maria Derrick, Virginia Hymes and Joan Manes for commenting on an earlier version of this paper.

Questions for discussion, study and further research

1. Write a short role-play aimed at teaching the distinction between *excuse me* and *I'm sorry*.

2. Do you agree with Borkin and Reinhart's analysis of *excuse me* and *I'm sorry*? Listen to the way people around you use these two forms, making notes on at least five occurrences of each form. Discuss your observations with reference to the analysis given here.

3. Observe the interactions which go on around you and try to write down, as unobtrusively as possible, five separate compliments along with the responses to them. Be sure to write exactly what you hear. Pool your data with other members of your class who have participated in the same exercise and try to work out the linguistic patterns you find. How many different syntactic structures and adjectives did you find and what were their frequencies? Are compliments formulaic in your speech community? Discuss.

4. Based on the Manes and Wolfson analysis and on your own data, develop a lesson aimed at teaching non-native speakers how to give and receive compliments. If possible, try teaching your lesson to an ESL class.

5. Observe an ESL class and take notes on how students of different language and cultural backgrounds interact with one another and with the teacher. Are there aspects of classroom behaviour which you would attribute to differences in sociolin-

guistic rules? Do you find any obvious examples of communicative interference? Discuss.

6. If you were to do research into the rules of speaking of your own speech community, where would you begin? What sorts of rules do you think it would be most interesting to study? Which would be most useful?

7. Watch a situation comedy on television and note down the sociolinguistic behaviour patterns which you think might be difficult for a non-native speaker to understand. Discuss.

Introduction to Chapter 4

Janet Holmes' paper is a further illustration of *rules of speaking* (in Wolfson's sense) and of pragmatic knowledge (as Fraser describes it in his chapter), and deals with one class of speech acts, *directives*, speech acts which have the function of getting someone to do something, such as *suggestions*, *requests* and *commands*, within a particular social setting (the classroom) and with a specific set of participants (teachers and pupils).

Holmes discusses how the forms directives may take in communication reflect the relationship between the speaker and the addressee, and their relative power. Such factors may effect the degree of directness of the directive. She then focusses on the forms directives tend to take in classroom settings, and shows how the successful interpetation of the teacher's directive by young children requires a matching of a complex variety of linguistic forms to the social rules governing interaction and learning in a classroom setting, a matching which is sometimes achieved through a process of negotiation. The acquisition of such skills is illustrative of the vast complex of different types of communicative and interpretive skills that underlie successful communication.

4 The structure of teachers' directives

Janet Holmes

'OK bus people' said the teacher, and immediately a small group of children got up and ran out of the classroom. One child, a new entrant, stood hesitantly, looking anxiously at the teacher. 'Are you going home on the bus Stephen?' she asked. He nodded. 'Off you go then', the teacher said, and he scampered off with relief towards the door.

The meaning of the teacher's first utterance was unambiguous to the more experienced pupils, who were familiar with classroom routine. They interpreted it as clearly directive in function, despite its elliptical form. The new entrant, however, his sociolinguistic competence in the classroom as yet undeveloped, needed a more explicit form of the directive before he was sure of its meaning and hence of the appropriate response. This paper examines the relationship between linguistic form and the functions of speech, focussing in particular on teachers' directives to elementary or primary school children.

Speech functions

A number of researchers have focussed on the social functions of speech, investigating the purposes for which language is used, and the variety of forms by which different functions may be expressed. Linguists, such as Halliday (1973 and 1975), sociolinguists, such as Hymes (1964a, 1967, 1974), conversational analysts, such as Sacks and his colleagues (Sacks 1972a; Sacks, Schegloff and Jefferson 1974), and linguistic philosophers, such as Austin (1962) and Searle (1965 and 1969), have all contributed from very different backgrounds to such research. The result has been a vast array of descriptive labels for different speech functions, some clearly overlapping, and some differing in their level of generality or abstraction.

Hymes (1974), for example, in a relatively parsimonious description of what he calls 'common broad types of functions' (p. 23), identifies eight functions of speech, deriving them from a theoretical framework which focusses on the components of communicative events: expressive (addressor), directive (addressee), contact or phatic (channel), metalinguistic (code), contextual (setting), poetic (message form), referential (topic) and metacommunicative (event). At a very different level of abstraction Austin (1962) suggests there may be up to ten thousand 'illocutionary' acts expressing different speech functions, and he also claims there are over a thousand different verbs in English denoting such acts: e.g. 'apologize', 'criticize', 'command', 'promise', 'forbid', 'plead', etc. Austin proposed a classification of illocutionary acts into five basic categories, but his taxonomy is criticized by Searle (1976) as follows:

> . . . there is a persistent confusion between verbs and acts, not all the verbs are illocutionary verbs, there is too much overlap of the categories, too much heterogeneity within the categories, many of the verbs listed in the categories don't satisfy the definition given for the category and, most important, there is no consistent principle of classification.
>
> (pp. 9–10)

Searle (1976) provides clear criteria for a reclassification into what he calls 'the basic categories of illocutionary acts' (p. 10) namely, representatives, directives, commissives, expressives and declarations. (Editors' note: see also the similar categories identified by Fraser, this volume.) Such categorizations suggest a solution to the overlap of labels and confusion of levels of abstraction which bedevil speech function analysis. They suggest a hierarchical relationship between the macro-level speech functions described by writers such as Jakobson (1960), Hymes (1964a, 1967, 1974) and Halliday (1973 and 1975), and the micro-level speech acts listed by Austin (1962) and others (e.g. Wilkins 1973; Dobson 1979).

A similar, although very differently derived, hierarchical structure is proposed by Sinclair and Coulthard (1975) in an analysis which relates three major 'transaction' types at the highest level of analysis ('informing', 'eliciting' and 'directing'), to twenty-two speech acts at the lowest level of analysis (e.g. 'nominate', 'acknowledge', 'evaluate', 'prompt'), by means of a clearly described system of elements in a 'consists of' relationship to each other. Although Sinclair and Coulthard's 'acts' are defined by their function in the discourse, and are therefore different in kind from Searle's and Austin's, the overall aim of identifying the functions of speech is common to both approaches. Moreover Sinclair and Coulthard's classification, has the additional advantage of being empirically based, being 'the only descriptive system which claims to describe a spoken text exhaustively' (Coulthard 1977, p. 25).

There would seem then to be both theoretical and empirical justification for positing a hierarchical relationship between speech functions (such as 'informative', 'directive', etc.) and speech acts (such as 'assert', 'claim', 'command', 'request', etc.) although the exact nature of the relationship remains an area for further research. In addition, within any speech function, Searle's (1976) article suggests a number of 'dimensions of variation in which illocutionary acts differ from one another' (p. 2). Speech acts might be organized then on scales involving dimensions such as the degree of commitment of the speaker to the truth of a proposition, the degree of force with which the proposition is presented, and so on. Schmidt and Richards (1980) discussing this notion point out, for example, that 'Suggestions, requests and commands are all directives. They differ in the force of the attempt, but all are attempts by the speaker to get the hearer to do something' (p. 4). One might represent such relationships diagrammatically in this way:

Speech function:	**Directive**	**Informative/representative**

Speech acts:	command, order	swear
	request	assert, state
	advise, recommend	claim
	invite	
	suggest	suggest
	hint	hypothesize

increasing force   *increasing commitment to truth of proposition*

The validity of such taxonomies, however, cannot be established without thorough empirical investigation, despite their intuitive appeal. Nor can the degree of overlap between categories be ascertained without further ethnographic research. As Corder (in press) points out, attempts to devise a universal and comprehensive set of categories are 'at the stage of what has been called botanizing – the pre-theoretical or natural history stage in the development of a science. . . . we are still concerned with "ethnography of speaking" '. Matters are complicated further by the fact that, as Schmidt and Richards (1980) note, 'It is probably not true that all languages name the same speech acts with illocutionary verbs (does every language recognize a *suggest: insist* distinction?), but again, no research has been reported' (p. 11). And, of course, any such classification must also take account of a variety of social constraints, such as the relative status of participants in an interaction, which will affect the interpretation of the function of utterances in different social contexts: 'beg' and 'command', for example, imply quite different relationships between the speaker and the hearer.[1] One of the main aims of this paper is to explore the relationship between social factors and the form of directive utterances in the classroom.

An initial and basic decision for the researcher investigating the functions of speech concerns the criteria to be used in classifying a particular utterance as a realization of one speech act rather than another. The most widely adopted criterion, and the one used in the analysis below, is the purpose of the utterance from the speaker's perspective: i.e. the speaker's intentions. This approach is not, of course, without its problems. Any utterance may be deliberately ambiguous or multifunctional, as this example from Searle (1969) illustrates:

> . . . suppose at a party a wife says, 'It's really quite late'.
> That utterance may be at one level a statement of fact; to
> her interlocuter, who has just remarked on how early it
> was, it may be (and be intended as) an objection; to her
> husband it may be (and be intended as) a suggestion or
> even a request ('Let's go home') as well as a warning
> ('You'll feel rotten in the morning if we don't'). (p. 70)

And how does the analyst correctly identify the speaker's intentions, since they are not available for examination? In the face of such problems conversational analysts like Sacks and his colleagues have argued that the illocutionary force of an utterance should be defined as what the listener understands by it, rather than what the speaker intends, since 'the listener's interpretation is evident in his response and it is this which determines the progress of the interaction. (Coulthard 1977, p. 19).[2] Most researchers, however, seem to have followed Austin (1962), using speaker's intention as the basis for classification.

Much research on speech functions in recent years has focussed on investigating the strategies available to speakers wishing to express particular meanings. Linguists have, of course, always been interested in the complex relationship between the function of an utterance and the form or structure by which it is expressed. The fact that an interrogative form, for example, such as 'Do I have to tell you, again?', is more likely to be a realization of the speech act 'warning', than a request for information, has been generally recognized. More recently researchers have begun to examine written texts and analyse spoken interaction in order to empirically establish the forms used to realize different semantic functions. While written texts have so far been the main source of information on conceptual categories, such as time, space, quantity, causation, etc. (e.g. Kennedy 1978 and 1979), spoken interaction has, not surprisingly, provided the chief source of data on the syntactic realizations of what Wilkins (1973) has called social or 'communicative categories': i.e. speech acts such as 'apologize', 'agree', 'approve', etc. The directive function of speech, in particular, has received considerable attention, and a brief summary of some of the relevant research will serve to illustrate the complexity of the relationship between form and function in linguistic interaction, as well as providing a background for the analysis of teachers' directives which follows.

Directives

Searle (1976) includes in the class of directives all speech acts whose primary function is that they count as attempts by the speaker to get the hearer to do something. His is a very broad classification in that he includes questions, commenting that:

> Questions are a species of directives, since they are
> attempts by S (speaker) to get H (hearer) to answer – i.e.
> to perform a speech act. (p. 11)

Elsewhere (1975) he has described one type of directive, requests, in some detail. He calls these 'indirect directives', and discusses how listeners correctly interpret such indirect speech acts, categorizing the available ways of producing them. His categorization is based primarily on the content of requests, although he provides illustrations of the syntactic forms by which they may be realized. He suggests, for example, that one of the strategies for making an indirect directive is by asking whether or stating that a preparatory condition concerning the addressee's ability to do A obtains: e.g. 'Can you pass the salt?'.

Searle (1976) discusses the formal linguistic features of speech acts more explicitly, suggesting that speech acts which are classifiable as directives, for example, are characterized by 'directive syntax', and proposes that:

> . . . such sentences as 'I order you to leave' and 'I command you to stand at attention' have the following deep structure:
>
> I *Verb* you + you *Fut Vol Verb* (NP) (*Adv*)
>
> I order you to leave is thus the surface structure realization of 'I order you + you will leave' with equi NP deletion of the repeated 'you'. (p. 17)

Identifying the surface structure forms by which directives may be realized is one of the main aims of work by sociolinguists such as Ervin-Tripp (1976 and 1977) and Mitchell-Kernan and Kernan (1977). Unlike Searle's work, these analyses are data-based, drawing on a wide range of empirical observations in a variety of different social contexts. Ervin-Tripp (1976), for example, argues that the specific form which is selected varies systematically with social factors such as age, presence of outsiders, familiarity, rank, territorial location, difficulty of task, whether or not a duty is normally expected, whether or not non-compliance is likely, and so on. She identifies six different types of directives which she orders 'approximately according to the relative power of the speaker and addressee in conventional usage and the obviousness of the directive' (p. 29).

1. *Personal need or desire statements*: e.g. 'I need a match.' Directed downwards to subordinates primarily.
2. *Imperatives*: e.g. 'Gimme a match'; 'a match'. Directed to subordinates or familiar equals.
3. *Imbedded imperatives*: e.g. 'Could you give me a match?' Directed most often to unfamiliar people, or those differing in rank.
4. *Permission directives*: e.g. 'May I have a match?' Rare in her sample. Possibly addressed upward more often than downward in rank.

5. *Question directives*: e.g. 'Have you gotta match?'
   This form is most common when the listener might not
   comply, so the question turns on the likely obstacle.
6. *Hints*: e.g. 'The matches are all gone.'
   Employed when speakers could rely on shared understandings of rules in transactional interactions, such as
   in office or classrooms, or of habits and motives in personal
   interactions such as within families.

Ervin-Tripp, unlike Searle, excludes questions aimed at eliciting
a verbal response from her analysis of directives. Her definition
of a directive would seem to be similar to Sinclair and Coulthard's
(1975) 'to request a non-linguistic response' (p. 41).[3] Although the
classification is based primarily on the social distribution and relative explicitness of the different types of directive, she provides
some structural description, and numerous examples to distinguish
between them. Imbedded imperatives, for example, are described
as follows:

> In these cases, agent, action, object, and often beneficiary
> are as explicit as in direct imperatives, though they are
> imbedded in a frame with other syntactic and semantic
> properties. (p. 29)

The importance of social context in the interpretation of directives
is very clear from such research. Utterances such as (1) 'Sal you
make a good door.' or (2) 'This analysis has to be done over.' are
unambiguously interpreted as directives in the appropriate social
context, despite their declarative form, and despite the fact that
in (1) the required act, and in (2) the required agent, is not
specified.

Other writers have also insisted on the need to take account of
social factors such as the relative status of participants, their role-
relationships and corresponding rights and duties, in assigning a
particular functional interpretation to an utterance. Leech (1977),
for example, in an interesting discussion of a proposed addition
to Grice's maxims – the maxim of Tact – suggests that tact is concerned with the avoidance of conflict, and hence clearly related to
such social variables as participants' rights and duties. In general,
he points out, indirectness of utterance in English is a tact marker
and thus 'the more tactful a directive is, the more indirect and
circumlocutionary it is' (p. 19). He provides (hypothetical) examples of utterances characterized by increasing tact:

(1) Give me some money.
(2) I want you to give me some money.
(3) Will you give me some money?
(4) Can you give me some money?

(4) is the most tactful form, he claims, because it involves the most complex conflict-avoidance strategy by the speaker, and the most complex inductive strategy on the part of the listener, to work out the force. Hints are obviously characterized by an even greater degree of tact in Leech's terms. He suggests that relative power, relative social distance and relative 'cost' of the proposal interact in determining the appropriate choice of directive-type in any interaction (Leech 1977, p. 24). It is interesting to note that Ervin-Tripp's empirical findings, based on data observed in work and home settings, are not inconsistent with Leech's proposals.

Some researchers have formulated rules for interpreting directive utterances. Labov (1972b), for example, provides a precise rule accounting for the interpretation of an imperative form as a request for action. Sinclair and Coulthard (1975), on the other hand, do not regard the relationship between imperative and 'command' as causing problems in their data, but they do provide rules accounting for the interpretation of declarative and interrogative forms as commands. Ervin-Tripp (1977) refines their rules on the basis of her data and produces what appears to be a very general and powerful rule for the interpretation of directive utterances:

> Those utterances will be interpreted as directives which break topical continuity in discourse, and which refer to acts prohibited to or obligatory for addressees, mention referents central to such acts, or give exemplars of the core arguments of understood social rules. Examples would be 'Somebody's talking', 'I see chewing gum', and 'Where does your dish go?' (p. 169)

This rule avoids reference to specific linguistic forms, and, unlike Sinclair and Coulthard's rules, accounts for examples where the required action is not made explicit. It defines directives in terms of crucial features of the social situation in which they occur, and provides a very useful basis for examining the use of teachers' directives in the classroom.

Teacher's directives in the elementary school

In most classrooms, even at elementary level, whatever the arrangement of space, the teacher is physically the central focus of pupils' attention for most of the school day. Until recently class-rooms have tended to be very clearly definable as 'status-marked' settings within which 'transactional' rather than 'personal' inter-actions are appropriate.[4] Although changes have occurred in many infant rooms to de-formalize the physical layout, and encourage freer interaction amongst pupils, and between pupils and teacher, many of the features of classroom interaction remain unchanged.

The teacher-pupil relationship is an asymmetrical one; the teacher is older and more knowledgeable than the pupils. The teacher is expected to be in control, to preserve an appropriate social distance from pupils, and to instruct and inform the children: to teach them the body of facts and skills the society values. Indeed Waller (1965) has described the teacher as 'a paid agent of cultural diffusion'. It is within this social context that one must consider the language used in classroom interaction.[5] An utterance such as 'Someone's chewing gum' may function as a request for a piece of gum addressed to an equal outside the classroom. Inside the classroom it will be unerringly interpreted as a command to stop by all but the newest arrivals. Ervin-Tripp's rule, quoted above, provides a very satisfactory account of why such an inter-pretation is appropriate in the classroom context.

It is possible, using Searle's definition of directives (which includes elicitation questions), to regard a great many of the teacher's utterances as directive in function. In order to limit the scope of the discussion, however, the term 'directive' is restricted in the analysis below to utterances intended to elicit a non-verbal response, 'to get the pupil to do but not say something' (Sinclair and Coulthard 1975, p. 50). The material used as the basis for the analysis has been collected in elementary school classrooms in New Zealand and Britain. Much of it has been contributed by graduate students in the form of tapes and transcriptions.[6]

The analysis can only be suggestive, since there are obvious weaknesses in the data. Recording often began, for example, at the point where the observer considered the lesson had 'really' started, thus excluding much of the organizational lan-guage, which tends to be predominantly directive in function. It seems likely, moreover, on the basis of the data examined, that variables such as class size, content of lesson, task required of pu-pils, personal preference, and even advice given in teacher training, would need to be considered in any statistical analysis. The main aim has therefore been to describe the various forms by which directives are realized in the classroom, rather than to provide detailed frequency data. Some reference is made, however, to general tendencies which were consistently observable throughout the data.

The directives are divided into three major categories on the basis of their form: imperative, interrogative or declarative. Within these categories syntactic variants and modifications have been discussed using formal and explicit criteria as far as possible, and the social correlations of forms have been noted where relevant. The categorization is followed by a discussion of the implications of the data for children's comprehension and their acquisition of sociolinguistic competence in the classroom.

1 Imperatives

Imperative forms were the most frequently occurring realizations of directives in the data. This is not surprising, firstly because they are relatively explicit, and secondly because, as Ervin-Tripp (1976) demonstrates, they tend to occur as realizations of directives in address to subordinates. Six structural variants of imperatives were identified in the data.

(*i*) *Base form of verb*: e.g. 'Speak up.'
This, the simplest form of the imperative, can be exemplified by 'Listen', the single most frequently occurring directive form in the data as a whole. Its frequency reflects its function – to remind children of their obligation to attend to the teacher's talk which has been shown to occupy 70 per cent of classroom time (Flanders 1970). In infant classes it was often preceded by a clap or a number of claps by the teacher, and in some cases quite clearly the clap substituted for this attention-getting imperative. Other examples of this simple imperative form, selected from a large number in the data are:

> 'Speak louder.'
> 'Put your hands down.'
> 'Have a look at the picture.'
> 'Come over here by me.'
> 'Don't shout out.'
> 'Don't all talk at once.'
> 'Don't draw on the folded piece.'

Imperatives were often used to make explicit the 'rules' of classroom interaction, e.g. 'Don't interrupt.', 'Don't shout out.', a point which is discussed further in the last section of the paper.

(ii) You + imperative: e.g. 'You look here.'
Though this form did occur in the data it was not very frequent, and was generally addressed either to a small group of children, or to an individual child: e.g.

> 'You just see the picture.'
> 'You go on with your work.'

The function of the explicit 'You' seemed to be either to distinguish between groups or children, or to add emphasis to the directive. 'You' is also explicit in the forms 'Away you go.' and 'Off you go.', but these more idiomatic forms were used much more freely, and were distributionally and functionally more similar to base form imperatives than *You + imperative* forms.

(iii) Present participle form of verb: e.g. 'Listening.'
This may be a distinctly New Zealand variant of the imperative. It is difficult to be completely certain about its classification, but, despite the fact that it is often accompanied by rising pitch, it has been classified as imperative rather than interrogative in form.

The main reason for this is that (1) 'I want you V-ing . . .' provides a more intuitively satisfying approximation to the underlying structure than (2) 'Are you V-ing . . .?', the interrogative alternative. The similarity of (1) to the commonly accepted deep structure of imperative forms provides the justification for classifying examples of this form in the imperative category.

Present participles are fairly frequently used by New Zealand teachers, particularly in new entrant classrooms, but they have never been noted outside the school domain. Examples from the data are:

> 'Just listening.'
> 'Looking at me.'
> 'Looking this way.'
> 'Sitting up straight please.'
> 'Sitting on the mat please.'
> 'Standing still.'

(*iv*) *Verb-ellipsis*: e.g. 'Hands up.'
The examples in this category share many of the features of what
Ervin-Tripp (1976) defines as 'elliptical forms'. She comments
that:

> In situations where the necessary action is obvious, it is
> common to produce elliptical forms specifying only the new
> information – the direct or indirect object. These will all be
> considered imperatives. (p. 30)

In the classroom the specified information sometimes involved the
inclusive agent 'everyone', and a place adverbial: e.g.

> 'Everybody on the mat.'
> 'Everybody round the table please.'

Other examples in the data specified the direct object: e.g.

> 'Now this one.' (i.e. Now look at this picture.)
> 'Hands away from your mouth.'
> 'Hands not voices.' (i.e. Put up your hand rather than
> calling out.)
> 'Hands up.'

The last example, which occurred frequently in the data, is more
complex than its surface structure might suggest. A correct
response depends on knowledge of the shared system of rules for
classroom interaction, a point discussed more fully in the section
on children's comprehension below.

A distinctive variant of this category involved agent specification alone, in the form of a child's name usually with strong stress;
e.g. 'John!'. Names were frequently used as directives by teachers
when the necessary action was quite obvious, either from the
immediately preceding discourse, or from familiarity with the
classroom rules for appropriate behaviour. 'John!', for example,
may function as a directive to 'Stop talking.', if talking has been
proscribed, or to 'Come here.' if that is the appropriate action in
the context. Interpretation of such forms is hence entirely context-
dependent, and in many cases requires knowledge of the prohibited or obligatory behaviour peculiar to the classroom. Names
used as directives are often distinguishable from 'nominations'
(Sinclair and Coulthard 1975, p. 42) only by their function in
context, in that they require a non-verbal rather than a verbal
response. Further examples with glosses are:

'Jane!' (i.e. Pay attention.) Jane was gazing out of the
window while the teacher was talking.
'Lisa!' (i.e. Stop throwing blocks around.)
'John!' (i.e. Open the window.) This followed a directive
with a non-specific agent, 'Someone open the window'.
'Sally!' (i.e. Come and sit on the mat.) This followed
'Sitting on the mat please'. Sally had ignored the directive.

(*v*) *Imperative + modifier*: e.g. 'Children looking this way please.'
Ervin-Tripp (1976) notes a number of post-posed forms such as
'please', address forms, modal tags and 'OK', whose distribution
appears to be socially significant. The precise social meaning of
such forms varied considerably from one context to another. In
some interactions, for example, such forms seemed intended to
'soften' the effect of the directive: e.g. ' "please" was added to
orders by waitresses when they asked cooks to perform services
outside the cook's normal duties' (p. 31). In other interactions,
however, such forms were judged to function as distancing
devices. In the classroom data post-posed address forms and
'please' were relatively frequent, and seemed to function as 'soft-
eners' following an imperative directive. Address forms are distinguishable from names functioning alone as directives by their
final position within the same intonation contour as the imperative
form. Examples:

'Turn around please Jo.'
'Put your hands on your hips everyone.'
'Looking this way please.'

An interesting distributional difference was noted in the occurrence of 'please'. In a number of small group discussions examined
'please' never occurred following directives; its occurrence was
confined to teacher's directives to the full class. This may be due
to inadequate data, but it is perhaps worth pointing out that this
distribution is consistent with Leech's (1977) maxim of Tact. He
suggests that the more powerful and socially distant the addresser,
and the more 'costly' the required action to the addressee, the
more tact is required in expressing the directive (p. 24). The 'soft-
ening' effect of 'please' following directives to the whole class may
therefore be an illustration of the greater degree of linguistic tact
appropriate to more formal interactions compared with the less
formal small group interactions. In the small group discussions

observed, social distance between teacher and pupils seemed reduced, the teacher's power was rarely explicitly asserted, and in some cases was temporarily relinquished to a limited extent, and the 'cost' of the actions required was perhaps reduced in that the audience was smaller.

There were no examples of post-posed modal tags or 'OK' in the data. This may well be a deficiency of the sample but it seems possible that it is also a reflection of the fact that such relatively informal forms are likely to be less frequent in the classroom situation. Imperatives followed by 'OK' with rising pitch are very common in young children's speech to each other: e.g.

'Pretend you're the doctor OK?'

but there were no such examples following directives from the teacher in the classroom transcripts.

(vi) Let + first person pronoun
Leech and Svartvik (1978) describe forms introduced by 'Let me' and 'Let's' as examples of first person commands. 'Let me see' occurred occasionally in the classroom data, generally in individual interactions between the teacher and a child, where the teacher wished to evaluate or assist with the child's work.

More interesting were examples involving 'Let's' addressed to the whole class: e.g.

'Let's finish there.'
'Let's try.' (to identify specific items in a picture).

The use of the first person plural pronoun would seem to suggest that solidarity rather than power is being signalled and, indeed, in informal contexts 'Let's' appropriately introduces a suggestion to a friend: e.g. 'Let's go to the pictures tonight'. In the classroom, however, such forms are clearly directives with the force of a command rather than a suggestion, (despite the 'pseudo-participation' implied by the 'us') and children are well aware of this.

Another interesting form introduced by 'Let's' is exemplified by instances such as:

'Let's see if you can sort this out.'
'Let's see who can sit down quickly.'

and the related elliptical form: 'See if you can put your hands up'. These forms resemble Ervin-Tripp's (1976) 'imbedded imperatives' in that 'the agent and object are explicit, so that the forms preceding them are a kind of formal addition' (p. 33). The function of these 'formal additions' seems to be to 'soften' or tone down the command, producing a politer and more 'tactful' utterance.

2 *Interrogatives*

Although less frequent than imperative forms, interrogative structures functioning as directives were relatively common in the classroom data. Two major types of interrogative were identified: modal and non-modal forms.

(*i*) *Modals*: e.g. 'Would you open the window?'
Sinclair and Coulthard (1975) provide a useful interpretive rule for modal directives based on their analysis of classroom discourse. It can be regarded as a more specific form of Ervin-Tripp's general rule for the interpretation of directives:

> An interrogative clause is to be interpreted as a *command to do* if it fulfils the following conditions:
>
> (i)   it contains one of the modals 'can', 'could', 'will', 'would' (and sometimes 'going to');
>
> (ii) if the subject of the clause is also the addressee;
>
> (iii) the predicate describes an action which is physically possible at the time of the utterance. (p. 32)

Examples of such forms from the elementary school data are:

> 'Would you like to go and ask Mrs S for the staple gun?'
> 'Would you like to try this?' (i.e. a jigsaw puzzle)
> 'Rowena would you get some crayons please?'
> 'David will you read this page for me?'[7]
> 'Can you read what it says for me?'

All the examples in the data were addressed to individuals. This distributional feature seems to be related to the social implications of such forms. Ervin-Tripp (1976), for example, notes that they are frequently used when the task required is special or difficult, when physical distance lies between the speaker and the hearer, or when the person addressed was in his or her own territory. These features account for all the examples noted in the data: getting the crayons, for example, was a special task assigned to a particular child; directives to children to read could be regarded as requiring them to perform a relatively demanding task; and many of these forms occurred when the teacher had moved from her 'home' position to stand, sit or kneel beside a child in what could be considered the child's territory.

(*ii*) *Non-modal interrogative directives*: e.g. 'Have you tried it?' Like Ervin-Tripp's (1976) category of 'question directives' this category is identifiable by the fact that many of the forms are identical to information questions. However, in context, they are generally unambiguously directive in function. In the elementary classroom context they are often relatively explicit (unlike Ervin-Tripp's examples), referring in some cases to the desired activity and the agent: e.g. 'Have you tried it?' functioned as directive to 'Try it' in the context observed. In many cases the forms used, as well as explicitly indicating the desired activity, also implicitly directed children to refrain from the undesirable behaviour in which they were engaged instead: e.g.

> 'People at the back are you listening?' (Implied 'stop talking')
> 'Who can I see sitting quietly?' (Implied 'stop moving and talking').

Examples which more closely resemble Ervin-Tripp's less explicit forms are:

> 'Lynda do you know where the paints are kept?' (i.e. Go and get the paints.);
> 'Whose maths is good?' (i.e. Count the items in the picture.);
> 'What are you meant to be doing?' (i.e. Stop what you are doing.)

Such samples were rare in the elementary school setting, however.

The social features of these forms in the classroom differ from those used between adults in Ervin-Tripp's data. She describes them as frequently used in situations where the listener might not comply with the directive; in such cases, treating the directive as an information question provides the addressee with an escape route: e.g.

> [Daughter to father]:
> 'You ready?'
> 'Not yet.' (Ervin-Tripp 1976, p. 38)

There were very few examples of children responding to an interrogative directive as if it were an information question, and, where they did occur, such responses seemed to be due to the child's inexperience of such directives from the teacher, rather than being deliberate strategies to avoid compliance: e.g.

T: Lynda do you know where the paints are kept?
L: Yes. (without moving)
T: Would you like to get them?
L: Yes. (without moving)
T: OK. Away you go.

The teacher moves from a non-modal interrogative directive to the modal form, and finally to the fully explicit imperative form, before the child comprehends the directive force of the teacher's utterances. The example illustrates Leech's maxim of Tact very neatly: the politest or most tactful form is also the least direct and, for the child, the most difficult to interpret correctly. This suggests one possible explanation for the infrequency of such forms in the data. The elementary school child's ability to detect directive intent in functionally ambiguous structures such as these, is perhaps not yet sufficiently well developed for the teacher to use such forms frequently with success.

3 Declaratives

Declarative directives in the classroom fell into two contrasting categories according to their relative explicitness and the amount of inference required to interpret the directive intent. Ervin-Tripp's (1976) closely related categories of 'need statements' and 'hints' reflect precisely this contrast.

(*i*) *Embedded agent*: e.g. 'I'd like everyone sitting on the mat.' Declaratives in this category can be identified by the fact that the agent and usually the required activity are expressed explicitly in an embedded or subordinate clause. And in many cases the main clause was introduced by 'I want' or 'I'd like'. Examples of these forms were relatively frequent in the data:

'I want you to draw a picture.'
'I'd like Arnold's group on the mat now.'
'I'd like to have everyone sitting really comfortably and not touching anyone else.'

According to Ervin-Tripp (1976) such forms occur most typically in two types of setting:

(a) 'the transactional work setting, where who is to do what
is very clear and a statement of need (or desire) by a
superior implied an obligation on the part of the
subordinate';
(b) 'in families, when solicitude on the part of the hearer
could be assumed' (p. 29)

The classroom is clearly a transactional setting, and thus statements of wish or desire by the teacher function as clear directives
to the pupils.

The extent to which pupils are expected to please teachers, by
responding to their wishes, is reflected by the fact that even such
forms as 'I wonder' and 'I think' may be used to introduce directives if they are followed by descriptions of feasible activities.
Thus, despite their apparently tentative form, the following examples clearly belong in this category:

'I wonder who can put their hand up without speaking.'
'I wonder if Larry could find us the right books.'
'I think we'll have everyone sitting on their bottoms.'
'Perhaps if each person could come back to the
middle . . .'
'It might be better if you sat right down.'

(ii) Hints: e.g. 'Kelly's hand is up!'
Although for convenience this label refers to intent rather than
structural features, it is possible to identify the formal characteristics of examples: the required agent and/or the required activity
is not explicit in the surface structure of these declarative directives. Hints require addressees to infer what is required from their
knowledge of the rules for appropriate behaviour in the context.
Many of Ervin-Tripp's (1976) examples are very oblique and
require considerable sociolinguistic competence from addressees.
They are thus more vulnerable to misunderstanding.

Perhaps for this reason, hints in elementary classrooms tended
to be more direct, and often took the form of praise for pupils
who were doing what the teacher required of the whole class. By
this means teachers could refer explicitly to the desired action,
while avoiding both an overt command and a reprimand to those
not conforming. In the process positive feedback is given to the
obedient pupils. Examples from the data are:

'I can see some nice sitting up.'
'Helen is sitting nicely.'

'I like the way you've got your hand up Anita.'
'I like the way you stood up quickly Neil.'
'Kelly's hand is up.'

In all these examples the required action, but not the agent of the directive, is explicit.

A second group of examples in this category took the form of descriptions of undesirable or proscribed behaviour, with an implicit directive to revert to desirable activities. In these cases the agent but not the required activity is quite explicit. A correct interpretation depends on knowledge of appropriate and expected behaviour in the context. So, for example, while 'Paul you're very quiet' can be interpreted as praise in a context where silence is required behaviour, it will function as a directive to contribute in a context where talk is expected and the addressor is in control. Examples from the classroom data are:

'John you're calling out.' (Pupils had just been told to put up their hands.)
'Sally you're not saying much.' (i.e. Make a contribution.)

There were also a few examples of forms where neither the agent nor the required activity were explicit. Such forms obviously make the greatest demands on the inductive abilities of pupils, but they were rarely misinterpreted since the intended directive was generally quite clear from the context and the pupil's role in relation to the teacher: e.g.

'I'm not going to do it by myself.' (i.e. Help me.)
'There's another piece of chalk over there.' (i.e. Bring it.)
'I do think that's enough noise with the chairs.' (i.e. Stop the noise.)
'You're too clever you are.' (i.e. Let someone else answer.)

The last example was the most complex found in the data, and it is doubtful whether in this case its directive function was recognized by the child to whom it was addressed. Only the word 'too' prevents it from being interpretable as unmitigated praise, and, in fact, its form may well have reflected the teacher's ambiguous feelings about a child who was performing her 'duties' perfectly, but, in the process, preventing others from doing so. This example indicates the subtlety of some of the rules underlying appropriate classroom behaviour, and suggests the kind of problems facing new entrants who need to acquire these rules to function appropriately in classroom interaction.

Children's comprehension of teacher's directives

Shatz (quoted in Coulthard 1977) provides evidence that two-year-olds interacting with their mothers in the home can correctly interpret directive intent both from explicit forms, such as imperatives, and from less explicit forms, such as interrogative directives. And Reeder (quoted in Coulthard 1977) demonstrated that children aged three to four were successful most of the time in interpreting indirect realizations of directives. Coulthard (1977) points out that contextual cues are probably very important in the correct decoding of functionally ambiguous forms, such as interrogatives. He suggests that where misinterpretations occur 'children's problems may lie in interpreting the context' (p. 165) and that this may present problems even for children as old as twelve, as an example from Sinclair and Coulthard (1975) illustrates:

> TEACHER: What are you laughing at?
> PUPIL: Nothing?
> The pupil interpreted the teacher's interrogative as a
> directive to stop laughing, but that was not the teacher's
> intention . . . he realized that the pupil's laughter was an
> indication of her attitude, and if he could get her to explain
> why she was laughing he would have an excellent opening
> to the topic. (p. 30)

The pupil here had misunderstood the situation, not the sentence, and hence had misconstrued the function of the utterance as a directive and its force as a 'command to stop'. Similarly children may treat a genuine question as a 'command to do' if the action referred to is feasible and appropriate, and especially if it is uttered by a statusful addresser: e.g.

> TEACHER: Are you going swimming today?
> PUPIL: (moves towards the door)
> TEACHER: It's not time yet. I just wanted to know if you
>   were going.

Ervin-Tripp (1976) notes that,

> Coming from a teacher, even a lexical reference to required
> or prohibited school activities is heard as a directive. How
> could so general a rule work as a processing device?
> Perhaps by creating a kind of semantic marker on these
> activity names, or their conceptual domain, activated when
> occurring in the context of the teacher. (p. 59)

This suggestion also provides a possible explanation for the correct interpretation of elliptical utterances such as 'OK bus people', and 'Hands not voices'.

It is quite clear from examples of misunderstandings of directives in the data that context is crucial in interpreting them appropriately. Children in the new entrant class need to acquire from experience many of the rules for successful classroom interaction. Some rules are made quite explicit: e.g. 'Don't shout out', and, once established, less direct forms such as 'You're shouting out', and 'Simon!', can be recognized as directives, whatever their form. Other rules are more subtle, and it may take the child some time to correctly interpret implicit directives based on such rules.

An excellent example of a complex rule is the rule for indicating that you wish to make a verbal contribution to a full class interaction. The child must learn to 'bid' for a speaking turn by raising one hand. Often the teacher will give a 'cue' (e.g. 'Hands up') to the children that they should bid for the right to respond to a question.[8] The correct interpretation of this directive is often very difficult for a child inexperienced in the linguistic etiquette rules of the classroom. Children frequently raise their hands in response to 'Hands up' whether they think they can respond or not. This is revealed by their subsequent confusion if they are nominated by the teacher. They misinterpret 'Hands up' as a directive to the whole class hearing it as similar to 'Stop talking' or 'Don't shout out'. This confusion is doubtless increased by the frequent use of 'Hands up' as an indirect means of reprimanding children who are shouting out responses. The misinterpretation is based on a failure to recognize that the meaning of 'Hands up' is embedded in the discourse structure of the classroom. 'Hands up' might be more fully explicated as:

> Put one hand up (1) if you are able to make an appropriate verbal response to my last elicitation, or (2) if by doing so you are providing an appropriate non-verbal response to my last elicitation.

((2) covers such elicitations as 'How many of you want to go swimming?')

Imperative forms are usually, however, explicit enough to prevent misunderstandings. The only cases of misunderstandings occurring in this category were directives realized as elliptical forms such as 'Hands up' or children's names. Directives taking the form of individual names are clearly potentially ambiguous in the classroom. Teachers use a child's name most commonly to signal that he or she should make a verbal response to a preceding or following question: i.e. to allocate a speaking turn. Thus directives realized by the same form are sometimes misinterpreted by young children: e.g.

> T: Someone open the window. John!
> P: Yes miss. (without moving)

In this case the child anticipated that something more would follow. In other cases children responded with confused silence, suggesting they assumed they were expected to answer a question they had not heard. Of course, teachers sometimes exploit this ambiguity directing an address form following a question to a child who is talking; it then functions both as a directive to stop and as a nomination allocating the child a speaking turn which he or she is in no position to take. Interpreting the function of address forms appropriately is then another sociolinguistic skill the new entrant must develop.

Non-modal interrogative forms functioning as directives may also be a source of confusion for new entrants in the classroom context, as the example on p. 105 illustrates very clearly. Another similar example was also observed in a new entrant class:

> T: Jason why have you got your raincoat on inside?
> P: (smiles)
> T: It's not raining inside.
> P: (no response)
> T: What are you going to do about it?
> P: (no response)
> T: Go and hang it up.

The teacher's interrogative directives elicit no response (and not surprisingly, neither does her hint) so she is finally forced to make the directive explicit using an imperative form.

Learning to respond to such indirect forms by performing the appropriate act is a skill which children acquire relatively quickly however. As the example quoted earlier illustrates, by twelve this interpretive rule is so well internalized that genuine information-seeking interrogatives may be interpreted as directive if they refer to required or proscribed activities. And utterances intended by the teacher as suggestions, such as 'Would you like to do a puzzle?', will almost certainly be heard as commands, given the social constraints on classroom interaction and the form of the social relationship between teacher and pupil. At elementary level, then, interpretive problems tend to derive from lack of familiarity with the context and the social and behavioural expectations of the teacher, rather than with the linguistic forms used.

The only other examples of misinterpretation in the data also illustrate the relevance of contextual factors in interpreting directives. Imperatives and need statements are maximally explicit, and hence they generally present no problems for the elementary school pupil. When they make complex contextual demands on the child, however, they may be misinterpreted: e.g.

> T: All right, stop, listen. You children who are still writing carry on writing. Put your chairs up very quietly you others. Do that then come back and sit on the mat. All right sit down please on the mat.

Children can follow strings of directives addressed to the whole class, but this example demands they distinguish which group each directive is addressed to, and follow only those applicable to the group to which they belong. In this case some children who were writing stopped and then followed the directives for those who had finished writing. Others responded only to the final directive and went straight to the mat. This latter response may be partly explained by Sinclair and Coulthard's (1975) observation, on the basis of their analysis of classroom discourse, that: 'In any succession of statements, questions and commands the pupil knows that he usually only has to respond to the final one' (p. 35). When the pupil has to follow several directives, or distinguish those which apply only to him, then misinterpretation is possible. An even more complex example of such contextually dependent directives is this one:

> T: First of all I would like to keep Robert's group on the mat. Sharon's group Miss H. is coming after maths to take you. So now you may go to the writing table. There is a puzzle table if you would like to go there. There is a crayon and dye table. Benny you could finish your sign. And Robert's group are on the mat. Away you go everyone.

Little wonder that few children proceeeded to the crayon and dye table after such a barrage of directives and such a range of directive types!

No examples were observed of cases where the linguistic complexity of the directive form led to interpretive problems, although relatively complex forms did occur. Imperatives preceded by 'if' clauses, for example sometimes functioned to select specific groups of children to whom the directive was addressed: e.g.

'If you did a painting today please go and get it.'
'If you've brought your own lunch go and get it now.'

Despite the apparent linguistic complexity of these forms neither seemed to cause any problems, perhaps because the appropriate response was quite clear in the context: i.e. children who had not done paintings or brought lunch could not follow the directive, even if they did not thoroughly understand that its form specifically excluded them.

Overall, then, although teachers' directives may be realized by a wide variety of forms, miscomprehension seems relatively rare. Children apparently acquire the necessary sociolinguistic competence very rapidly, and do not often misinterpret the function of the forms they hear. Nor do they often mistake the force of teachers' directives. They soon recognize the power and the pervasiveness of the teacher's control in the classroom. At one level teachers control all the relevant knowledge in the classroom and the way it is disseminated. At another they control the quantity, content and quality of classroom talk, and even the form it takes (Stubbs 1976a; Holmes 1978). Teachers constantly monitor pupils' contributions, correcting, evaluating, editing and summarizing (Stubbs 1976b). Pupils learn their role in such interactions by experience. The values and attitudes concerning appropriate pupil behaviour, about what comprises relevant knowledge and how it is to be transmitted, about what constitutes an appropriate response to teachers' directives and elicitations, are all aspects of what the child must learn in the role of pupil, and are elements of what Jackson (1968) has called 'the hidden curriculum'.

Since at least a quarter of the teacher's classroom talk is devoted to organizing and disciplining pupils by explicit statement (Boydell 1974; Delamont 1976) the ability to understand such talk is obviously crucial. A correct interpretation of teachers' directives requires that the child recognize the controlling role and powerful status of the teacher in the classroom, and the rights associated with that role and status. Children seem to learn to scan all teachers' utterances for potential directive function. And they soon recognize that forms which, in other contexts, would be correctly interpreted as 'advice' or 'suggestions' carry the force of 'commands' in the classroom situation. The effect of role and status differences on the interpretation of the force of an utterance is particularly clear in the case of expressions of personal desire. A declarative such as 'I want a pencil' is a clear command spoken by the teacher, but it will be treated as a request if addressed to the teacher by a pupil. Some teachers demand that children make its request status quite explicit by adding 'please', and address forms, such as 'Miss' or 'Sir', or even by reframing it as a 'permission directive' or modal interrogative (e.g. one teacher responded to 'I want a pencil', by saying to the child 'Please may I have a pencil Mrs F.'). The relevance of social features, such as setting, status, role, and the rights and duties of participants is undeniable in correctly interpreting the functional meaning and illocutionary force of utterances.

The reason why children so quickly acquire the sociolinguistic competence to perform their roles as pupils is perhaps, as Willes (1975) suggests, that their motivation to please the teacher is very high, and the classroom setting provides continual opportunities to demonstrate this. Teachers obviously exploit their pupils' desire to please, as demonstrated by the use of praise and condemnation as indirect directives. Hints similarly assume that pupils are anxious to conform to the teacher's wishes and, since they generally refer to expected pupil behaviour, such as sitting still, being quiet, responding to questions and so on, they are rarely misinterpreted. Given a strong desire to please, then, children soon become very skilled at accurately interpreting directive intent in teachers' utterances. Teachers may avoid ostentatious demonstrations of authority by using less explicit directive forms, but children soon learn from experience that the teacher's every wish is their command.

Notes

1. The effect of status differences on the interpretation of speech acts is mentioned by Searle (1976), and the social implications of choice of form for expressing directives are discussed in some detail by Ervin-Tripp (1976 and 1977) on the basis of empirical observations. This point is more fully discussed later in the paper.
2. Some of the implications of these different approaches are helpfully discussed in Coulthard (1977).
3. 'Non-linguistic' responses presumably do not include, however, head nods substituting for 'yes', or head-shakes substituting for 'no': i.e. conventional non-verbal tokens of linguistic responses.
4. These terms are defined by Ervin-Tripp (1969) and Blom and Gumperz (1972), and are useful basic sociolinguistic concepts.

5. See Stubbs (1976a and 1976b), Edwards (1976) and Holmes (1978) for a more detailed discussion of the formal nature of much classroom interaction, and the effect of this on the language of the classroom.
6. I would like to thank Juliet Burman, Jim Denton, Marion Smyth, Jocelyn Tarrant and Anna Thompson for providing transcriptions of tapes of classroom interaction which have been used in this analysis.
7. Although such directives are not strictly aimed at eliciting a non-verbal response, they are included here since they are clearly not 'questions'. Reading aloud in the classroom is perhaps more appropriately regarded as an activity than a 'reply'.
8. 'Cue' and 'bid' are technical terms used by Sinclair and Coulthard (1975) in their analysis of classroom discourse.

Questions for discussion, study and further research

1. On page 91, a number of speech acts are arranged in scales under the speech functions *directive* and *informative*. Do you agree with the relative positions of the speech acts on the scales? What effect do social constraints such as the status of the participants and the context of speech have on the force of speech acts? Can you think of other speech act labels you would want to include on these scales?

2. To what extent and in what ways do you think the variables class size, content of lesson, task required, etc., mentioned on page 97 are likely to affect the structure and frequency of directives used by teachers to pupils? Can you think of any other variables which might need to be considered when comparing the directives used by different teachers?

3. Leech's maxim of Tact, mentioned on pages 95, 101 and 105, suggests that the more powerful and socially distant the addressor and the more 'costly' the required action to the addressee, the more tact is required in expressing the directive. In what ways might degrees of tact be realized linguistically?

4. Consider the function of questions in different contexts. What are the non-linguistic characteristics of contexts in which questions tend to have directive force?

5. Directives which depend for comprehension on a shared social or cultural background between teacher and children may present problems for minority children. Consider whether any of the types of directives described in this article might be difficult for minority group children to understand.

6. Keeping other social variables constant, classify directives used by (a) children to parents, (b) parents to children, (c) children to unfamiliar adults, (d) between unfamiliar adults, (e) unfamiliar adults to children. Note any differences in the frequency of particular types of directives in different interactions.

7. Hints often refer indirectly to the hearer's duties or the speaker's rights. Collect examples of hints, noting their structure, and consider the extent to which they involve shared understandings which are not made explicit in the utterances.

8. With the teacher's permission observe in a classroom, noting down all directives used by the teacher (a) to the whole class (b) to small groups or individual children. Are there any differences in the structure or frequency of the directives addressed to the different groups?

9. With the teacher's permission observe in a new entrant classroom and note examples of directives used by the teacher which are not understood by the children. Which types of directives tend to be misunderstood most frequently? How does the teacher rephrase such directives to ensure comprehension?

Introduction to Chapter 5

From the micro-perspective on directive speech acts within speech events in Holmes' paper, in this chapter we turn to a macro-perspective on conversation as a speech event. Research on the analysis of conversational behaviour is reviewed, and conversation is seen as an activity which is directed to social goals (e.g. the establishment of roles, presentation of self) as well as the linguistic goals (communication of meanings). How do speakers recognize and conduct conversation? Speakers and hearers are seen to share assumption about the goals and processes of conversation which enable them to interact with each other and to interpret conversation as an ongoing, developing and related succession of utterances. Such a movement is constructed from strategies for the introduction of topics, openings and closings, the pairing of utterances in conversation and turn-taking conventions. Conversation is seen to have not only linear structure but hierarchical structure, topics being created within topics, for example, or topics mentioned at one point in a conversation, serving as assumed background knowledge for things said twenty minutes later. The acquisition of conversational skills is dependent upon not only these linguistic aspects of conversational discourse, but a knowledge of the social constraints within which they operate in a particular culture.

Canale's concept of *strategic competence*, is here illustrated through the discussion of conversational repair, and its effect on conversation in both a native and second language is illustrated.

Implications for the teaching of language through the use of conversation-like activities (e.g. dialogues) are discussed.

5 Conversational analysis[1]

Jack C. Richards and Richard W. Schmidt

Human beings spend a large part of their lives engaging in conversation and for most of them conversation is among their most significant and engrossing activities. Similarly, researchers from a great many academic disciplines have looked at conversation as an object of inquiry, and none have failed to be fascinated. Our understanding of how people conduct conversations has been enriched by observations by psychologists and linguists (generally working under the banner of 'discourse analysis'), among others. There is a widely used model for the analysis of conversation by Bales (1950), which involves coding conversational material into categories such as 'shows tension', 'shows solidarity', 'shows antagonism' for the study of small group behaviour. In this chapter, however, we will focus primarily on the work of a small number of sociologists, including Erving Goffman (1974, 1976), whose insistence on viewing conversation and talk in general as social interaction within a social frame has been widely influential, and those sociologists who are often grouped together under the label of 'ethnomethodologists', e.g. Garfinkel 1971, Psathas 1979, Sacks 1972a , Schegloff 1968, 1971, 1972, 1979, Schenkein 1978a, b, Sudnow 1972, R. Turner 1974.

1 The ethnomethodological perspective

In most sociological theorizing, values, norms, roles, interest coalitions and the like are assumed to have an external reality. One way of approaching the study of conversation (an obvious one) is to study the correlations between such facts of social order and features of talk. The perspective of ethnomethodology is quite different, however, since it looks less to objective social reality than to the methods or efforts that people use to actively and continually create and sustain for each other the *presumption* that the social world has a real character (J. H. Turner 1974, pp. 321–31). For ethnomethodologists, the social world is an *achievement*, and the content of that world is not as interesting as the character of work that societal members do to maintain or alter it. Ethnomethodologists are interested in societal members' knowledge of their ordinary affairs and their own organized enterprises, in practical reasoning and everyday practices. All of these are viewed as accomplishments, so ethnomethodologists frequently speak of 'accomplishing ethnicity', 'doing talk' (R. Turner 1974, cf. everyday, non-technical '*making* conversation'), or doing 'topicalization work' (Winskowski 1977, p. 77), as opposed for example to 'talking about a topic'. This interest in everyday social activities has led to a great deal of research on carefully transcribed natural conversations, focussing on some of the most mundane features of talk, but oriented to delicate and unexpectedly complex features of the unfolding activity. While this attention to conversation did not arise because of any initial special interest in language use *per se*, ethnomethodologists have pointed out that 'none the less, the character of our materials as conversational has attracted our attention to the study of conversation as an activity in its own right' (Schegloff and Sacks 1973, p. 289). In recent years, the ethnomethodologists – together with those linguists, applied linguists, psycholinguists and philosophers whose ideas have cross-fertilized with theirs – have produced the most significant input to the study of conversation.

The term 'conversation' is used somewhat ambiguously in current literature, referring sometimes to any spoken encounter or interaction and sometimes, more restrictedly, to:

> . . . talk occurring when a small number of participants come together and settle into what they perceive to be a few moments cut off from (or carried on to the side of) instrumental tasks; a period of idling felt to be an end in itself, during which everyone is accorded the right to talk as well as to listen and without reference to a fixed schedule; everyone is accorded the status of someone whose overall evaluation of the subject matter at hand . . . is to be encouraged and treated with respect; and no final agreement or synthesis is demanded, differences of opinion to be treated as unprejudicial to the continuing relationship of the parties.   (Goffman 1976, p. 264)

As Goffman points out, all talk is grounded in its surroundings, but what we call conversation is more loosely anchored to the world than other kinds of utterances. Moreover, in everyday terms we often orient to '*a conversation*' as a kind of event, as when we report, 'I had an interesting conversation with Ted today.'

(1) A: Hi.   (2) A: You ready to order?
     B: Hi.   B: What's your soup and sandwich?
                      A: Uh, it's a corned beef salad sandwich and uh beef noodle soup, I think.
                      B: No, I'll take a club sandwich. And coffee.
                      A: OK.

In both (1) and (2) what is spoken may be treated as *conversational*, but neither exchange constitutes *a conversation* in the more restricted sense, though (1) might have led to one and (2) might conceivably have incorporated one.

Hymes (1972a) uses the term *speech event* for activities that are directly governed by norms for the use of speech. As speech events, conversations can be contrasted with other types of speech events such as lectures, discussions, sermons, courtroom trials, interviews, debates and meetings. We recognize each of these speech events as distinct by virtue of differences in the number of participants who take part in them, as well as through differences in the type and amount of talking expected of the participants. Speech events also have identifiable rules for proper beginnings, middles and ends, violations of which are noticed and reportable: 'Then Susan came over and interrupted our conversation'; 'so, he just left in a huff'. The characteristics and conventions of conversation as a kind of speech event are learned by language learners and ought to be describable. It is to this which we now turn. For the most part we will be concerned with conversation in the more restricted sense, as an event, though we will point out instances where generalizations may be extended to other speech events that qualify as talk but not specifically as conversations, as well as instances where findings may apply even more restrictedly, for example only to telephone conversations.[2]

2 The cooperative principle

Conversation is more than merely the exchange of information. When people take part in conversation, they bring to the conversational process shared assumptions and expectations about what conversation is, how conversation develops, and the sort of contribution they are each expected to make. When people engage in conversation they share common principles of conversation that lead them to interpret each other's utterances as contributing to conversation. Consider the following example:

(3) A: Where did you buy that shirt?
    B: And he shouldn't say it anyway because that's what he does.

Is this a conversation? For B's sentence to be interpreted and understood, we need in some way to be able to link it to A's question. One of the assumptions we make when we take part in conversation is that if I ask you a question, whatever you say will somehow be interpretable as constituting an answer to my question. In this case, this does not appear to have taken place and the resulting exchange is uninterpretable. We would, if faced with such a reply, repeat our question to make sure the other party had clearly understood it, or ask the other party to repeat their utterance to see if we had understood it properly. If we experienced repeated exchanges of this sort from a conversational partner, we could justifiably enquire into the state of our partner's mental or psychological health.

Now consider another example:

(4) A: How much did you pay for that blouse?
    B: Do you like it? I got it at Metro.

In this case, although B doesn't answer A's question, the avoidance of the requested answer is interpretable as an answer. It is equivalent to, 'I don't want to tell you that,' The reply is thus seen as coherent.

The philosopher Grice has described four Maxims or Principles of Cooperative Behaviour which speakers observe in conversation (see Fraser, this volume). These are:

1. Maxim of Quantity: Make your contribution just as informative as required.
2. Maxim of Quality: Make your contribution one that is true.
3. Maxim of Relation: Make your contribution relevant.
4. Maxim of Manner: Avoid obscurity and ambiguity. Be brief and orderly.

(Grice 1975)

By the Maxim of Quantity, Grice refers to the assumption that if a speaker has access to information required by the hearer, he or she is expected to communicate that information to the hearer. Consider this example:

(5) A: Where is your mother?
    B: She is either in the house or at the market.

As Keenan (1976) points out, B's utterance conversationally implies that the child doesn't know specifically where the mother is located, but only that she is in one of two places. If the child did in fact know in which of the two locations the mother was located, the maxim would have been violated by failing to provide the information required.

The Maxim of Quantity also accounts for the fact that we normally give sufficient, but not more information than is required. We can thus compare the following conversations. In example (6), sufficient information is given. But in example (7), the child has not yet acquired the conventions associated with the maxim and so gives more information than an adult conversationalist would be expected to give:

(6) A: Where are you going?
    B: I'm going to the bathroom.
(7) A: Where are you going?
    B: I'm going to the bathroom to do wee wee.

The second maxim, the Maxim of Quality, accounts for the fact that in conversation we normally act on the assumption that our partner is not being untruthful or is not deliberately trying to deceive us. If not, it would be extremely difficult to maintain conversation with our partners.

The Maxim of Relation is illustrated in this exchange:

(8) A: I'm out of writing paper.
    B: There's a shop around the corner.

Acting on the assumption that B's reply is relevant, A will assume that the shop is open and that it sells writing paper. B has implicated as much. Imagine that A went round the corner and found that the shop was a clothing shop and did not sell stationery, and so confronted B:

(9) A: You said I could get paper at the shop around the corner.
    B: No, I didn't. All I said was that there was a shop around the corner. I didn't say what kind of a shop it was.

A would be justifiably annoyed, because B was not playing the rules of the conversational game and was not observing the Maxim of Relation.

Clark and Clark (1977) discuss similar examples of how rules of conversational implicature, dependent on manipulating the four conversational maxims, can be used to express sarcasm, irony, criticism and a range of other types of inferential meaning. For example, consider the following exchange between two university lecturers:

(10) A: How did you find Jones' thesis?
     B: It was well typed.

By choosing not to be as informative as required, B is suggesting that the other qualities of the thesis were not worth commenting on. B has thus communicated through rules of conversational implicature that it was a bad thesis.

From the examples we see that conversation is more than a series of exchanges; it consists of exchanges which are initiated and interpreted according to intuitively understood and socially acquired rules and norms of conversational cooperation, which can in turn be manipulated to create a wide range of meanings beyond the level expressed directly by the utterances in the conversation themselves.

While the examples given so far illustrate the importance of Grice's maxims of conversation for understanding short, mostly two part exchanges, these maxims are also operative in the interpretation of individual utterances and in the organization of much longer stretches of discourse. Consider, for example, a long telephone conversation in which friends exchange bits of information, tell stories about themselves and mutual friends, and generally engage in gossip not directly aimed at accomplishing some specific interactional goal. Even such an apparently amorphous or aimless conversation can often be seen as highly structured in terms of the maxims, especially the maxim *be relevant*.

Conversations often take the form of stories told in rounds, and in such cases the smooth flow of conversation requires that each story told be relevant to the one preceding. If the maxim of relation is broken, if I listen to your story about an interesting play you have seen and counter with a story of my own about my new car, with no apology for changing the subject, you are likely to consider me rude, and if I do this often enough you may begin to wonder whether I am mentally or emotionally disturbed. My failure to follow your stories with ones that are detectably relevant can be seen as a failure to understand your stories, or perhaps as rejection of you and your experiences.

Frequently, relevance is established by the obvious incorporation of elements from the first narrative into the second. If you tell me about your troubles in trying to park your car before going to class at the university, I can safely follow this with a story about my own parking problems. If you tell about an accident, I can tell about one I have seen or been in; if you tell about learning how to swim, I may tell about the time I almost drowned as a beginning swimmer; if you tell me about a trip to Europe, I can tell a story about similar events that have happened on my travels. In all these cases, the relevance of what follows to what has preceded will be transparent and the conversation will progress happily.

While relevance may be obvious, speakers very frequently make use of discourse markers to signal (and assert) that what they have to say is relevant. Phrases like 'that's like what happened to me when . . .' establish relevance that might not be immediately clear. In examining a transcript of a long telephone conversation, Schegloff (1971) found abundant use of such linking devices:

(11) A: Oh, right.
      B: And then decide, but uh   } redundancies
      A: Right.   indicate the
      B: Ehh, who knows?   conclusion of
      A: I know.   previous story
      B: You know. . . SO, I got some lousy courses this term too.

In the last line of example (11), the significant discourse markers used by B are *SO* (said rather loudly), indicating that a new topic or story is being introduced, and the deictic *too*, which claims relevance to something said earlier by A. In this particular case, the *too* refers back to a statement by A that 'I have a lotta tough courses', which occurred fifty interactional turns previously. So the story about to be told is being claimed to be relevant not to the immediately preceding story but to one much earlier.

Stories or narrative turns in conversation are usually made relevant not just to the immediately preceding story or topic but to a broader theme or controlling topic for the conversation as a whole. While the conversation just quoted from consists of a great many stories and short exchanges, almost all of these are related implicitly or explicitly to the controlling topic introduced at the beginning of the conversation by the caller: 'How's school going?'

Once this overall frame is established, each story is related to it, primarily through the use of academic temporal and spatial referents. A friend is referred to as someone 'in my abnormal class', a story is told about someone who died 'in the middle of the term' (rather than 'in October', which might be equally true but less relevant), events are related that happened 'at the end of class' (rather than at 10.30 a.m.) or 'on the way to the bookstore'.

When a story is told or a topic introduced that is not relevant to either what has just been said or to the overall continuing topic, some sort of recognition of this lapse from the maxim of relevance is usually made:

(12) A: Oh, my mother wanted to know how's your grandmother?

In introducing this topic, the only one in Schegloff's transcript that does not deal with 'how's school going?', A recognizes and implicitly apologizes for the break in relevance through her use of *Oh*. She further justifies the obvious topic switch by attributing the question to her mother rather than to herself. As Ryave has pointed out, the relations displayed between stories 'are not capricious and happenstance, but are instead the products of the conversational participants' attention and careful management' (Ryave 1978, p. 121).

The relevance of Grice's Maxim of Relation, as well as the other conversational maxims, to conversation in a second language is dependent on the degree to which such maxims are universal or language specific. While it is clear that conversation in any language is dependent upon these conversational maxims, the specific form they take may vary across cultures. Keenan points out, for example, that there may well be differences across cultures in the degree to which members of a society are expected to conform to the Maxim of Quantity, that in some cases 'meeting another's informational needs may be relatively unexpected or marked behaviour' (Keenan 1976, p. 69). She discussed how in Malagasy society conversationalists regularly provide less information than is required by their conversational partners, even though they have access to the necessary information. For reasons that have to do with local customs and belief, speakers in that society may avoid identifying people in their utterances. They will obscure the identity of a child in referring to it in conversation for example, for fear of tempting a malevolent force to intervene by doing so. By not observing local variants of conversational postulates, Keenan observes, foreigners speaking Malagasy appear brusque and impolite and much too direct.

3 Speech act and interactional acts

The principles and maxims of cooperative behaviour illustrate
some of the assumptions people bring to conversation. But for
what purposes does conversation take place? Lane (1978)
describes some of the concerns of conversation as 'exchanging
information, maintaining social bonds of friendship, kinship, etc.,
negotiating statuses and roles and deciding and carrying out joint
action' (Lane 1978, p. 58). Conversation can thus fulfil many
different functions.

One approach to the analysis of language functions is through
speech act theory. When people converse, they may make promises, give praise, flatter, criticize, or issue invitations and warnings.
A crucial goal for conversationalists is to interpret the intended
speech act appropriately. The following example of a telephone
conversation between a professor and a foreign student illustrates
the student's failure to interpret the intended act:

(13) A: Hello, is Mr Simatapung there please?
     B: Yes.
     A: Oh . . . may I speak to him please?
     B: Yes.
     A: Oh . . . are you Mr Simatapung?
     B: Yes, this is Mr Simatapung.

Here B answers A's question as if it were an existential question
rather than a request to bring the named person to the phone
(see Schmidt and Richards 1980).

The question then arises whether it would be useful to consider
conversation as a sequence of speech acts and proceed to write a
grammar of discourse by focussing first on the smallest units
(speech acts) and gradually working out the possible combinations. Certainly there are some speech acts that allow us to predict with reasonable certainty what other speech act will follow.
For example, 'How are you?' is frequently followed by 'I'm fine'.
Here the first utterance can be characterized as a question, a type
of 'directive' in the classifications of Searle (1976) and Fraser (this
volume). The second utterance can be called a report, or 'representative'. However, we could not claim that all or even most
directives are followed by representatives, or that any other general speech act category is necessarily followed by an utterance
from another general speech act category.

One of the limitations of traditional speech act theory (Austin
1962, Searle 1969) for conversational analysis is that speech acts

are usually defined in terms of speaker intentions and beliefs, whereas the nature of conversation depends crucially on interaction between speaker and hearer. Goffman has claimed that:

> . . . the expression of claims regarding inner states is not what takes up most of the individual's speaking time. Nor is much time actually spent in giving orders, announcing decisions, declining requests, making offers, and the like. And when any of these possibilities do occur, they often do so indirectly, operating through something else; they are an effect that is produced, but an effect that tells us little about the details of the strip of activity that produces it.
>
> (Goffman 1974, p. 503)

Labov and Fanshel have taken the same position, asserting that conversation is not a chain of utterances (speech acts), but rather 'a matrix of utterances and actions bound together by a web of understandings and reactions' (Labov and Fanshel 1977, p. 30). According to Labov and Fanshel, it is not such speaker based acts as requests and assertions that propel conversation and establish coherence of sequencing in conversation, but rather such *interactional acts* as challenges, defences and retreats, which have to do with the status of participants in the conversation, their rights and obligations.

A similar distinction between the speech act (or illocutionary act) and the interactional act is given by Edmondson (1981):

(14) A: Promise me you'll come.
    B: Okay.

In this example the utterance *Okay* may be viewed as a 'promise' as a speech act, but as an interactional move might be more aptly characterized as compliance or, in Edmondson's terms, a 'satisfy' or 'resolve'.

A second reason to modify the 'chain of utterances' notion of conversation is that many, perhaps most, speech acts are multifunctional. A student who asks a teacher, 'Would you speak more slowly, please?' is simultaneously requesting action, asserting that the teacher is speaking too fast and reporting difficulty. Labov and Fanshel point out that speaker and hearer react to these speech acts at many levels of abstraction. Brown and Levinson have pointed out that we may carry out our social intentions at different levels of abstraction as well, giving the example of a boss reproving an employee for not doing a job. Knowing that the employee has neglected a batch of correspondence, the boss asks one by one whether each piece of work has been done, and receives a series of negative replies. An intention to criticize is accomplished through the use of a series of utterances (unit speech acts), none of which are clearly analysable as criticisms when taken separately. Brown and Levinson conclude that conversational plans are hierarchical, and 'conversational understanding is achieved by reconstruction of levels of intent beyond and above and integrative of those that lie behind particular utterances or sentences'(Brown and Levinson 1978, p. 238).

A final motivation for seeing conversation as a form of interaction rather than merely a sequence of utterances comes from considerations of 'framing' (Goffman 1974). The type of activity or speech event being undertaken, as well as the situation in which this is embedded, largely determines the kinds of speech acts that can occur (cf. Holmes, this volume). As Levinson (1979) has pointed out, the application of Grice's maxims may also be dependent on the nature of the activity (speech event) in which talk or conversation is embedded. In an interrogation, for example, neither party assumes the other is fulfilling the Maxims of Quality, Manner, and especially Quantity:

(15) A: Did you see last week's *Newsweek*?
    B: Part of it.
    A: Did you read that part of it?
    B: I'm not sure whether I did or not.

In ordinary conversation we would assume that the questioner is more interested in the content of a magazine than in its layout or visual form (possible, of course, for example if the interlocuters are graphic designers) and that it would be uncooperative to understand the question in a more specific way. We would normally take the answer 'part of it' to implicate that B had *read* that part of it and not just *seen* part of it, making our inference on the basis of Grice's Maxim of Quantity. In an interrogation, however, we cancel the implication from *seen* to *read* since we know it is not in the interest of defendents to cooperate fully (Levinson 1979, p. 373).

4 Adjacency pairs

If we take the central problem of conversational analysis to be the discovery of connections between utterances and interaction, we may begin to uncover the coherence of conversation by identifying sequencing rules which apply to utterances as interactional acts. One way in which meanings are communicated and interpreted in conversation is through the use of what has been called adjacency pairs. Adjacency pairs are utterances produced by two successive speakers such that the second utterance is identified as related to the first as an expected follow-up. The two form a pair, the first utterance constituting a *first pair part* and the next utterance constituting a *second pair part*. Coulthard (1977) describes adjacency pairs as 'the basic structural unit in conversation.' Some examples of adjacency pairs are:

(a) Greeting-Greeting   A: Hello.
                                    B: Hi.

(b) Summons-Answer   A: Jimmy!
                                    B: Coming mother.

(c) Question-Answer   A: Is that what you mean?
                                    B: Yes.

(d) Farewell-Farewell   A: OK, see ya.
                                    B: So long.

According to Schegloff and Sacks (1973), the basic rule of adjacency pair operation is that when a speaker produces a recognizable first pair part, that speaker should stop talking and the conversational partner should produce a recognizable second pair part. Adjacency pairs thus provide for turn-taking, and also prescribe the type of talking that the next talker can do. Questions are to be answered, and usually are. When a speaker fails to provide the proper second pair part, this is often noticed and commented on, as in the following example from Sacks (1972a):

(16) WOMAN: Hi.
       BOY: Hi.
       WOMAN: Hi, Annie.
       MOTHER: Annie, don't you hear someone say hello to you?
       WOMAN: OK, that's okay, she smiled hello.
       MOTHER: You know you're supposed to greet someone, don't you?
       ANNIE: Hello. (Hangs head)

The examples given so far are tightly constructed, with strong limitations on what counts as a proper second pair part, although the woman in (16) indicates some tolerance for a non-verbal response ('that's okay, she smiled hello'). For other adjacency pairs, there is much more freedom for conversationalists responding to first pair parts, with several options available as second pair parts:

(e)	Compliment-Acceptance	A:	That's a nice shirt.
		B:	Thanks.
	-Agreement	B:	It is quite nice, isn't it.
	-Rejection	B:	Well, I think it makes me look old.
	-Shift	B:	Judy found it for me.
	-Return	B:	Thanks, I like yours too.
(f)	Complaint-Apology	A:	You ate the cake I left in the fridge!
		B:	Sorry.
	-Denial	B:	No I didn't, it must have been Susan.
	-Excuse	B:	You shouldn't have left it there.
	-Justify	B:	I was hungry. It was just a small piece anyway.
	-Challenge	B:	So what?
(g)	Offer-Accept	A:	Like a lift?
		B:	You saved my life.
	-Reject	B:	Thanks, but I'm waiting for my friend.
(h)	Request-Grant	A:	Can you mail these for me please?
		B:	Sure.
	-Put off	B:	Sure, but I won't have time today.
	-Challenge	B:	Why do you always ask me to mail them *for* you?
	-Refusal	B:	Sorry, but I won't be near the Post Office.

For language learning and teaching there are several possible areas of difficulty with adjacency pairs. First is the fact that a particular utterance may be intended as one of several first pair parts of adjacency pairs. 'Hello' may be a greeting, or a summons ('Hello . . . anybody home?'), or an answer to a summons, as when answering the telephone. Questions may be information questions, or requests for action ('Could you do that for me?') or criticisms ('Why did you do that?'), etc. In language teaching, we tend to treat all questions, particularly yes/no questions, as if they belonged to a single adjacency pair, namely Request for Information-Answer (Richards 1977). Thus we teach students to reply to yes/no questions with *yes* or *no* plus repetition of the verb or auxiliary used in the question:

(17) A: Are these apples fresh?
     B: Yes, they are.

What is consistently lacking in language courses is the opportunity to practice other adjacency pairs, such as Request-Grant:

(18) A: Are these apples fresh?
     B: I just bought them. Help yourself.

As a consequence, many students are only capable of short stilted replies such as *Yes, I can* or *No, I can't*, which while grammatically correct, may be conversationally inappropriate as second part constituents of adjacency pairs. Students need a large stock of adjacency pairs and practice in using them in a wide range of situations if they are to be comfortable conversationalists.

Non-native speakers are often considered overly passive in conversation with native speakers. One explanation for this is that non-native speakers may easily fall into the trap of consistently providing only second pair parts and leaving all first pair parts to a native speaking interlocuter, answering questions with *yes* and *no*, acknowledging compliments or offers with *thanks*, responding but never initiating. This is an easy trap to fall into, since as Sacks (1972a) has pointed out, questioners have the right to talk again after the other party has answered the question. This leads to a possible conversation consisting solely of Q-A-Q-A-Q-A exchanges, with one party initiating all questions. Coulthard (1977) points out that this seldom happens in conversation, although such sequences are common in doctor-patient interviews and courtroom discourse. They are also common in conversations between native and non-native speakers. Holmes and Brown (1976) have suggested some ways in which the situation could be improved. Instead of simply answering a question, non-native speakers can learn to answer a question, give some extra information and ask another question:

(19) A: Are you a student?
    B: Yes, I've come to study commerce. Are you a student?

Students can practise evading a question by giving a vague answer and then changing the topic:

(20) A: Are you feeling homesick?
    B: I'm not sure. Many things are very different here. Have you ever lived in another country?

We have given here only a structural description of some adjacency pairs, but some of the most difficult problems for non-native speakers arise because realizations of these pairs are subject to *ritual constraints*, which have to do with 'how each individual ought to handle himself with respect to each of the others, so that he does not discredit his own tacit claim to good character or the tacit claim of the others that they are persons of social worth whose various forms of territoriality are to be respected' (Goffman 1976, p. 266). While adjacency pairs such as Greeting-Greeting are closed sets, formulaic and easily learned, the question of whom one can greet and when may vary across cultures. In the Western United States, complete strangers may greet each other (or not) when passing on the street. This is often shocking to visitors from some countries, for example Japan, where such greetings would be considered presumptuous and highly offensive. For the more open-ended pairs, such as Complaint-Apology/Denial/Excuse/Justify/Challenge (there may be other options as well for compliment responses – see Pomerantz 1978), the problem is intensified. Edmondson (n.d.) asks how far a teacher should be expected to uphold the social values of the institution and the society in which teaching occurs and how far a student should be expected to conform with the social norms assumed to operate in the target language community, and states that this is ultimately a political issue. Holmes and Brown (1976) and many others have argued that students at least need to learn the resources available in the target language to say what they want to say.

5 Openings and closings

Conversations do not simply begin and end. The openings and closings of conversations and other types of speech events are organized and orderly accomplishments by conversationalists. We can imagine a non-native speaker who in his lessons has recited simple exchanges like 'Good morning', 'How are you?', 'I'm fine', etc. But when the learner is confronted with actually having to make a practical opening like this to a native speaker, 'the very same sentences become the basis for an occasion of social interaction and for possible further conversation. He is doing much more than using linguistic skill at producing acceptable and recognizable sentences; he is entering the arena of social action and exploiting some available procedures for social organization by doing so' (Speier 1972, p. 402).

For the native speaker as well, openings and closings are problematic. By this we do not mean simply that there are occasions when it is difficult to initiate conversation with a particular person or some conversations that are difficult to get out of, but that all transitions from a state of non-talk to talk, or from talk to non-talk, require engineered solutions.

Openings and closings are speech event-specific. For many speech events, there is an initial summons (the ringing of a church bell, a memo calling a meeting), and participants assemble over time before the occasion actually begins. There may be a specified setting (e.g. church, courtroom, clinic) and the persons who assemble are oriented to as specified category members (e.g. as members of the family or 'persons' at dinner table; as bride, groom, minister, guests, etc. at a wedding; as doctor, nurse, patient in surgery). Some events require a specified number of participants before the events may properly be seen as beginning, such as a quorum at a meeting (Turner 1972).

Some speech events may begin as soon as the required persons are present, for example a cocktail party, which begins with the presence of a host and a guest, even if the guest is 'early'. There may be some ambiguity about category membership (some guests may take on co-host functions), but there is no requirement that for example 30 per cent of the guests must arrive before drinks may be offered. Other speech events require formal markers before the event properly begins. When members assemble for a meeting, there may be background noise and conversations may be in progress, but the meeting itself has not properly begun until an authorized person uses some sort of attention-attractor or floor holder or other formal marker: banging a gavel, saying 'right', or 'OK, folks, are we ready to go again?', etc. The chairman of the meeting may then commence the meeting proper, often by setting out an agenda:

(21) (*general background noise*)

CHAIRMAN: Right, er . . .

(*general background noise, 4 sec. pause, general background noise*)

CHAIRMAN: Are we ready to go again now?

(*background noise, 3 sec. pause, background noise*)

RAY: Yes.

(*background noise*)

CHAIRMAN: Good, Ray's ready. Er, can I just mention um . . . just – just mention one more thing before I go round the table and then I really have got a batch of points. Ray has . . .

(*background noise ceases*)

CHAIRMAN: . . . just reminded me might as well bring this one up as well, just to mention it.

(Atkinson, Cuff and Lee 1978, p. 134)

Turner (1972) points out that in group therapy the session itself does not commence simply on the co-presence of patients and therapist, or even with the first instance of therapist talk (THERAPIST: 'Look, before we start . . .'), but given the presence of the therapist and some approximation to clock time, participants orient to the closure of pre-therapy talk. Silence is often seen as the boundary between pre-therapy and therapy talk, or the therapist may announce the beginning of the session with 'Well, we might as well start', or 'Well, I think what we had better do is start'. A classroom lecture may begin in a similar way, or the lecturer may open with 'last week we were talking about . . .' and end with, 'Well we'll return to this topic tomorrow'.

A conversation is quite different from many other speech events in that it has no specified setting, no time or place (except for the absence of other speech activity, in which case it is heard as an interruption), no required roles other than 'persons' (though some external roles such as professor/student may not be shed), no pre-specified agenda, and a quorum of simply two or more. Like other speech activities, however, conversations must be opened, and commonly this is done through the use of an adjacency pair such as Greeting-Greeting, Request-Grant, Question-Answer, or Statement-Response (Ervin Tripp 1964):

(22) A: Good morning.
      B: Hi.

(23) A: Got a match?
      B: Sure.
(24) A: How do you like our show?
      B: You have some beautiful paintings here!
(25) A: That was a terrible lecture!
      B: Yeah, I wish he could speak in normal English.

Such adjacency pairs provide for the immediate participation of both parties to a conversation and also allow for the possibility of further talk (e.g. questioners have the right to ask another question), but none of the examples above consist of openers that must inevitably lead to a full conversation. Greetings exchanged on the telephone (ANSWERER: Hello; CALLER: Hi, Bill) do inevitably lead to further talk, but that is because the answerer's *hello* is a response to the caller's summons (the ringing of the telephone) and it is the responsibility of the caller to provide at least one topic of conversation to justify having made the summons (Schegloff 1968). In face-to-face interaction we might consider such greetings to be pre-conversational, invitations to further talk. By means of the flow of additional turns a conversation may or may not get built (Speier 1972).

Closings, like openings, do not just happen, but must be made to occur by coordinated activities of the conversationalists. While a role-played conversation in a classroom might be declared finished by a teacher ('OK, that's fine, now let's see how _____ and _____ would do that'), real conversations must be closed by participants in such a way that 'one speaker's completion will not occasion another speaker's talk, and that will not be heard as some speaker's silence' (Schegloff and Sacks 1973, p. 294). Again, the simplest solution is the use of an adjacency pair, specifically a terminal exchange such as an exchange of goodbyes. These are not the only possibilities, however. 'Thank you', 'you're welcome', 'OK' and other utterances also occur as last utterances in conversations. Since these are not unambiguously terminal exchange parts, there must be other signals indicating that conversation is ending. It turns out that considerable prior work by conversationalists is required to set the stage for a proper closing.

Sacks and Schegloff point out that closings are preceded by *possible pre-closings*, such as 'well', 'OK . . .', 'So-oo' (with downward intonation). When these occur at the analysable end of a topic (signalled by the use of an aphorism or proverb in the following example), the pre-closing may lead to a terminal exchange:

(26) A: Uh, you know, it's just like bringing the blood up.
　　　 B: Yeah, well, things always work out for the best.
　　　 A: Oh certainly. All right.
　　　 B: Uh uh.
　　　 A: Okay.
　　　 B: G'bye.
　　　 A: Goodnight.

Possible pre-closings do not always lead to closings, of course, since this is also a device used to indicate that only a *topic* is being closed, and additional topics may then be introduced. It is only when neither party in the conversation lays any further claims to these opportunities for introducing new topics that a complete closing section is realized. Moreover, closing sections may include much more than the example in (26). Conversationalists may set up for closing by referring to their own interests ('Well, I gotta go.') or to the other party's interests ('Well, I don't want to keep you any longer.'). The routine questions that often occur at the beginnings of conversations ('What are you doing?') can provide material for moves towards conclusion ('So, I guess I'll let you get back to your books.'). Reinvoking the reasons for entering a conversation ('So, well, I just wanted to know how you were doing.'), and making arrangements for future conversation ('Yeah, OK, so we should get together soon.') are among the resources available for making conversations reach closure smoothly.

Both openings and closings can present difficulties for second language learners. There may be different conventions operating in the mother tongue and target language, and transference of rules and expectations from one language to another may create confusion. While there has been little cross-cultural research in this area, Wolfson (Chapter 3, this volume) reports differences in the openings of telephone conversations in the United States, France and Egypt. Closings pose special problems for non-fluent language users, and some of the difficulties of foreign learners in interpreting sincere vs. ritual invitations reported by Wolfson are probably attributable to the 'making arrangements' strategy for closing conversations. Second language learners may entirely miss the intention behind pre-closing moves like 'Well, I guess you have got lots of things to do' and may have difficulty themselves in easing towards closings. They may be too abrupt, as with a foreign student who ended a telephone conversation in the following way:

(27) I have nothing more to say, so goodbye.

6 Topic

The way topics are selected for discussion within conversation and the strategies speakers make use of to introduce, develop, or change topics within conversations constitutes an important dimension of conversational organization. Coherent conversation respects norms concerning the *choice* of topics, for example. Children learning to speak their first language eventually learn that they mustn't ask their parents why the sun is in the sky, who made God, how deep the Atlantic ocean is, or questions on a host of other topics that are not an acceptable part of older child or adult conversational interaction. Coulthard comments: 'an initial question is what sort of things can and do form topics in conversation? Some topics are not relevant to particular conversations... and the suitability of other topics depends on the person one is talking to. We experience, see, hear about events all the time . . . Some are tellable to everyone, some have a restricted audience, some must be told immediately, some can wait and still retain their interest' (Coulthard 1977, pp. 75–76).

What is tellable of course depends heavily on cultural norms. But even within a particular culture, topics are constrained by the speech event or activity in which talk occurs. The topics which may be raised in a meeting are limited (references to one's children or other aspects of one's personal life are disallowed unless these are made relevant to the business of the meeting), and may be specified in advance through a printed agenda which can be added to only at the beginning of the meeting. Given that ordinary conversation permits the mention of more things than the business meeting, the possibilities for topics and who may introduce them are not quite unlimited. Norms for how one conducts oneself vis-a-vis specific categories of persons are still in effect, and not only are we constrained from talking about certain things with certain people there may also be requirements about what we *should* talk about. R. Turner (1974) suggests that when related parties meet the conversational possibilities may be limited by the need to bring one up to date or, as in reunions, to talk over old times.

We want to look briefly now at some additional facts about the organization of conversation to see more closely how initial sequences such as adjacency pairs in conversational openings evolve into longer stretches of discourse. We have already mentioned that one adjacency pair, Greeting-Greeting, gives talkers an opportunity (an obligation for telephone callers) to introduce a first topic.

Part of the structure of openings also has to do with the positioning of topics within the conversation, as Schegloff and Sacks (1973) point out. The participants select a topic as first topic through a process of negotiation. The first topic, however, may be held back until the conversation develops to a point where it can be appropriately introduced. For example, a conversation may open:

(28) A: What's up?
      B: Not much. What's up with you?
      A: Nothing.

Later, possibly after additional preambles, one of the participants may go on to introduce a topic such as a new job, which could have been offered in direct response to 'What's up?' As Goffman points out, conversationalists might want to 'talk past' some topics initially, waiting until a much later time to introduce a sensitive issue, 'all of which management requires some understanding of issues such as delicacy' (Goffman 1976, p. 268). Schegloff and Sacks have also pointed out that in telephone conversations we often find a pre-first-topic closing-offering, an utterance such as 'Did I wake you?', 'Are you busy?', etc., which if declined becomes a pre-sequence for topic talk.

We need now to point out that while adjacency pairs consist of two utterances each spoken by a different speaker, it is clear that longer stretches of speech are functionally related in a similar fashion. An adjacency pair Criticize-Apologize has an expected additional response of Forgive. A Request that is followed by a Reject may precipitate a Repeat Request, which could again be rejected, side-stepped, ignored, etc. A question may not be followed immediately by its expected second pair part of Answer, but may be answered by another Question, resulting in embedding:

(29) A: Can you come by for dinner tonight?
      B: What time?
      A: About 7.
      B: Sure, love to.

In addition, we should recognize once again the hierarchical nature of conversation. An answer to a question might not consist of a simple utterance but rather a long story, the point of which answers the question. In these and other ways (see for example Jefferson 1972, on side sequences and Merritt 1976, on eliding and chaining), turns lead to future turns, and within these turns topics may be dealt with.

Winskowski (1977, 1978) refers to topicalizing behaviour, by which is meant bringing up topics, responding to other people's topics, mentioning something, avoiding the mention of something, carrying the discussion one step further, and so on – the creation of topic in the activity. With this focus on topic as process, we can see that topic behaviour often consists of rounds of topical turns which are reciprocally addressed and replied to, as in the following example:

(30) A: Oh nothing, we're just cleaning up, we had dinner. What's new?
      B: Nothing much. I still got a cold.
      A: Oh, has it improved at all, hopefully?
      B: Yeah, it's gotten better, it's gotten better. It'll be all right tomorrow. It better because I'm going out tomorrow.
                                                (Winskowski 1977, p. 86)

With 'what's new?', A presents a general purpose topic opener, to which B responds by initiating, raising or nominating a topic ('I still got a cold'). A's next move ratifies or accepts the topic. A's ratification move ('Oh, has it improved at all, hopefully?') is functionally similar to comments such as 'yeah, I know' or 'uh-huh', which intersect another participant's talking turn and whose function may be interpreted as giving encouragement to the other speaker without claiming the floor for talk. However, by using a question as her move, A is using an even stronger device to return the floor to B. B's answer to A's question expands on the topic, as requested by A. Each move then responds to the previous move and at the same time sets up transactional obligations regarding the following move, defining the topic all the while. Winskowski claims that even the boundary markers between topic are defined in this way:

(31) A: And the world isn't understanding.
      B: Nope. Uh, I just wanted to listen to somebody who is in a better place than me. What are you doing?
      A: I'm working with Margaret.
                                                (Winskowski 1977, p. 88)

A's first turn in this example offers an evaluative comment on B's prior move (this is a continuation of the conversation in (30)). B responds with agreement to the evaluation ('Nope') and identifies the current topic (her state of health) as her reason for calling. In the same turn, she goes on to identify a new topic by orienting to what A may have been doing. This move then defines 'Nope . . . I just wanted to listen to somebody . . .' as having been the terminal move for the previous topic.

While topics may be dealt with extensively or briefly and exhibit degrees of complexity, the most common recurrent features are probably topic nomination, ratification (acceptance), elaboration and comment (by the listener). This four part sequence can be seen in such varied types of discourse as children's riddles and adult brief mentions:

(32) A: What's red, carries a sack of toys and falls down the chimney?
    B: I don't know. What?
    A: Santa Klutz
    B: Yuk!

(Roberts and Sloan 1978, p. 22)

(33) A: Oh, my mother decided not to come for Christmas.
    B: Why?
    A: Well, I think she just doesn't want to make another trip so soon.
    B: Too bad.

Topic nomination may not consist of raising an entirely new topic, but remind the listener of a previously discussed one:

(34) A: You know Sherman?
    B: That asshole.
    A: He got a new job, selling time sharing.
    B: Suits him.

Atkinson (quoted in Hatch 1978) calls such examples as 'You know Sherman?' topic priming, a way of establishing topic reference before giving new information. Hatch points out that this careful establishment of topic is particularly important in native-non-native conversations.

Structure has been identified for some longer stretches of discourse as well, such as narratives, reports of past experiences in which the order of mention reflects the order in which events occurred, by Labov and Waletzky (1967), Labov (1972a) and Labov and Fanshel (1977). Briefly, a fully formed narrative shows an *abstract*, often a general proposition which the narrative will exemplify; an *orientation*, mention of time, place, persons; a *complicating action*; an *evaluation* (what's the point?); a *result*; and a *coda* (e.g. 'That's what happened', 'It was so funny'). Linde and Labov (1975) have also looked at descriptions of apartments. They found that although many different types of descriptions are possible, the great majority of such lay-out descriptions took the form of imaginary tours which transformed spacial layouts into temporally organized narratives. Hatch and Long (1980) note the similarities of such descriptions to principles familiar to composition teachers and call for comparative analyses of the planned and unplanned narratives of native and non-native speakers.

Hatch (1978) emphasizes that fluent conversationalists in a second or foreign language need a wide range of topics at their disposal. Initially learners may depend on 'canned topics'. They may get by with the ability to answer questions about recurring topics such as how long they have been in the country, their reactions to the country, what school courses they are taking, their occupation and so on. However, to move beyond the stage where discourse is predictable with familar and practised topics, learners need practice in introducing topics into conversation:

> They should practise nominating topics about which they are prepared to speak. They should do lots of listening comprehension for topic nominations of native speakers. They should practise predicting questions for a large number of topics . . . They should be taught . . . elicitation devices . . . to get topic clarification. That is, they should practise saying *huh*, echoing parts of sentences they do not understand in order to get the rest of it recycled again, *pardon me, excuse me, I didn't understand*, etc . . . Nothing stops the opportunity to carry on a conversation quicker than silence or the use of *yes* and head-nodding when the learner does not understand.
>
> (Hatch 1978, p. 434)

Learners also need to be able to follow the flow of a topic through a conversation. Knowledge of the real world, as Hatch comments, is one source of information the learner can make use of, predicting and anticipating questions and related discourse for certain topics. Learners will also need to be able to recognize the discourse functions of such phrases as *anyway, well, by the way,* which may mark a shift of topic. New topics may be linked to previous topics with such phrases as *that reminds me of the time, now that you mention it, speaking of that,* and attempts to return to a previously nominated topic with *to get back to what I was saying,* or *what I was trying to say was.* . . . Topic shift may also have illocutionary effects signalling for example, refusal to answer a question:

(35) A: How old are you?
     B: I'm a very wise person.

7 Turn taking

Conversation by definition involves two or more people. But the distribution of talking among the participants is not merely random. It is governed by turn-taking norms, conventions which determine who talks, when, and for how long. A speaker with poor management of turn-taking rules is one who 'doesn't let you get a word in edgeways'. A speaker who doesn't contribute to a conversation arouses negative evaluations too, or may make the conversation terminate abruptly. Sacks, Schegloff and Jefferson (1974) describe the way turns take place in conversation. One of the basic rules is that only one person speaks at a time. A speaker may select the next speaker through the use of an adjacency pair, such as when a challenge is followed by a denial:

(36) A: You look tired.
     B: I feel fine.

Alternatively, the next speaker may self-select a turn:

(37) A: I must tell you what happened to me yesterday.
     B: I'll call you back. I've got a visitor.

Participants in conversation are involved in ongoing evaluation of each other's utterances, to judge appropriate places to take up the turn to talk. Rules for turn taking differ according to the type of speech event. In classrooms, a child raises a hand to talk. In debates, the chair allots turns. In some families, 'Don't talk unless you're spoken to' is a maxim of table etiquette for children. Even in informal conversation turn taking is somewhat affected by rank, and assertion of the right to talk is an indicator of the power or status of the speaker and the degree to which the participants in the conversation are of the same or different ranks. Turn taking is one way in which roles and statuses are negotiated in conversation.

Turn-taking rules may vary from culture to culture and may cause problems for the non-native speaker attempting to engage in conversation. Lein and Brenneis (1978) compared the turn-taking behaviour of American black and white children with Fiji Indian children and found that when arguing both black and white American children were very strict in their attention to each other's turns, with minimal overlapping. The Fiji Indian children displayed a considerably different attitude towards turn taking:

> . . . simultaneity did not stop a sequence; in fact, there was a great tolerance for overlap, with as much as thirty seconds of mutual speech found in some arguments. These overlaps were not the results of unintentional poaching on another's time but of deliberate attempts to overwhelm the other speaker.   (Lein and Brenneis 1978, p. 307)

Turn taking is closely related to topic nomination, since one reason people take a turn at talking is when they have something to contribute to the topic, or when they wish to change the topic. Turn-by-turn talk is also essential to the expansion of a topic, since for example when telling a story the teller needs to know what the recipient has made of the story so far and thus what the story has amounted to. Jefferson (1972) has pointed out that listeners display appreciation and show understanding of stories at possible completion points, though tellers can indicate that a response was premature ('No, wait, there's more.'). At the next possible completion point, recipients again have an opportunity to respond via their new understanding of the story.

8 The good conversationalist

While sequencing of moves may be the major analytical problem of conversational analysis, there is more to talking than taking one's turn at the appropriate time and more to being a conversationalist than simply knowing the structural rules of conversation in a particular culture. Conversation is frequently recognized as an art or as a skill that can be polished and refined so that we recognize some native speakers as being better at it than others. Guidebooks for the 'improvement' of conversation are available for native speakers, but like prescriptive grammars, these books frequently stress things that one should *not* do in conversation. One author, discussing the art of story-telling in conversation, makes the following recommendations (among others):

Don't stare at your listeners.

Don't look at the ceiling.

Don't let yourself be hurried.

Don't tell a story that is long, pointless or inappropriate.

Don't tell a story until you are sure of it.

Don't begin a story unless you can go through it without stopping.

Don't digress. Omit unnecessary detail.

Don't add anything after you have made your point.

Don't attempt dialect stories unless you know the dialect.

Don't be first to laugh at your own story.

Don't tell too many stories.

Don't tell tactless stories about mothers-in-law, stammerers, etc.

Don't pun.

Don't explain that the story is really true.

Don't attempt repartee unless you have had a great deal of practice.

(Eichler 1928, pp. 187 and 188)

While such a long list of commandments would probably be inhibiting to the non-native conversationalist if presented in such a negative form, the etiquette approach to conversation has some usefulness for non-native speakers and might be referred to by materials writers. For example, Post (1975) has a major section devoted to 'the art of conversation'. While the emphasis is on manners for formal situations and contexts in which native speakers most often feel uncomfortable, there are some acute observations on American norms, such as the requirement for introductions whenever two strangers meet in the company of a mutual friend. Post comments that 'the worst sin is to make *no* introduction', which would be surprising to Japanese learners of English, who normally do not introduce in such circumstances. Paulston (1974) has pointed out the difference between the American norms and those in Sweden, where at a party Swedes do not wait to be introduced by a third party, but go around the room, shake hands with everyone and introduce themselves to those they have not met.

If we take the ethnomethodological perspective of seeing talk or conversation as an achievement, then we are perhaps prepared to say something more about skills that are probably exhibited in most native speaker conversations but which might be manipulated more or less effectively by some conversationalists. Goffman (1974) argues that talkers do not just provide information to recipients but present dramas to an audience, employing means that are essentially theatrical:

> . . . what the individual spends most of his spoken moments doing is providing evidence for the fairness or unfairness of his current situation and other grounds for sympathy, approval, exoneration, understanding, or amusement. And what his listeners are primarily obliged to do is show some kind of audience appreciation. They are to be stirred not to take action but to exhibit signs that they have been stirred.
>
> (Goffman 1974, p. 503)

In a warmly animated conversation, the talker does not tell tales as simple reportings of past events or bald statements of fact, but recounts a dramatic *version* of what happened, using dramatic devices such as irony, innuendo, sarcasm, humour and suspense. Suspense especially is often achieved through recognizable structural means. The sequence of topic nomination, ratification, expansion and comment often involves suspense in the form of a puzzle as the first move:

(38) A: We used t'have a good time around the   PUZZLE
        ginny.
     B: The ginny?   PASS
     A: Yeah, the ginny. People'd jump in it 'n SOLUTION
        get all nice 'n cooled off, and-duh,
        v'course it was no place t'get caught
        skinny dipping since ol' man Walters was
        church council president r'something heh
        heh, but we, y'know managed t'spend
        part of every hot day dipping in the
        ginny hehh hehh heh.
     B: Sounds like fun.   COMMENT

                                    (Schenkein 1978b, p. 69)

A similar example, expanded to six turns by the insertion of a second puzzle and pass:

(39) A: I'd love to come, but-tuh, I'll be down at   PUZZLE
        Mullard all week*end*.
     B: At Mullard?   PASS

A: Y'know Mullard Space Lab in London.   SOLUTION/
We're we're in the middle of a sort of a –   PUZZLE
– experiment there.

B: A sort of experiment?   PASS

A: Yes, y'know they've launched this   SOLUTION
orbiting observatory carrying three
grazing incidence uh X-ray telescopes,
and this weekend, uhh, some important
data from a, uh supernova's coming in.

B: Bernice will be very unhappy about it   COMMENT
y'know that don'tchu . . .

(Schenkein 1978b, p. 71)

In the next example, a puzzle is an essential part of the story, and the story-teller re-creates the puzzle in the telling of the story for the benefit of the listener:

(40) A: Yeah . . . this fella I have uh *fe*lla this *man*, he had uh
f- who I have for linguistics is

B: Hm hm.

A: Really too much.

B: Mm.

A: I didn't notice it but there's a woman in my class who's
in nursing. She said to me she s'd 'didja notice he has a
*han*dicap' an' I said 'What?' y'know I s'd 'I don't see
anything wrong with him'.

B: Mm

A: She says 'his *hands*'. So the next class fer an hour 'n
f'fteen minutes I sat there 'n I watched his hands.

B: Why whatsa matter with 'm?

A: He ca- he doesn't have f- full use of his fingers or
something 'n he- he holds the chalk funny an'

B: Mm

A: He- his fingers don't bend.   (Schegloff 1971, p. 6)

Although we cannot be sure, it seems unlikely that the original conversation between A and the nurse ended with the nurse simply indicating 'his hands'. More likely she explained further; but the point of the story is that A was perplexed, and she uses the conversationalist's dramatic licence to create the same perplexity for the listener.

The conversational technique of embodying elements of 'what

happened' in the performance of a story is a general one. Talkers regularly include direct quotes from story characters, sometimes mimicking accent or intonation as well. More subtle is the device of embodying one's *characterization* of an event in the telling:

(41) A: And it's like a Mickey Mouse course. It's a joke. It's speech.
    B: Speech.
    A: It's the biggest joke going, it really is. I figure I'm gonna start talking with a lithp and by the end of the term I'll get an A because I haveta improve.
    B: Hahh.

In this example, A characterizes a course as a 'joke' and proceeds to tell a joke. Her joke refers to lisping, and she lisps in the telling (Schegloff 1971 transcript).

In everyday conversations, where there is an easy exchange of speaker and hearer roles, techniques of dramatic appreciation are as important as those of presentation. As everyone knows, to be a good listener is crucial. We have already indicated some of the ways in which conversationalists listen and demonstrate that they are paying attention. They ratify topics which have been nominated and they 'pass' when presented with a puzzle. They allow current talkers to complete narratives and indicate comprehension with appropriate comments. They follow the maxim *be relevant* by responding as expected to first pair parts with second pair parts and by making next stories detectably relevant to last stories. While the other party is holding the floor, they provide frequent feedback in the form of *uhuh*'s, *mm*'s, *oh*'s and *yeah*'s. Occasionally they indicate comprehension more actively:

(42) A: Because but uh oh my my North American Indian class is really it's *so* boring.
    B: Yeah.
    A: I- y'know this *guy* has not done anything yet that I understand. And no one no one else in the class understands him either. We all sit there an' we laugh at his jokes.
    B: Yeah I know.
    A: An' we nod when he wants us to say yes an'
    B: Yeah.
    A: We raise our hands when he wants to take a poll 'n
    B: Mm.
    A: Y'know but when we walk outta the class

B: Nobody knows what went on.

(Schegloff 1971)

The irony of this piece of conversation is that while A is telling a story about *pro forma* responses to a professor, B is giving *pro forma* replies such as *yeah* and *mm* to A. Whether A or B are aware of this irony, the final collaborative utterance by A and B together ('Y'know but when we walk outta the class . . . nobody knows what went on') indicates that B has been listening attentively and has in fact understood the point of A's story.

Since feedback and comprehension-indicating devices for informing on reception are among the basic requirements of a communication system, we may expect a large degree of universality in their use, including the presence of the semi-linguistic and non-verbal responses Goffman has called bracket-confirmations: 'the smiles, chuckles, headshakes and knowing grunts through which the hearer displays appreciation that the speaker has sustained irony, hint, sarcasm, playfulness or quotation across a strip of talk' (Goffman 1976, p. 262). Universal presence does not imply universal form or distribution, however, and careful comparative work is required to uncover the parallels, similarities and differences between English conversational devices such as *I know, yeah, right, uhuh*, etc. and their counterparts in other languages.

9 Repairs

The process of conversation involves monitoring to ensure that intended messages have been communicated and understood, and this involves correction of unsuccessful attempts where necessary. The term *repair* refers to efforts by the speaker or the hearer to correct trouble spots in conversation (Schegloff, Jefferson and Sacks 1977). Repairs may be initiated by either the speaker or the hearer. Speaker-initiated repairs are termed *self-repairs*:

(43) Is a dollar all right or will I need more than that for the p . . . to cover the postage?

Other repairs are repairs carried out by the hearer:

(44) A: She married that guy from Australia . . . what was his name? . . . Wilson . . . Williams?
    B: Don Wilson.
    A: Yeah, Don Wilson.

Not all repairs succeed, however:

(45) A: Can you tell me . . . do you have any records of whether you . . . whether you . . . sent . . . oh shit.
    B: What did you say?
    A: I'm having the worst trouble talking.

In conversation between a second language learner and a native speaker, there may be requests for other repairs when the non-fluent language user signals that he or she hasn't understood something. *Echoing* is one technique which is sometimes used, whereby the speaker repeats a word or phrase which is not understood and the conversational partner explains it or replaces it with an easier item.

(46) A: We're going mountaineering tomorrow.
    B: Mountain . . . ee . . .?
    A: Mountaineering. You know, to climb up the mountain.

Phrases such as *huh, what, one more time, I'm sorry*, may also be used to signal the need for repair. Facial expressions, gestures and eye movements are also important. Schwartz (1977) describes two non-fluent language users whom she recorded on video tape.

> Self-initiated repair was marked by both linguistic and extralinguistic means. To mark self-initiated repairs, the second language learners would often pause, say 'uh,' turn their eye gaze away from the auditor and look either up or down, frown with eyebrows pulled together, and/or flutter their eyelids . . . broken eye gaze signalled a breakdown in the interaction and seemed to serve both as a physical sign of emotional distress when the speaker was having trouble, and as a warning to the auditor that repair would take place
> (Schwartz 1977, p. 110)

The concept of repair in second language communication can be extended to include what Tarone (1977) and others have referred to as *communication strategies*. These are self-initiated repairs and requests for assistance which occur when the speaker is trying to express concepts for which target language vocabulary is lacking. They include:

(a) *approximation*. Lacking a word in the target language, the speaker may choose an approximate word, such as a synonym, e.g. *shop* instead of *department store*.

(b) *word coinage*. A word may be made up in an attempt to fill out a gap in knowledge of a target language item. For example in the following utterance the speaker lacked the word *ice breaker*.

(47) Helsinki produces a lot of *ice crushing ships*.

(c) *circumlocution*. A paraphrase or description of a word may be used when a word is unknown. For example the speaker may lack *bookshelf*:

(48) Does the room have . . . *a place for books*?

(d) *borrowing*. A word from the mother tongue may be used when the target language word cannot be remembered:

(49) A: I felt very . . . *malu* . . . you know?
    B: You felt very *shy*?
    A: Yes, shy.

(e) *mime*. The speaker may act out a word:

(50) A: Then the plane . . . (mimes a plane taking off)
    B: It took off?
    A: Yes.

(f) *topic shift*. A speaker who doesn't possess sufficient vocabulary or confidence to discuss that topic in the target language may change the topic.

(g) *topic avoidance*. The speaker may avoid introducing certain topics because of lack of sufficient vocabulary to discuss them. The ability to carry out self-repair and to elicit repair from one's conversational partner is an essential skill for a second or foreign language learner. In signalling the need for repair, the conversational partner is often forced to use a simpler word or structure, or to shift the topic to the beginning of the sentence where it may be easier to identify:

(51) A: Did you enjoy the ballet?
    B: Huh?
    A: The ballet . . . the dancing, on Friday night. Did you enjoy it?

10 Implications

The categories discussed so far represent some of the dimensions of conversational discourse that second language learners need to master. While the learner has intuitively acquired the principles of conversational discourse in his or her own language, conversational competence is just as important a dimension of second language learning as the grammatical competence which is the focus of much formal language teaching. Transfer of features of first language conversational competence into English, however, may have much more serious consequences than errors at the level of syntax of pronunciation, because conversational competence is closely related to the presentation of self, that is, communicating an image of ourselves to others. For this reason the study of cross cultural differences in conversation constitutes a vital study of interethnic communication (see Scollon and Scollon, this volume).

The teaching of conversation is hence a much more basic and comprehensive activity than is sometimes assumed, and implies far more than the parroting of dialogues. It must focus on strategies of conversational interaction. The traditional concern of teachers with complete grammatically correct sentences may not be well directed when it comes to the teaching of conversation, particularly at the intermediate and advanced levels. Jakobovits and Gordon (1980) have argued that the technique of teaching talk lies in the art of *not* teaching language.

Whether conversation can be taught directly is a controversial issue. Jakobovits and Gordon point out that first language verbal fluency is not taught within the 'instructional register' of formal education, but is the natural outcome of the socialization process. For second language learners they argue against such activities as role-playing because the cues of *actual* talking spring spontaneously from involvement in real relationships and because individuals can learn to talk only by being treated as talkers. They insist that the student should be treated as a talker or social participant rather than as a learner or inadequate social participant, and see the teacher's role as one who creates or engineers the social occasions for talk:

> The teacher has many available techniques, as provided by the sociocultural and classroom frames; namely: initiate exchanges, create happenings, make declarations and announcements, make requests and assignments, group individuals and direct them to work on a particular activity, invite visitors and volunteers, and so on. In other words, the teacher is in a position to create the hustle and bustle of the classroom social and interactive milieu. It is through these exchanges and engineered happenings that the teacher controls the talk in the classroom: not necessarily its topical

content, nor its particular formative features that a trained orientation in grammar may focus on; but instead, it is through engineering the social directives that the teacher thus comes to *control the CONTEXT for emerging talk.*

(Jakobovits and Gordon 1980, p. 14)

Others interested in the pedagogical implications of conversational analysis argue for more direct instruction. An attempt to deal systematically with turn taking, topic nomination, openings and closings as components of conversational proficiency in a second language course is described by Keller (1976), who has developed a series called *Gambits* which practises these aspects of conversational interaction.

Gambits are conversational tools for introducing what we are about to say. We use them every day and in a variety of situations. For instance, when we want to state an opinion, we can say, 'I think that . . .' or 'In my opinion . . .'. When we want to introduce something unsavory, we can say, 'Whether we like it or not . . .' and when we want to bow out of a conversation we can try, 'Well, it was nice talking to you'. If our conversation partner couldn't take the hint, we can also hammer it home with, 'Sorry, I've really got to go now'.

(Keller 1976, p. 19)

An example of a *Gambits* activity developed by Keller and colleagues is the following, which is described as the 'interrupting game'. The students have a list of phrases which are described as:

(a) Attention-getting openers – interrupters (Sorry, but . . . Excuse me for interrupting, but . . . I might add here . . . I'd like to comment on that . . . May I add something . . . May I say something here . . . I'd like to say something . . . May I ask a question . . .)

(b) To return to the topic (anyway . . . in any case . . . to return to . . . to get back to . . . where was I . . . going back to . . .)

A speaker starts talking on a selected topic. The students practise taking a turn using one of the phrases given. The speaker answers, then tries to get back to the topic as quickly as possible. And so the game continues. For example:

(52) A: Last night I went to a hockey game . . .
B: Excuse me for interrupting, but which one?

A: The one between the Boston Bruins and the Montreal Canadians. Anyway, so I went to the game and got to my seat . . .

C: Sorry, where was your seat?

A: In the red section. As I was saying, I got to my seat . . .

Like drilling or any other form of language activity, the resulting conversation may not be completely natural, and this particular example practises turn-taking formulae more typical of teacher-student (or parent-child or interrogator-defendent) discourse than face-to-face conversational interaction between equals, but it does demonstrate how turn taking can be practised in a language class. For some students the exchanges so practised may be available for use in real encounters.

One pedagogical result of recent interest in conversational analysis, the discovery of the orderliness of ordinary speech and the contrast between real conversation and the traditional dialogue has been an increased use of (more or less) authentic conversational material in language classes. Old dialogues are re-scripted to appear more 'natural', though it is debatable whether many writers can actually write (i.e. invent) authentic dialogue. Some recent texts, e.g. James, Whitely and Bode (1980, 1981), and O'Neill and Scott (1974), do use actual, unscripted conversations, including hesitations, interruptions and even natural grammatical errors for listening comprehension and speaking practice.

In evaluating students, the question is often asked by whose norms performance is to be judged. Since conversation is a social activity, when we evaluate an actual communicative act, 'we are evaluating both the utterance as a social act and the speaker as a social member' (Edmondson ms.). A more appropriate focus for the teacher's attention might be on the coherence of the learner's conversation, and this in turn will depend on the learner's control of the various features of conversation we have discussed here: fluent second language users will thus use the conversational maxims and speech act conventions of English to express and interpret conversations on a wide range of topics. They will make use of adjacency pairs, openings and closings, turn taking and repair strategies to initiate and develop conversation with skill and confidence, without however drawing attention to the mechanisms by which they engage in the conversational process.

Notes

1. Portions of this chapter previously appeared in the *TESOL Quarterly* (Richards 1980). We would like to thank Richard Day and Leon Jakobovits, who provided useful comments on an earlier draft. Responsibility for the interpretations given here is, of course, our own.

2. It should be noted that some speech events may contain other speech events. A joke may occur within a conversation, which can be embedded within the frame of a cocktail party. There may be specifiable principles behind such hierarchical organization, but we are not sure at this time how many levels of organization there may be, whether it would be useful to recognize categories of 'supra-speech events', etc.

Questions for discussion, study and further research

1. The claim that talkers do not simply report events in conversation but present a *version* of 'what happened' may be illustrated by the contrast between a teenager's report of 'how the party went last night' to a peer as opposed to a parent (Jakobovits and Gordon 1975). Observe and describe your own versions of a reported event on several retellings. Specify the features which vary according to the person you are talking to. Are specific relationships the only source of variation?

2. Hawaiian Telephone Company sent the following notice to its subscribers:

Some things you always wanted to know about the telephone company.

Why do I experience a delay in conversation when making certain long distance calls?

The delay that occurs is due to the distance the signal must travel.

Most calls between Hawaii and the mainland today are by satellite. Your voice travels 22,300 miles to an orbiting communications satellite, then back down an equal distance to reach the called party. That one-way trip through the satellite takes about 3/10ths of a second. So when you stop talking you must wait more than half a second before you will hear the other person's reply . . .

(Hawaiian Telephone 1980)

Why would a telephone company find it necessary to send such an explanatory note to customers? What effect is the satellite delay likely to have on telephone conversations? In more general terms, what is the relationship between telephone (or other communications systems) design and the requirements of conversation?

3. Choose a person whom you consider to be a skilled conversationalist and tape-record that person in conversation with several other people, either friends or new acquaintances. Do the factors of good conversation described here contribute to an understanding of your subject's skill? What else is involved?

4. Tape-record several conversations of non-native speakers of English with either native speakers or other non-native speakers. Analyse your data to see the extent to which these non-native speakers exhibit the skills described in this chapter. Do conversational skills appear to correlate with or be largely independent of linguistic proficiency? Compare your data with either (a) native speaker behaviour or (b) patterns of conversational interaction in the native language of your subjects.

6. Jakobovits and Gordon (1974, 1980) have argued that simulated dialogues in language texts are always artificial. Examine some texts and compare them with real talk to see the extent to which this claim is defensible. Jakobovits and Gordon further argue that dialogues are a basically inauthentic kind of conversational practice and that the necessary and sufficient condition for authentic conversational practice in the language classroom is that the pupil must *enact himself in the conversation*. Do you agree or disagree?

7. Can you find examples of different conventions for the opening and closing of face-to-face conversations and telephone conversations between different languages?

8. What implications does the study of conversation have for second and foreign language teaching?

Introduction to Chapter 6

Scollon and Scollon broaden yet further the perspective taken on language and communication in previous chapters and see communicative style as a major issue in cross-cultural communication. Communication is crucial for a variety of important social transactions and differences in communicative style can have serious consequences, particularly for minority groups. Communicative style includes rules for the distribution of talk between participants, topic selection, the presentation of information within discourse (i.e. its *information structure*), and the presentation of self or face. They make the important point that differences in linguistic conventions associated with such features of communicative style (e.g. differences in length of pauses between turns, taciturnity, or in conventions for signalling given and new information) are often interpreted in interpersonal terms (i.e. as threats, challenges, disagreements, etc.), and often lead to stereotyping.

The effect of strategies for the presentation of self (i.e. how one communicates how closely one wishes to identify with other participants in a conversational interaction, and how the participants perceive their status, and power) is discussed in terms of the communication of 'politeness', drawing on the work of Brown and Levinson. Their discussion of politeness strategies complements Wolfson's discussion of rules of speaking and Fraser's analysis of speech acts. They illustrate a fragment of a grammar for rules of speaking, which accounts for levels of formality or informality in communicative style according to the power of the speaker, the social distance between speaker and hearer, and the degree of 'weight' (i.e. threat) involved in a particular speech act. They also suggest that such systems may differ significantly across cultures and even within a single language (e.g. British English versus American). This paper thus presents a powerful analysis of the sociolinguistic dimensions of communication and suggests a framework for contrastive discourse analysis.

6 Face in interethnic communication

Ron Scollon and Suzanne B. K. Scollon

1 Interethnic communication in the modern world

Since World War II interethnic communication has emerged as a fact of the modern world. Pluralism in communicative style is found throughout world and national technological, business, legal and educational bureaucracies. Whether it is a multinational corporation or an international student exchange, differences of language and communicative style will be found as a central issue to be understood and to be taken into account. Within nations and even much smaller jurisdictions, the social and geographical mobility of the post-war period coupled with the concern for extending the privileges and duties of modern citizenship to all citizens has caused multi-ethnic communication to become the rule rather than the exception. The modern sense of a world that is rather small and where competition for limited material and energy resources is keen has focussed differences in communication as a problem that can no longer be treated as temporary or inconsequential. Redistributions of technological mastery and resource control have quite recently emphasized that no group may unilaterally declare its mode of communication to be the preferred, universal model.

Unfortunately, cultural, social and communicative pluralism is rarely found in simple contacts between two parties. Bilingualism for example is most often multilingualism. Where a bureaucratic system must deal with multiple codes it is rarely just two. This means then that communicative problems cannot be solved by the obvious but too simple solution that each group learns the other's code. Since multiple groups and multiple codes are typical, solutions must be sought at a level higher than that of communication between two groups.

1.1 *Gatekeeping encounters*

With social, economic, and geographical mobility in the modern world has come the need for technological, business, educational, legal, and other institutions to control movement into and within such institutions. Erickson (1976) has identified gatekeepers as individuals who have been given the authority to make decisions on the behalf of institutions that will affect the mobility of others. Counselling sessions, job interviews and legal trials are typical of gatekeeping encounters in their objectivity, the value placed on focussed face-to-face interaction, and in their significance far beyond the time of the encounter. The interaction of a quarter of an hour may affect a lifetime of experience for the individual as well as some aspects of the life of the institution. Furthermore, the opportunity for redress or reparation is severely limited by the focussed nature of the interaction. Typically, where redress is sought, it is controlled in further gatekeeping encounters.

Because gatekeeping encounters have been seen as critical for the institution in controlling access and mobility and critical for the individual in determining major aspects of life experience, many institutional and legal constraints have been placed on their operation. These encounters are designed to be as objective as possible with each gatekeeper receiving equal training and briefing and with each applicant being given equal evaluative treatment. As Erickson has pointed out, though, this objectivity breaks down in two significant areas. Where the gatekeeper shares with the applicant membership in some group, there is a marked correlation with improved outcomes of the encounter for the applicant. This is the sort of 'leakage' that is treated as conflict of interest in the attempt to create objectivity and fairness of treatment.

The second form of leakage in gatekeeping encounters is caused by communicative style. Erickson (1976) and Gumperz (1978) have shown that differences in communicative style may result in a negative outcome for the applicant. Differences between the gatekeeper and the applicant in their way of speaking or in their body placement, movement, and rhythm may produce miscommunication of intent. While the basic message may be understood clearly enough, the interpretation may be muddled or wholly misconstrued. These failures of the interpretive process result in the discrimination against certain applicants that the objectivity of the gatekeeping encounter is designed to prevent.

Because communicative style is so intimately associated with one's identity both as a person and as a member of a group, and because one's own style is used largely out of one's own awareness, leakage from communicative style is a particularly insidious source of misinterpretation. Where the misinterpretation or misunderstanding is overt, it is quickly and easily acknowledged and both participants in an interaction can seek to correct it. Where it is out of awareness it is not corrected but directly interpreted. This direct interpretation of difference in communicative style often leads to ethnic stereotyping and the negative outcomes of these encounters.

While Erickson (1976) found differences of communicative style between all ethnic groups in his study, he argues that some concept of 'pan-ethnicity' is necessary to deal with the gatekeeping encounter. That is, while there were differences between Black, Mexican, Puerto Rican, Polish, Italian, and Irish Americans, the first three groups formed a class he termed 'Third World' and the second a class he termed 'white ethnic'. The differences between these two 'pan-ethnic' classes were qualitatively different from the differences within 'pan-ethnic' classes. It is our opinion that ethnic stereotyping operates more strongly for 'pan-ethnic' groups. For that reason, we find it of greater concern to identify major sources of such stereotyping than to seek closely refined descriptions of any particular ethnic group.

1.2 *Communicative style as discourse*

In this paper we will make a somewhat arbitrary choice to focus only on discourse in our discussion of communicative style. Communicative style naturally includes much more than speech. As we have mentioned above, body movement, placement and rhythm are central aspects of communicative style. Our choice is motivated partly out of convenience in an attempt to limit the scope of our treatment. This particular limitation is useful, we feel, because of the amount of recent work on discourse. The work of Gumperz (1977a, 1977b, 1978); Gumperz and Roberts (1978); Tannen (1977, 1979a, 1979b); Darnell (1979) and Kochman (1979) has pointed to the centrality of discourse in the communication of ethnicity. Of course, language has always been thought to have had a central role in any human communication. Recently, however, it is becoming clearer that the focus on grammar and pronunciation may well be misplaced if what we are seeking to understand is communication between different groups.

The central issue is that of what Bateson (1972, 1979) has called metacommunication, which he in turn attributes to the insights of Whorf (1956). In his view, every message is a double message. Simultaneous with the basic message is a metamessage. This second message gives information about the interpretation of the primary message. In this view, communication goes wrong more often when speakers can determine *what* was said but not *why*. These metamessages that tell us *why* someone is speaking and *how* it is to be interpreted are communicated largely out of awareness as an integral aspect of the communicative style of the speaker. In looking at discourse we are interested in untangling the interwoven strands of message and metamessage that are themselves interwoven with communicative style.

2 Four aspects of discourse

While many aspects of discourse have recently received attention in the literature, we will look at just four of these. We look at the distribution of talk or how speakers exchange turns at speaking and how the topic of a conversation is determined. We use 'information structure' to encompass prosodic, grammatical, and morphological systems of marking givenness, contrastiveness, perspective, grounding, definiteness, and topicality. We will also make brief reference to the work in artificial intelligence and cognitive science which deals with frames, schemata, and scripts. Finally, we will elaborate most fully on the presentation of self or 'face'.

2.1 *Distribution of talk, turn exchange*

When people talk to each other in conversation they normally do not all speak at once. They usually take turns at speaking. The exchange of turns usually takes place smoothly with a minimal amount of confusion about whose turn it is to speak. Listeners can tell when it will be possible to take a turn and manage their entrance as speakers without difficulty. While this process of exchanging turns seems very natural, on closer look it is a process that is based on a mutual agreement among the participants on conversational conventions. Sacks, Schegloff and Jefferson (1974) have shown just how complex this process is even in its 'simplest' characterization.

Our concern here is with looking at what happens when there is some disagreement among the speakers about such conversational conventions or principles of discourse. Sacks, Schegloff, and Jefferson speak of 'transition relevance places' (TRPs) at which the speech of a participant will be heard as finished for that turn and it becomes possible for another speaker to take the floor. At this point there may be a pause or at least some delay while the first speaker decides whether or not someone else is going to claim a turn at talk. If no claim is made the first speaker may continue.

These points at which turns are exchanged are highly susceptible to disagreement in spite of the ordinary and expected successful management of these exchanges. As a result, this agreement among speakers can be used as a measure of their general social agreement. People can interrupt or talk at the same time as others as a way of showing their unwillingness to go along with the presumed social agreement. Of course, speaking simultaneously does not in itself indicate a positive or negative relationship. As in other social communications, what is an insult in one context may be an expression of friendship in another. A person may interrupt another either out of hostility and disagreement or to show how closely the two participants can trust each other as friends. What is important is that because orderly exchange of turns is taken to be the norm, any interruption, simultaneous speech, or very long silences will be interpreted as saying something about the relationship of the speakers.

Problems arise when for any reason two or more speakers approach the conversation with different expectations about something as simple as the speed at which turns should be exchanged. A person who has just gotten himself out of bed to answer the phone and finds the other party calling from another time zone and wide awake may have to account for his slowness in speaking. He may even be accused of hostility or coldness.

The speed of turn exchange becomes critical in interethnic communication because of the fact that there are often differences between groups in their expectations about turn exchange. Where members of two different groups interact and their expected pause between turns differs, the results are very predictable. The 'faster' one concludes a turn, waits a 'normal' length of time, hears no response and so concludes that he may continue by taking another turn himself. Meanwhile the other speaker has waited his 'normal' length of time, a pause slightly longer than the other's, and just as he is planning to take his turn, the other has begun speaking and either he does not get to say anything or he finds himself coming in simultaneously with the other. This difference in timing may be very slight but it can be heard as highly significant. A 'faster' speaker hears a 'slower' one as reserved, withdrawn, without opinions of his own, unsure, or perhaps even hostile. The 'slower' speaker hears the 'faster' one as arrogant, egocentric, pushy, domineering, or impatient. In both cases the result of a small difference in timing can result in a big difference in attitude, in quite negative feelings about the other interactant.

It becomes important then in interethnic communication for each speaker to be aware that the other may be operating on an assumption of a different exchange period and to carefully avoid stereotyping the other speaker on the basis of this sort of misinterpretation.

2.2 *Topic control*

In a study of phone conversations, Schegloff (1972) found that the person who initiated the conversation controlled the introduction of the topic. He pointed out that the first 'move' in the conversational interaction was a 'summons'. This is a request made to the other party for the right to talk with him. It signals the desire to open communication. In the phone call the summons is the ring of the phone. In conversation it is the initial greeting.

The answer to the summons is typically open-ended. That is, the answerer grants the right to talk to the one requesting interaction and he grants it without restricting the possible topics. The originator then introduces the topic in the third turn of the exchange.

What is important about topic control work for us is that in the first place what appears to be a natural result of the initiation of conversation may not be treated the same in all cultural or ethnic groups. For example, we found at Fort Chipewyan, Alberta (Scollon and Scollon 1981) that conversations were opened with a summons that called for the answerer to introduce the topic, not the original summoner. Where two parties begin a conversation with these different assumptions, problems can occur. Each may either assume that he has the right to introduce the topic or that the other has that obligation. The possible misinterpretation is that the other is either egocentric if he insists on introducing a topic or evasive if he does not. Unless the two parties have this initial agreement, the interaction may falter on the question of whose topic should be discussed.

A second interest of this work is that topic control may interact with turn exchange. For example, the first speaker may be from a group that assumes that the first speaker controls the topic and that group also has a 'fast' turn exchange. The second speaker may assume the second speaker should introduce the topic and be also somewhat 'slower' in exchanging turns. If so, the result is predictable. The first speaker will call for the right to talk. The second will introduce his topic. The first will then introduce his own topic as he assumes it was his right to do. Then, because he continually regains the floor through his faster rate of turn exchange, he comes to dominate the conversation, speaking only about his own topic.

The potential for negative evaluations each of the other is obvious. The first speaker hears the second as withdrawn, insecure or hostile. The second hears the first as domineering and egocentric. Each of these evaluations is a straightforward, predictable result of the mechanics of the distribution of talk. All that it takes is some difference in the preliminary assumptions about the distribution of talk to produce these negative effects.

These negative evaluations that result from differences in the distribution of talk become ethnic stereotypes when people regularly experience them in communication with members of particular ethnic groups. Of course it is often easier to dismiss the miscommunication as evidence of the negative qualities of the other group than it is to re-examine the communicative situation. For each group on the other hand it is preferable to have a 'given' set of assumptions about the management of talk. These assumptions work to smooth communication within the group by reaffirming their interactional agreement. They also work to preserve and mark the boundaries between groups and so are not easily abandoned in spite of the potential for negative stereotyping in communication with other groups.

2.3 *Information structure*

In our preceding discussion we have treated talk as if it were an undifferentiated mass that came in units of 'turns' but no more delicately tuned to interactional considerations. Now we would like to briefly consider the talk itself more directly.

We are all aware of such things as 'tone of voice'. We find ourselves able to say, 'It's not *what* he said that bothered me but the way he said it!' It is largely the information structure that is communicating such perceptions. This can be done through the prosodic system of intonation, rate of speaking, loudness, or pitch placement. It may also be done grammatically with changes of word order or morphologically by the addition of small words, suffixes or prefixes to add emphasis.

It would be too much to illustrate all of these possibilities here. We would like to mention a few examples, though, of factors that are often important. Recent linguistic studies of discourse have mentioned among the dimensions of interest contrastiveness, givenness, definiteness, point of view, topicality (see for example, Chafe 1976), perspective and grounding (Scollon, to appear; Scollon and Scollon 1981).

In some languages contrast is shown with stress, that is, with a somewhat raised pitch and an increase in loudness. The stressed word (in *italics*) is singled out as contrasting with the listener's expectations for some reason. When we say, '*I* didn't forget to bring my briefcase', we signal a contrast. The person represented by '*I*' is contrasted with someone else who is not specifically mentioned. Of course, we may hear this sort of contrastiveness as an innuendo. It is suggested that someone else has forgotten and should not have forgotten.

In the same way, any element could be contrasted. 'I didn't forget *my* briefcase', could be taken as the suggestion that *you* did. 'I didn't forget my *brief*case', implies that I did forget my suitcase or some other case. In short, the use of stress can turn a basic message into quite a variety of messages. The derived messages may be heard as innuendoes or insinuations. By that we mean that the use of contrastive stress tends to suggest some impropriety, possibly on the part of the listener.

Gumperz and Roberts (1978) have shown that serious problems can arise from the fact that while contrast or emphasis is often indicated with stress in English, in other languages it may be marked morphologically. Indo-Aryan languages such as Hindi mark contrast with morphemes. Stress, though, is automatically placed on the second to the last or penultimate syllable. When people who speak Indo-Aryan languages speak English they often use the penultimate stress pattern (Gumperz 1977b). This means that the penultimate syllable is stressed automatically. The result is often heard by native British English speakers as contrastive stress and thus as innuendo or insinuation. Again, a rather mechanical outcome of discourse differences is misconstrued as an expression of attitude or relationship.

Another aspect we might mention is grounding. In any message some information is more important than other information.

While the purpose of communicating may be to present certain ideas, some background must always be given the listener. This distinction between foreground and background information has especially been noticed in storytelling. Labov (1972a) made a distinction between free and narrative clauses. Free clauses present background information, evaluation and orientation. Narrative clauses advance the action of the story. This distinction is basically the same as Hopper and Thompson's (to appear) distinction between backgrounded (free) and foregrounded (narrative) clauses.

There is reason to believe (Bobrow and Norman 1975; Clements 1979) that foregrounded information is remembered better than backgrounded information. In fact, it could be argued that that is just why the distinction is made in all languages that we know of. This distinction makes it possible for the speaker to signal to the listener what aspects of his whole message he should pay close attention to and which he should disregard or at least treat as less memorable.

The problem with grounding is that it is signalled differently in different languages (Hopper and Thompson, to appear). In English grounding is marked grammatically. Foregrounded clauses are independent, non-subordinated clauses. Backgrounded clauses are subordinated. Foregrounded clauses appear in normal temporal order. Backgrounded clauses may reverse temporal order or be atemporal. Hopper and Thompson (to appear) have argued that foregrounded clauses are high in 'transitivity', a complex notion involving verb tense or aspect, the number of participants in the clause and their case roles as well as other grammatical factors.

In Athabaskan grounding is signalled by an interaction between the grammar and the prosodic structure (Scollon, to appear). The foregrounded clause is the last clause before a juncture marked by the end of a sentence and a pause. All other clauses are backgrounded. A pause elsewhere does not mark foregrounding nor does the end of a sentence. That is, in Athabaskan the last clause in a prosodic-grammatical unit (a verse) is foregrounded.

What is true of grounding in Athabaskan is often true in the English of many Athabaskans. This creates the potential for confusion in interethnic communication. For the Athabaskan, transitivity and subordination may be irrelevant in determining grounding. For the English speaker the prosodic structure is likely to be irrelevant. In these cases what happens is that each party hears the other and perhaps clearly understands what is said in some literal sense. What is not understood is where the speaker is placing the emphasis. The result is the feeling that the other has not come to the point or has emphasized the wrong things. Each participant's memory of the communication may also have selectively retained and lost different aspects because of differences in the perception of grounding. Each may come away from the situation with a very different memory of what was said and what was accomplished. This then results in the potential for accusations of broken promises and deviousness.

There are many other ways in which the differential selection of aspects of the message for emphasis may cause misinterpretation. What is important for our purposes is to realize that much misinterpretation is the automatic result of the mechanics of the marking of information structure where the two parties approach the communication making different assumptions. And because the misinterpretation tends to produce a negative stereotyping of the other party, it is difficult to see through this process to the mechanical principles on which it is based to look for solutions.

2.4 *Frames, schemata, scripts*

We have looked at conventions speakers have for the distribution of talk and conventions for marking the information structure of that talk. At a more internal level there also appear to be social and cultural conventions for the interpretation of messages. Researchers in artifical intelligence, psychology, cognitive science, and linguistics are beginning to use the concept of frames (or schemata or scripts; different researchers prefer different terms) to understand how memory and cognition are organized (Bobrow and Collins 1975; Schank and Abelson 1977; Just and Carpenter 1977). As an example, Kintsch (Kintsch 1977; Kintsch and Greene 1978) has found that people approach a story with an expectation that it should have a certain number of parts. His subjects at the University of Colorado expected stories to have three main sections or episodes. This schema of three parts was found to affect their ability to understand and remember Athabaskan stories which were organized around groups of four sections. Kintsch's subjects either forgot one section or merged two into one to produce the three sections that would match their schema for stories. Where stories met that expectation, memory and comprehension were significantly better.

This work is new and as yet not well understood. It does suggest to us, though, that where people approach communication with different frames, schemata or scripts there is a serious potential for miscommunication. If one's expectation were for a story of four parts, a three-part story would sound incomplete. If one expected a three-part story, a four-part story would seem too long or to have some gratuitous content. In each case there is the potential for this failure of one's expectations to turn into a negative evaluation of the other party to the communication.

2.5   *The presentation of self*

Brown and Levinson (1978) present a theory of politeness strategies based on universal wants for negative and positive face. Depending on perceived dimensions of distance and power, both face wants are played off against each other in interaction using different strategies of deference and solidarity politeness. The core of Brown and Levinson's theory consists of the concepts of negative and positive face. When people interact in public they are concerned to preserve and present a public image that has two aspects. The positive aspect of a person's public face is his concern to be thought of as a normal, contributing member of his social world. Since the speaker's face is his public image, his positive face wants are to be seen as a supporting member of that public. At the same time, though, a person wants to preserve some sphere of his own individuality, his own territory within which he has the right of independence of movement and decision. Within his private sphere he wants the right not to be imposed upon. This aspect of face, because it asserts the right to be independent of the social world, is negative face. Social interaction in Brown and Levinson's view consists in each speaker playing off his own positive and negative face wants against those of other interactants. Politeness strategies are the codings of communication which provide in each case the carefully calculated balance of these wants which are continually under negotiation in public communication.

Another dimension to be considered is the idea that any act of communication is an imposition on the hearer's face. Since some communications are relatively innocuous, they do not require much delicacy. They may be presented directly without undue consideration of the hearer's face. Other impositions are so serious that they cannot be broached at all. Between these two extremes lie the majority of communications.

Brown and Levinson (1978) distinguish five categories of politeness strategies. These range from those which involve very little risk of loss of face, their first strategy 'bald on record', to the strategy of not saying anything because the risk is too great, their fifth strategy. The second category of strategies they call positive politeness. These strategies emphasize the commonality of the speaker and the hearer. These strategies are addressed to the hearer's positive face, that is, to his desire to be thought of as a supporting member of the society.

We prefer to call this category of politeness strategies 'solidarity politeness' as a way of reminding ourselves that the emphasis of these strategies is on the common grounds of the participants' relations. Lying behind solidarity politeness is the assumption that there is little distance (−D) between the participants and that there is also at most a slight power (−P) difference between them. Among the strategies that Brown and Levinson give for solidarity politeness are these (1978, p. 107, our numbering):

1. Notice, attend to H (earer)
2. Exaggerate (interest, approval, sympathy with H)
3. Claim in-group membership with H
4. Claim common point of view, opinions, attitudes, knowledge, empathy
5. Be optimistic
6. Indicate S knows H's wants and is taking them into account
7. Assume or assert reciprocity

Brown and Levinson then go on to elaborate these and other sub-strategies with examples from three languages, English, Tzeltal, and Tamil. They show that there are striking parallels in the linguistic forms used to express these and the following deference politeness strategies in these three wholly unrelated languages. We could not give examples of each strategy in each situation in a paper of this length. Instead we will just refer in general to the strategies as Brown and Levinson have summarized them.

We can now recall that Erickson (1976) found that in gatekeeping encounters co-membership provided significant 'leakage' in that it provided improved access to social and institutional mobility for the applicant. Here we can now rephrase this finding. Co-membership emphasizes low distance (−D) and low power difference (−P). This configuration (−P−D) is a concomitant of solidarity politeness strategies and allows the communication of impositions with a relatively low risk of loss of face. We think it is this low risk of loss of face, especially for the gatekeeper, that facilitates the conduct of the gatekeeping encounter in a way that favours the applicant.

Brown and Levinson (1978) call the third category of politeness strategies negative politeness. This is because these strategies are directed to the negative face of the hearer, to his right to be free from imposition. The essence of negative politeness is deference and so we prefer to call these strategies deference politeness strategies. This helps to remind us of the emphasis on deference as well as to avoid possible negative connotations in using the word negative.

Unlike solidarity politeness, deference politeness emphasizes the distance (+D) between the participants. The speaker, out of respect for the hearer's negative face, advances his imposition with care. He seeks to give the hearer 'a way out' in case the hearer regards the imposition as too great. This respect for the independence of the hearer from social obligations results in the strategies for deference politeness given by Brown and Levinson (1978, p. 136, our numbering).

1. Make minimal assumptions about H's wants, what is relevant to H
2. Give H option not to do act
3. Minimize threat
4. Apologize
5. Be pessimistic
6. Dissociate S, H from the particular infringement
7. State the F(ace) T(hreatening) A(ct) as a general rule

Deference politeness acknowledges the seriousness of the imposition in the act of making it. Solidarity politeness, though, is directed more to the general nature of the relationship between interactants.

The fourth category of politeness strategies treats impositions as so great that they are advanced only 'off record'. By this we mean that the communication is ambiguous. It may be taken either as an imposition or not. The decision is left up to the hearer.

2.5.1 *Global politeness systems*

There are three factors that determine what kind of politeness strategy will be used, power, distance and the absolute seriousness or weight of the imposition. Brown and Levinson suggest that different groups may typically treat these factors differently. If one group for any reason should place a value on maintaining distance (+D) between individuals, this will create an overall deference politeness system. If another group should place a value on emphasizing the common grounds of social interaction, this will create a system of solidarity politeness. These two types of system are symmetrical in that both speaker and hearer use the same strategies in their interaction. The symmetry of the system reflects the assumption that there is little difference in power between the participants. These two types of system can be graphically illustrated as below:

−P+D, *deference politeness*   −P−D, *solidarity politeness*

Speaker$_1$ ⇌ Speaker$_2$ STRATEGIES: 3 (deference politeness) 4 (off record) 5 (not said) imposition assumed high

Speaker$_1$ ⇌ Speaker$_2$ STRATEGIES: 1 (bald on record) 2 (solidarity politeness) imposition assumed low

Where there is a strongly asymmetrical power relationship (+P) a different set of strategies is used by each speaker. The more powerful speaker uses low numbered strategies, especially the first one, 'bald on record', in speaking 'downward'. The less powerful speaker uses strategies of deference (3, 4, and 5) in speaking 'upward'. This situation can be shown as below:

+*P* +*D*, *asymmetrical*

Speaker$_1$	STRATEGIES: 1 (bald on record) 2 (solidarity politeness)
Speaker$_2$	STRATEGIES: 3 (deference politeness) 4 (off record) 5 (not said)

These global politeness systems reflect the overriding values on distance (D) and power (P) differences held by members of particular groups. In any particular case, of course, because of individual differences, differences in the imposition being advanced, or differences in the context, any strategy might be used by a speaker. For example, even where two speakers are in a very asymmetrical relationship the 'lower' one does not need to show deference in an emergency. A shout to 'get out of the way', if it is offered in the interest of saving a life, can be taken as no loss to face even if in other contexts it would be heard as rude.

Our general interest in this discussion of global politeness strategies is to argue that the way a person speaks will always reflect underlying assumptions about the relations of distance and power between himself and his listener. Brown and Levinson's insight has been to provide us with a theoretical framework within which we can discuss the face relations between speakers as a matter of deep assumptions about relationship that are encoded in the politeness strategies of deference and solidarity.

2.5.2 *Taciturnity and volubility*

It is often noticed about people that some like to talk more than others. We also know that any of us enjoy talking in some situations better than in others. In the past decade or so there have been reports of cultural, ethnic, and other social groups in which talk is either highly valued such as for American Blacks in some contexts (Labov 1969; Kochman 1979; Mitchell-Kernan 1972) or in which talk is avoided at least in some contexts such as the Paliyans of India (Gardner 1966), the Apaches of Southwestern United States (Basso 1970), or the Quaker religious group (Bauman 1974).

In order to understand how people come to value much talking, volubility, or the avoidance of talking, taciturnity, we need to consider Goffman's (1976) claim that the reason people talk is to test and negotiate their view of the world against that of others. This would mean that someone who was interested in negotiating his view of the world would be more inclined to talking than one who was not. Of course this willingness would vary from time to time, from context to context, and from person to person. We suggest that the willingness to negotiate one's view of the world is another expression of the desire for positive face. This willingness is expressed with solidarity politeness strategies. These strategies imply an underlying assumption of low power difference (–P) and low distance (–D). They may also be heard as volubility because they are more diffuse in the sense that they address the general relationship, not the specific imposition.

Deference politeness strategies include not saying the imposition. This tie to taciturnity is a natural expression of the underlying assumption of a high distance (+D) between participants. This assumption of high distance is another expression of the disinclination to negotiating one's view of the world or expecting one's interactants to do the same.

In this theoretical framework then we can see that taciturnity reflects an assumption of deference politeness and volubility reflects an assumption of solidarity. The relative amount of talk then is directly reflective of the assumed face relations of the participants. The potential for miscommunication lies in the dimension of power (P). If two speakers disagree in their underlying assumptions about distance, one will approach with deference (+D) while the other expresses solidarity (−D). This solidarity may be heard by the other person, though, as expressing an asymmetrical power relationship (+P) where the other is exerting power over him. The deference of the first would be appropriate to an asymmetrical relationship which only confirms the potential power relationship. What this means is that an initial simple difference in the assumed distance (±D) can easily turn into the assertion of power (+P) by the speaker who has assumed solidarity face relations. The irony is that it is the speaker who has assumed the closeness and solidarity of the two that ends up in a dominating position. While this may not be his choice, the situation becomes difficult to unravel unless he begins to assume high distance (+D) and express deference politeness. Since he has begun with solidarity politeness, this withdrawal of the assumption of common grounds may feel like the development of hostility and further impede the progress toward agreement.

2.5.3 *Bateson and Mead's end linkage*

Bateson (1972) and Mead (1977) have suggested that we can understand the way different groups relate to each other by looking at typical patterns of relationship within each group. In their view, each group will have conventional ways for people in dominant-submissive relationships to treat each other. When they come into contact with members of other groups they will rely on their own conventional patterns to deal with the others, even where those patterns may turn out to be inappropriate. Miscommunication between people of different groups comes from an inappropriate use of conventional patterns of communication.

An example that Bateson and Mead use comes close to our interests here. They discuss the dimension of dominance and submission and the dimension of spectatorship and exhibitionism. They claim that different groups may 'link' these two dimensions in different ways. One group may 'link' the dominance end of the one dimension with the exhibitionism end of the other dimension. The person in the dominant position would be assumed to be the one who should exhibit or display. The other person, the one in the subordinate role, would be the spectator. This is what they mean, then, by 'end linkage'. The example we have just mentioned Bateson and Mead say is typical of British fathers in the family as well as British lecturers, editors and others in dominant roles. They are expected to exhibit or display while others watch as spectators.

Bateson and Mead then say that the linkage is different for Americans, presumably at least since the Second World War. Dominance is 'linked' to spectatorship and submission is 'linked' to exhibitionism. The result in British-American communication is that the British speaker, if he is dominant, expects to display while the American, as subordinate, also expects to display. If the two accept the asymmetry of power in favour of the British member, each will display. The British member will then feel the American is asserting dominance when in fact he is seeking to express submission.

On the other hand if each assumes an asymmetry of power that favours the American, each will expect the other to display. The absence of displays from the British member, while expressing submission, will be taken as assertions of power. The result is that each, while trying to show submission, will show dominance to the other; each, while trying to show dominance, will show submission. Where two speakers agree on the relationship, they will unconsciously express disagreement; where they disagree they may express agreement. It will be difficult for either to reassess the situation since the misinterpretation will tend to reconfirm already held stereotypes of the other group.

We feel that Bateson and Mead's concept of end linkage is a very useful tool for understanding interethnic communication. There are several difficulties with it that we feel can be eliminated by rephrasing end linkage in terms of universals of politeness phenomena. The three difficulties that crop up most often have to do with individual differences, with contexts, and with the values placed on role distance. While it is possible to describe British and American patterns as Bateson and Mead have, it can always be pointed out that such and such a Briton does not behave that way. Does that make him less British or more American? That is, are these generalizations definitive?

It is also pointed out that, given the right situation, any Briton or any American may switch roles. An American may of course play a British role without becoming a British citizen in the process. But more centrally, in some contexts an American in a clearly dominant position may be seen to display or exhibit for the spectatorship of others. How else may we take the displays of lecturers, musical performers, or politicians?

Finally, it seems clear that in some societies the dominance-submission roles are sensed more strongly as roles than in other societies. In such a 'role distancing' society there is nothing incompatible about a person enacting a dominant role in one context and a submissive role in another. Can it be assumed that all dominance and all submission is treated as the same in all roles that any individual enacts? Or is display associated with one kind of dominant role and not with another?

We feel that we can retain the best of Bateson and Mead's concept while avoiding the difficulties by first considering their dimension of dominance-submission as the relationship of asymmetrical power (+P). Their distinction between exhibitionism and spectatorship we can rephrase as one between solidarity and deference. If we look at the comparison they make between the British and the American family, a comparison close, in fact, to their own home and perhaps the principal source of their observations, we can characterize the British family as assuming asymmetrical relations between the father and the children. This assumption, (+P), implies that the father will use low numbered politeness strategies (bald on record, solidarity) in speaking to the children while they will use higher numbered strategies (deference, off record, silence) in speaking to him. The father's low numbered strategies we have already associated with volubility and we have associated the children's strategies of deference with taciturnity. We see then that the assumption of an asymmetrical power relationship is all that is needed to predict the volubility or exhibitionism of the father in relations with his taciturn or spectating children.

In the American family Bateson and Mead suggested that the relations were reversed with children displaying and the father observing. We think that it is not a simple reversal of the British situation. It does not feel right intuitively to us to say that Americans express deference to their children even while it does seem fair to say that there is a higher expectation in America that children will be more voluble in such contexts. We believe that the American family setting is better expressed as a symmetrical solidarity politeness system. All family members are treated as close (−D) and there is little acknowledgement of a power disparity. Americans, at least the ones being typified by Bateson and Mead, feel the family is a communicative system of solidarity relations (−P−D). This is characterized by high volubility, expression of common grounds for interaction, and impositions of members on each other are treated lightly. To the British perception, the American family has reversed roles because of the high volubility in the displays of children. To the American perception, the British family is an unpleasant power structure of domineering father and submissive (but potentially rebellious) children. In both cases the perception of individuals and the strategies for communication are determined by underlying values placed on power (P) and distance (D).

If we move away from the family into more public settings such as the lecture, we can see how difficulties with Bateson and Mead's concept can be avoided. The volubility of the lecturer and the silence of the audience make us suspect that the relationship between lecturer and audience is like that of the father and his children in the British configuration. The lecturer appears to be in a relation of dominance (+P) over his audience. This does not square with two observations. The first is that anyone could distinguish a tape-recorded lecture from tape-recorded dinner table talk with children, even without cues from the topics. The style of a lecturer is simply not the same as the style of a father. Our view of communication is that any difference in style communicates a difference in relationship. This suggests that there is something wrong.

The second observation that causes problems is that both British and American lecturers display or exhibit for their audiences. Bateson and Mead's view would imply that American lecturers were treating their audiences as their superiors, that they were showing submission through their displays. We do see some value in Bateson's (1972) observation that Americans tend to use hesitation and faltering syntax as an expression of sincerity. Brown and Levinson (1978) give this sort of 'hedging' as an expression of deference. On the level of the speech act then we can see the American lecturer showing some deference to his audience. The British lecturer, Bateson claims, does not falter and is heard as arrogant by American audiences. Our view, though, maintains that overall the lecture is nevertheless a display, an exhibition, and we must account for that.

To do so we need first to consider role distancing. Several writers, notably Ong (1977), and Foucault (1977), have pointed out that we must always distinguish between the real author and the implied author of a work. The real author is the biological, historical individual responsible for doing the writing. The implied author, though, may consist of a highly complex set of relations between the real author and the text. This essay is an example. There are two real authors and an implied plural author. One person, however, at each stage of handling the manuscript works alone. One person is writing on a page at the moment this is written. The plurality of the real authors' ideas is practically reduced to the physical activity of one of them and then in turn grammatically phrased as a plurality, now implied by the 'we' of authorship. This implied author exists in relation to the text and may continue to exist, unchanged, whether the real authors are living or not. It is because in the essay this relationship is so easily buried or fictionalized that we often mistake the real author for the implied one.

What is true of authors is also true of readers. The implied reader of this text is assumed to have certain knowledge, certain interests, and certain prejudices. There is no doubt that all real readers will not share all of these. It is the text, in fact, that creates and mediates a fictionalized relationship between the implied author and the implied reader. What the real author(s) and real reader(s) do is quite independent of the roles created by the text.

We would like to suggest that the role of lecturer or in fact any public performance role is like authorship in this respect. A clear distinction must be understood to exist between the real lecturer (or author or singer) and the implied performance role. We have learned to accept this role distance for some performance roles but we need to understand lectures as structurally similar.

Returning then to our point we would say that the relationship between the lecturer and his audience is one of solidarity politeness. This is because it is a relationship between fictionalized roles, the role of implied lecturer and implied listener. It makes no difference that the listener's mind is on yesterday's ballgame or tomorrow's shopping trip, the lecturer (implied) treats the listener as if he is all there and attending to the lecturer. Of course wherever the listener has gone in his mind, it is highly likely that he will seek to enact the implied role of an attentive, understanding listener with his physical presence.

We see the lecturer as giving solidarity displays because of his implied role of solidarity with the audience. The underlying assumption is low distance (–D) and a low power difference (–P). In these displays of solidarity politeness the lecturer resembles the father in the British family as well as the father in the American family. The difference is that the British children are expected to show deference, children should be seen and not heard, while the American children are expected to reciprocate in shows of solidarity. The audience to the lecture as an implied audience is assumed to be fully in accord with the lecture and potentially capable of responding in kind with voluble and considered questions.

The central difference between the British and American cases seems to lie not in the dimension of spectatorship-exhibitionism but in the overall value placed on distance. Brown and Levinson (1978) have suggested that the British have a deference politeness society while Americans, especially in western areas have a solidarity politeness society. What this means is that the British prefer to maintain distance between individuals in public while Americans prefer to emphasize the common grounds on which individuals may build relationships.

To the extent this is true then we see Americans as seeking to express and maintain solidarity relations (–P–D) in all contexts, family, lectures, authorship, and in public face-to-face encounters. The British on the other hand express a greater degree of flexibility in social relations. In family contexts relations are asymmetrical, in public face-to-face encounters relations are symmetrically deferent and in public performances relations between fictionalized roles are symmetrically solidarity relations.

The implication of these differences between British and Americans is that the British will experience Americans as always 'in performance'. The American emphasis of solidarity will resonate with the British enactment of performance roles to produce this perception. On the other hand, the British expression of multiple relations depending on the context will strike Americans as insincere, cold, and indifferent. Americans will see the British as playing roles and in fact 'in performance'. The difference, then, has to do with the acceptance or rejection of role distance or differentiation as a group value. In a group that accepts or values the expression of multiple communicative roles, it is possible for each role relationship to have a distinct system of politeness relations. Solidarity or deference is felt as a relationship between roles, not persons. In a system such as the one that seems to be developing in America since the war, role differentiation is viewed as a negative quality, as devious or even as pathological. In such a system all roles will tend to be expressed with a single communicative style, solidarity politeness.

2.5.4 *A comment on education in America*

As an example of how problems may arise through either different communicative systems coming into contact or from changes within a single system we would like to comment briefly on American education as a politeness system. We have just advanced the notion that in America there has been a tendency, we think since the war, for the whole society to move into a global solidarity politeness system. This has been motivated by the best of democratic interests in creating equality of educational opportunity. For the educational system as a whole, equal educational opportunity has come to mean a de-emphasis on differences between groups (–D) as well as an equalization of power differences (–P). As an expression of this mood of equality of opportunity, teachers have often adopted solidarity politeness strategies. As we have tried to argue, solidarity politeness is a more or less automatic communicative outcome of assuming low power difference (–P) and low distance values (–D). The move toward solidarity politeness strategies in the classroom has been an unconscious communicative expression of the basic goals of the educational system. As a result, classroom communication is expected to reflect symmetrical solidarity politeness.

Unfortunately, behind the expression of solidarity lies a significant power differential. At the very least, it is the difference between the teacher's power as an adult and representative of the school and the student's power as an immature and single member of society. In some cases the power difference is very much greater as when the teacher also represents an ethnic or social group of economic or technological dominance and the student represents a minority ethnic or social group.

The condition thus created is a classical double bind (Bateson 1972). The teacher, from an asymmetrical position of power (+P), uses low numbered strategies (bald on record, solidarity) while simultaneously requiring the student to treat them as symmetrical expressions of solidarity. If the student responds to the expression of power (+P) with the universally appropriate and respectful deference, he may be punished for being silent, withdrawn, indirect, vague, or even hostile. If the student responds to the expression of solidarity, (–P–D), with the universally appropriate and respectful reciprocal solidarity politeness he may be punished for being too pushy, 'uppity', and disrespectful of the teacher's authority and position.

In our opinion the only viable response to such a situation from the point of view of the student is a complete withdrawal (Jacob and Sanday 1976; Ogbu 1974). Of course, in many cases that response is also prohibited by law and leaves, in fact, no viable response for the individual. This is the double bind. The basic message is that there is a power difference of significance (+P). The metamessage is that this basic message should be ignored. Then where the individual realizes this conflict and responds to it he is punished for attacking the system. Bateson used this concept as a way of gaining insight into the development of schizophrenia in individuals as members of groups such as families. We believe that the same communicative dynamics are operating in many cases within the American educational system with tragically similar results.

2.5.5 *Selected displays: boasting and bragging*

As a final view of the presentation of self in interethnic communication we would like to look now at a particular kind of presentation, the presentation in exaggeration called boasting or bragging. It is possible to draw fine distinctions among behavioural complexes that might be called boasting such as Kochman (1979) has done for comparisons between American Blacks and Whites. Kochman argues that boasting and bragging are different activities for Blacks. Boasting is taken as non-serious or humorous self-display which is not necessarily backed up by tests of ability in the real world. This sort of display is positively valued. Bragging, though, is understood to be serious and disapproved, at least until the braggart can make his claim good. In that case the display is no longer understood as bragging. Kochman feels that White Americans do not distinguish boasting from bragging and generally disapprove of either.

This difference between Black and White views of boasting and bragging is the source of misunderstanding between the two groups. We believe that it is also confounded by a third behaviour that we will call 'putting your best foot forward'. This sort of display is approved in contacts between strangers or generally in public contexts. We suggest that it falls short of the negative aspects of boasting/bragging for White Americans by avoiding exaggeration and hyperbole. In public one does show off one's best but in a somewhat 'reduced' way. That is, one leaves some room for the other party to praise oneself. Pawley and Syder (n.d.) have called this 'the reduction principle'.

We would like to consider this 'reduction principle' or 'putting your best foot forward' but with modesty to be an expression of solidarity politeness. It expresses optimism on the part of the speaker, the optimism of knowing that your best will be well accepted and approved by other interactants. In its reduction it allows the other parties to the interaction to express their solidarity by showing or even exaggerating interest, sympathy and consideration.

We are especially interested in the orientation to the future taken by 'putting one's best foot forward'. In job interviews, for example, it expresses the assumption that one will be hired and that one's employment will be profitable to both the institution and to oneself. In educational contexts solidarity politeness expresses the assumption that one will succeed within the terms laid down. One expects a positive and continuing future involvement with the goals and outcomes of education. In legal contexts 'putting your best foot forward' expresses solidarity with the philosophy of the law, the assumption that however out of line one's behaviour had been to bring one into the legal sphere, one's intentions are to remain in solidarity with the social world that one has threatened to violate. Deviance and violation are treated as temporary aberrations in a career of solid social membership.

There are clear differences between American Blacks and Whites on these expressions of boasting, bragging, and 'putting your best foot forward' and we believe these differences are the source of misunderstandings between the groups. Two considerations, though, lead us to treat these differences as relatively minor. The first is that, as Kochman (1979) has said, members of the two groups are belatedly coming to understand each other through at least the mass media if not through increased face-to-face contacts. Thus the differences, while still present and important are better understood. This understanding allows people to make some compensation in their own expectations in interactions with the other group.

Our second consideration is more important. We believe both Black and White displays in this range are expressions of solidarity politeness. Where Blacks and Whites misunderstand each other it is more likely caused by a disagreement on the amount of real solidarity underlying the communicative expression. We will argue below that an expression of solidarity can go very wrong if there is an underlying assumption of distance (+D).

Before considering this possibility we need to first sketch out the expression of deference politeness in contexts similar to those we have just mentioned. One of the strategies of deference politeness is to express pessimism (Brown and Levinson 1978). From this point of view one cannot 'put one's best foot forward'. Such presumption on the opinions and attitudes of the listener is out of keeping with the deference being shown. In a job interview, for example, someone expressing deference would not presume that he was going to receive the job, that would be up to the interviewer entirely to decide. One would not display knowledge, skills, past achievements, that would presume that he knew just what would please the interviewer. Again, this would be too great an imposition on the face of the interviewer. In educational contexts, deference politeness is, again, expressed by making minimal assumptions about the outcomes of the process. One assumes that the teacher knows best and expresses pessimism about one's own potential. In legal contexts the same reticence about assuming a positive outcome is an expression of deference politeness. One is pessimistic, apologetic, leaves options in the hands of others and makes minimal assumptions about the hearer's wants, goals, or intentions.

2.5.6 *A legal example*

We would now like to close our discussion of discourse and face with a partly hypothetical example of a particularly significant gatekeeping encounter, the legal process. In fact the legal process consists of a series of 'gates' from the first observation of a violation to the final release from parole. Since this is only an example we will not be able to treat this highly complex process with the delicacy it deserves. It is our goal to suggest how considerations of face may enter into the legal process as 'leakage' of the type Erickson (1976) has described. We do not intend to do more than suggest where problems may lie and, if they do exist, what might be done. To provide a more careful, conscientious and accurate representation of the interactions we hypothesize here would require a major body of research that has yet to be undertaken.

In 1978 a report of the Alaska Judicial Council suggested that for certain classes of offences, jail sentences given in the state courts were consistently longer for Blacks and Alaska Natives than for Whites, given the same conditions of offence and prior record. The state court system, of course, has viewed this suggestion with caution and alarm, with caution because the study was based on a plea bargaining study which was not strictly and methodologically concerned with this issue, and with alarm because if this suggestion is found to be true it indicates serious ethnic discrimination within the state of Alaska's legal system.

This situation appears to be just the one described by Erickson and which we have outlined above in our discussion of gatekeeping encounters. The judicial system in the State of Alaska has made and continues to make every effort to restrict the possibility of discrimination in the state courts. It is simply not a situation that can be dismissed as racism in the courts on the one hand or as non-existent on the other hand. In any case, the situation is not to be treated lightly either by parties within the judicial system or by outside observers. The potential for discrimination exists, we believe, in 'leakage' from communicative style, or as we are now in the position to discuss, from differences in the presentation of self.

We will look at only one aspect of the legal process, the pre-sentence report. The report of the judicial council noted a significant difference in the pre-sentence reports written for Natives and non-Natives. Pre-sentence reports for Natives remarked on the absence of any expression of plans for the future. Overall these reports reflected a pessimism that we associate directly with deference politeness. In contrast, both Blacks and non-Black non-Natives (a category which may include other ethnic groups than Whites) expressed the intention of returning to a job or return to school. That is, they expressed the desire to improve themselves. They put their 'best foot forward'. This expression of solidarity politeness strongly contrasts with the expression of deference politeness of Natives.

Without further analysis of the actual interactions that went into the writing of these reports and of the reports themselves, we must be careful not to draw too many conclusions. Here we would like to suggest, though, that these expressions of solidarity politeness and deference politeness are sufficient, if everything else is equal, to produce the results reported by the judicial council.

It is clear from the literature we have cited above that American Blacks and Whites may be fairly characterized as assuming solidarity politeness relationships in at least some contexts. One of these contexts is before the law. Whatever experience there may be to the contrary, we believe that American Blacks and Whites prefer to assume equality, and therefore solidarity (–P–D), relations before the law. Alaska Natives on the other hand appear to assume deference relations (+P+D, –P+D) before the law (Hippler and Conn 1972; Hippler 1973) as in many other contexts. And here we might add a comment on the usefulness of the 'pan-ethnic' category 'Alaska Native'. While very important differences exist among Native groups and within Native groups in Alaska, in this context before the law the assumption of deference relations seems to be quite characteristic of all Native groups. The pre-sentence reports appear to confirm this.

The court itself may be characterized as an asymmetrical system of high power difference and high distance (+P+D). The appropriate interactive strategies in such a system are low numbered (bald on record) 'downward' and high numbered (deference) 'upward'. We believe that most defendants understand this and in fact display the appropriate deference *while in court*.

The problem that surfaces in the pre-sentence reports lies between the original arrest and the court. The pre-sentence report is prepared, not in court, but in a somewhat less awesome, less formal context. The individuals involved in preparing these reports are not in the professional or formal position to command deference within the American legal system. These individuals in fact operate from the basic American assumption of solidarity politeness (–P–D).

So far then the result is that Blacks and Whites interact with the individuals who prepare the pre-sentence report on a mutual assumption of solidarity politeness. Whatever is actually said, it is interpreted as optimism, 'putting your best foot forward' and recorded in the language of solidarity politeness. This, in turn, expresses the underlying assumption of all parties of equality before the law which is heard, of course, as respect for the law, respect for the legal system. This at least supports if not fosters a favourable outcome.

We will need in a moment to reconsider the case of the Blacks. For now we would like to suggest that the deference politeness of Alaska Natives which is expressed as making minimal assumptions about the outcomes and rather full submission to the dictates of the law is heard by those preparing pre-sentence reports as an expression of guilt. Recall that the system in which one expresses low numbered strategies and the other deference is an asymmetrical system of high power difference (+P). The deference will sound like acceding power to the individual preparing the report which may result in some all-too-human exaggeration of the potential for the expression of power. This misperception of the polite deference of Natives may reflect itself in a report language of indifference, shiftlessness, or strong assumption of guilt. This sort of report could easily be translated into a more severe sentence than one expressing the assumed optimism of solidarity politeness.

What has happened structurally is that the assumption of symmetrical relations on both sides has been translated into an asymmetry because one expressed solidarity and the other expressed deference. This situation could be graphed as below:

REPORTER

+P+D

−P−D, solidarity $\quad S_1 \rightleftharpoons S_2$ $\qquad S_1$ (solidarity)

NATIVE DEFENDANT $\qquad\qquad\qquad \longrightarrow$

−P+D, deference $\quad S_1 \rightleftharpoons S_2$ $\qquad\qquad S_2$ (deference)

The problem that underlies this misunderstanding is the reporter's assumption of commonality (−P−D) before the law coupled with the Native's assumption of respect for the distance (+D) between himself and the reporter. Both are acting out of respect and concern for each other but the means of expression 'backfires' and produces quite contrary messages.

Now we need to return to the reports for Blacks which should result in a positive outcome given that both parties are assuming solidarity strategies for the interaction. There is a 'joker' in the system here which does border on racism but of a newer kind. We have said that both the Black defendant and the reporter are assuming solidarity as an expression of equality before the law. There may be in at least some cases an underlying assumption of high distance (+D) between him and the defendant. If this should happen, the opposite asymmetry would result. The distance (+D) of the reporter would be expressed, heard and even felt as deference politeness. If the defendant should choose to emphasize his equality before the law (−P−D) this would be reflected in a negative report. It might be thought that the defendant did not show appropriate meekness or remorse in the face of the law and an intimation of a need to punish this 'lack of remorse' might easily leak into the process.

This situation would be structurally just the opposite of the Native situation.

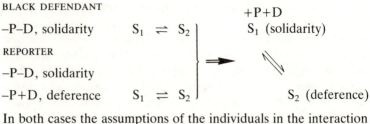

BLACK DEFENDANT

−P−D, solidarity $S_1 \rightleftharpoons S_2$

REPORTER

−P−D, solidarity

−P+D, deference $S_1 \rightleftharpoons S_2$

+P+D

S_1 (solidarity)

S_2 (deference)

In both cases the assumptions of the individuals in the interaction translate into communicative style through the expression of face relations. In both cases the potential for misunderstanding may translate into reports that reflect those misunderstandings as negative views of the defendants, one as too pushy, domineering, or as not showing remorse, the other as too meek, guilty, or perhaps shiftless. It is at least possible that such reports could influence the sentencing process.

Some of the factors that enter into this potential for discrimination through communicative style can now be identified. The first factor is the assumptions individuals make about basic face relations. Where these are different there is the potential for conflict. The second factor is assumptions individuals make about the legal process, solidarity relations out of court, deference relations within court. A third factor surfaces which should be considered in further research, the role of the non-professional in non-formal contexts. Sudnow (1967) found that in a large urban hospital, while policy prevented discrimination by hospital staff, decisions by ambulance drivers in approaching the emergency entrance affected the outcomes for the emergency patients they were delivering. Some patients were delivered with great urgency, including the sounding of the ambulance siren. Others were delivered slowly, with only the honk of the horn. The latter were treated with less urgency by the receiving staff. It was significant that those latter cases tended to be members of minority groups, the aged, or patients obviously under the influence of alcohol. An informal and unofficial decision by the ambulance driver was significant in determining what sort of treatment individuals would receive as patients in a public hospital.

3 Multi-ethnic gatekeeping, a recommendation

We have taken the position in this paper that multi-ethnic communication is a fact of the modern world. We see no reason why or how this should change in the predictable future. We have identified a significant situation, the gatekeeping encounter, in which there is a serious potential of discrimination against ethnic or other social groups by those who hold institutional, social, economic, or technological power. Following Erickson (1978) we have argued that the most serious potential for discrimination lies in 'leakage' into the situation from differences in communicative style. Communicative style we have seen as consisting partly of patterns of discourse, the ways in which speech and verbal interaction are integrated. While discourse consists of at least the distribution of talk, the information structure, cognitive frames, schema and scripts, and the presentation of self through talking, we have seen the latter, the presentation of self as the key to understanding interethnic communication.

The problem that we would now like to discuss is how differences in assumptions about face can be reconciled in a multi-ethnic framework. In both the comment we made on education and in the example just concluded of the judicial system, complications arose from the fact that one party had assumed solidarity politeness while the other had assumed deference politeness as the appropriate set of strategies for interaction. In other words, one party chose to emphasize the common grounds for interaction while the other party chose to emphasize fundamental differences between the individuals. There is an overriding problem with solidarity strategies in that they are structurally the same as those used in situations of asymmetrical power relations by the powerful member of the interaction. Solidarity strategies then carry with them the potential for creating a double bind. In gatekeeping situations, the situation itself defines the relationship as asymmetrical. One party has been invested with the power to make decisions that seriously impact on the lives of applicants at the 'gate'. When the gatekeeper uses solidarity strategies they can be heard doubly, either as expressions of power or as expressions of common grounds or solidarity. As Erickson (1976) has pointed out, co-membership will override ethnic difference in such encounters. The applicant is in a double bind. He is enticed into solidarity expressions by the hope that co-membership will work to his advantage. In using solidarity strategies he risks sounding disrespectful of the power of the gatekeeper. If he uses deference strategies he risks sounding withdrawn, unconcerned, hostile, or haughty and thereby jeopardizes his chances of success.

We believe that only the gatekeeper is in the position to remove the double bind, having access as he has to the sources of power and decision that control the situation. The only way to untie the double bind of interethnic gatekeeping encounters is for the gate-keeper to voluntarily use strategies of deference. The gatekeeper must assume a responsibility for understanding, accepting, and posi-tively valuing the differences presented by the applicants. As Erickson (1976) has also concluded,

> The obvious policy implication is that the personnel and the organizational context and structure of the institution of gatekeeping should be fundamentally changed to take into account ethnic, racial, social class, and other kinds of particularistic attributes of the statuses of persons meeting face to face. (p. 144)

Further intensification of the expression of solidarity relations by gatekeepers in multi-ethnic situations can only be interpreted as a wish to increase the double bind into which the power of the gatekeeper has placed the applicant.

We can see then that at the level of world communication the way to improve communication is not to adopt English, better English, Standard English, any other 'standard' form of language, or in fact any means of communication predicated on commonness of education or experience. Because of the complexity of world communication, we also cannot expect solutions based on every-one learning everyone else's communicative system. The only viable solution that we can imagine is the cultivation of an inter-national, interethnic, intercultural communicative style of def-erence politeness. We must assume at the foundation that communication is difficult and problematical, that we must mini-mize our impositions on others, that we must leave others the option of not acting on our impositions or acting as they choose, and that we can make only minimal assumptions about the wants, needs, relevancies, and priorities of others. The only common ground on which interethnic communication can be based without discrimination is the valued assumption of difference.

Questions for discussion, study and further research

1. The authors depict differences in communicative style as a cen-tral issue in interethnic communication. Can you cite examples of such differences with reference to (a) degree of talking expected of participants in different situations, e.g. meal talk, party talk,

conversing with strangers on a bus, (b) presentation of self, e.g. during a job interview.

2. The authors limit their discussion to linguistic dimensions of communicative style. Can you find examples of non-linguistic aspects of communicative style, and particularly those which differ across cultures?

3. Examine a tape recording of a segment of conversation. Identify some of the ways information structure is presented by looking for examples of contrastive stress, foregrounded clauses and backgrounded clauses.

4. Study the list of strategies for expressing solidarity politeness and deference politeness discussed by the authors on page 167, and then classify the utterances below according to the strategies they cite.

> I wonder if you can help me.
> Help me with this bag, will you mate.
> This food tastes sort of strange.
> Let's have something to drink.
> You'll have another drink, won't you.
> Could I see you for a second.
> Goodness, you cut your hair. By the way, I just came to borrow some flour.

5. Can you think of differences in address systems which confirm the authors' comments on differences between American and British professors' relationships with students?

6. Pick two groups representing linguistic and/or cultural backgrounds with which you are familiar and systematically compare them with respect to (a) turn taking, (b) grounding, (c) framing, (d) volubility, (e) the presentation of self, in general and in specific displays such as boasting. How does each group interpret the behaviour of the other? If you are yourself a member of one of the groups you have analysed, do you feel any differently about the other group after having done such an analysis?

7. Identify the gatekeepers in your society, considering as broad a range of institutions as possible. Do members of a particular ethnic group tend to occupy a disproportionate number of gatekeeping positions? Does Erickson's concept of leakage apply to gatekeeping encounters, or their outcomes? To what extent can

leakage be attributed to communicative style in the cases you examine?

8. As the authors point out, communicative style is closely identified with one's identity as a person, as well as as a member of a group. Consider differences in communicative style as an aspect of personality, varying within cultural or ethnic groups, by (a) comparing two individuals you know well with regard to their use of solidarity and deference politeness strategies, or (b) examining the use of discourse strategies reflected in the dialogue of several characters in a contemporary play.

9. Compare and contrast the communicative discourse styles used in your society by members of different groups such as politicians, businessmen, military, academics, etc. Can you find differences associated with occupational or professional groups? Do these seem to be more or less important than differences reflecting ethnicity and/or social class?

Introduction to Chapter 7

All of the papers in this volume indicate that our understanding of communication must include insights from outside the traditional realm of theoretical and descriptive linguistics. Pawley and Syder indicate some of the ways in which the study of conversational data requires modification of the linguistic paradigm itself, and thus make a significant contribution to linguistic theory and what Schegloff (1979) has called syntax for conversation. Pawley and Syder look at the related puzzles of nativelike selection and nativelike fluency: the ability of native speakers to convey meanings by expressions that are not only grammatical but also natural and idiomatic, and the ability of native speakers to produce fluent stretches of spontaneous connected discourse which exceeds human capacities for encoding novel speech in advance or while speaking. They argue that the linguist's view of native speaker knowledge must be expanded to include memorized sequences and lexicalized sentence stems in addition to the usual apparatus of linguistic description, i.e. productive rules plus lexicon. Such a modification of linguistic theory will require rejection of the principle of parsimony in the evaluation of grammars, but will more accurately reflect native speakers' real linguistic knowledge.

Pawley and Syder's concepts of memorized sentences and lexicalized stems are related to previously introduced terms such as holophrases (Corder 1973), prefabricated routines and patterns (Hakuta 1974), formulaic speech (Wong-Fillmore 1976) and gestalt vs. analytic language (Peters 1977). Pawley and Syder's identification of holistically stored sequences with a processing capacity vital to speaker's needs to compose and decode spoken discourse under tight time-bonding, with many discourse matters to attend to besides grammatical manipulation, suggests a more significant role for routines and patterns than that conceded by Krashen and Scarcella (1978), but one that can easily be accommodated by McLaughlin's (1978) reformulation of Krashen's acquisition/learning distinction in terms of controlled/automatic processes or the expanded model of monitoring presented by Morrison and Low in the next chapter of this book. If this is a satisfactory explanation of the way (or one of the ways) in which we process language, Nattinger has indicated some implications for foreign language teaching:

> Perhaps we should base our teaching on the assumption that, for a great deal of the time anyway, language production consists of piecing together the ready-made units appropriate for a particular situation and that comprehension relies on knowing which of these patterns to predict in these situations. Our teaching therefore would center on these patterns and the ways they can be pieced together, along with the ways they vary and the situations in which they occur.
>
> (Nattinger 1980, p. 341)

7 Two puzzles for linguistic theory: nativelike selection and nativelike fluency

Andrew Pawley and Frances Hodgetts Syder

1 Introduction

This essay discusses two linguistic capacities which we term *nativelike selection* and *nativelike fluency*.[1] The first of these is, roughly, the ability of the native speaker routinely to convey his meaning by an expression that is not only grammatical but also nativelike; what is puzzling about this is how he selects a sentence that is natural and idiomatic from among the range of grammatically correct paraphrases, many of which are non-nativelike or highly marked usages. The second is the native speaker's ability to produce fluent stretches of spontaneous connected discourse; there is a puzzle here in that human capacities for encoding novel speech in advance or while speaking appear to be severely limited, yet speakers commonly produce fluent multi-clause utterances which exceed these limits. Although the general nature and practical importance of nativelike selection and fluency are recognized, at least tacitly, by all second language teachers, these linguistic abilities present certain problems of formal description and explanation that have generally been overlooked. It will be suggested that in order to describe and explain them we must take a view of the native speaker's grammatical knowledge that is somewhat different from any that now has wide currency among grammarians.

Drawing on studies of English conversational talk, we will argue that fluent and idiomatic control of a language rests to a considerable extent on knowledge of a body of 'sentence stems' which are 'institutionalized' or 'lexicalized'. A lexicalized sentence stem is a unit of clause length or longer whose grammatical form and lexical content is wholly or largely fixed; its fixed elements form a standard label for a culturally recognized concept, a term in the language. Although lexicalized in this sense, most such units are not true idioms but rather are regular form-meaning pairings. The stock of lexicalized sentence stems known to the ordinary mature speaker of English amounts to hundreds of thousands. In addition there are many semi-lexicalized sequences, for just as there is a continuum between fully productive rules of sentence formation and rules of low productivity, so there is a cline between fully lexicalized formations on the one hand and nonce forms on the other.

The theory does not jibe well with the traditional compartmen- for explaining nativelike fluency and selection. In the store of familiar collocations there are expressions for a wide range of familiar concepts and speech acts, and the speaker is able to retrieve these as wholes or as automatic chains from the long term memory; by doing this he minimizes the amount of clause-internal encoding work to be done and frees himself to attend to other tasks in talk-exchange, including the planning of larger units of discourse. An utterance will be nativelike to the extent that it consists of a lexicalized sentence stem plus permissible expansions or substitutions. However, many such stems have a grammar that is unique in that they are subject to an idiosyncratic range of phrase structure and transformational restrictions; that is to say, by applying generally productive rules to these units one may produce an utterance that is grammatical but unnatural or highly marked.

The theory does not jibe well with the traditional compartmentalization of grammar into syntax (productive rules) vs. dictionary (fixed, arbitrary usages). Nor does it allow acceptance of Occam's Razor, or the principle of parsimony, in the evaluation of descriptions of the native speaker's linguistic competence. Insofar as many regular morpheme sequences are known both holistically (as lexicalized units) and analytically (as products of syntactic rules) it is necessary to specify these sequences at least twice in the grammar. Some possible implications of the lexicalized sentence stem hypothesis for the theory of grammar will be sketched in the final section of the paper.

2 The puzzle of nativelike selection

Although foreshadowed in earlier, structuralist work, the concept of a 'generative grammar' is due principally to Chomsky (e.g. 1957, 1965), as is the equation of knowledge of a generative grammar with 'linguistic competence'. Since the 1960s, at least, it has been widely accepted that one part of the language learner's task is to:

(1) learn a/the system of rules which enumerates the infinite set of sentences in the language, assigns correct structural descriptions to these sentences, and distinguishes them from ungrammatical sequences.

A focus on the creative power of syntactic rules has been one of the main attractions of the Chomskyan approach. Few linguists have quarrelled with the assertion that the possible sentences in any natural language are an infinite, or at least an indefinitely large set. The transformational-generative models developed in the late '50s and the '60s provided a plausible account of the grammatical basis of this particular kind of linguistic creativity. There are, of course, a number of different forms that a generative grammar might take. Lately there has been much debate on this matter, and on such questions as whether the domain of syntactic rules should be limited to the sentence, whether or not syntactic rules can in all cases be adequately described without reference to meaning, presuppositions, shared belief systems, coherence requirements on connected discourse, and other not-strictly-syntactic knowledge. Without quibbling over these issues, let us accept that a generative grammar is part of what a person must know in order to be a competent user of any language, and turn to another, little-studied problem.

The problem we are addressing is that native speakers do *not* exercise the creative potential of syntactic rules to anything like their full extent, and that, indeed, if they did do so they would not be accepted as exhibiting nativelike control of the language. The fact is that only a small proportion of the total set of grammatical sentences are nativelike in form – in the sense of being readily acceptable to native informants as ordinary, natural forms of expression, in contrast to expressions that are grammatical but are judged to be 'unidiomatic', 'odd' or 'foreignisms'. This assertion still holds, we believe, if the total set of sentences is restricted to those that make sense and do not exceed three clauses in length. Items (2) and (3) illustrate, contrasting a piece of narrative, spoken by a New Zealand man of about 70, recalling his family's circumstances at the outbreak of World War I, with a paraphrasing of the narrative in a style that is grammatical but generally unnatural:[2]

(2)   I had /four ⌊uncles–
   they /all /volun/teered to ⌊go a⌊way–
   and ah / that was ⌊one /Christmas–
   th't /I'll /always re⌊member––
   because ah–my /four /uncles /came ⌊round–
   They were /all in ⌊uni/form–
   an' ah /they are /goin' t' /have /Christmas ⌊dinner with /us––
   'n' /what w's /more im ⌊portant–
   /they're /goin' t' pro⌊vide it–
   'n' /that was /really ⌊something

(3)   The brothers of my parents were four
   Their offering to soldier in lands elsewhere in the army of our
   country had occurred.
   There is not a time when my remembering that Christmas
   will not take place,
   because of the coming of the brothers of my parents to our
   house,
   having put on their bodies the clothes of the army.
   The eating of Christmas dinner by them in our company was
   to happen
   and above that thing in importance
   the buying of the food by them was to occur,
   a thing that was indeed unusual and indeed good.

   If a language learner is to achieve nativelike control, then, he
must learn not only a generative grammar as this term is usually
understood – a set of rules specifying all and only the sentences
of the language. In addition he needs to:

(4)   learn a means for knowing which of the well-formed sentences
   are nativelike – a way of distinguishing those usages that are
   normal or unmarked from those that are unnatural or highly
   marked.

How this distinction is made is the 'puzzle of nativelike selection'.[3]
The special difficulties of acquiring this component of communicative competence will be appreciated by anyone who has learned
the rules of sentence construction in a new language from a grammar book, before he has had much exposure to the language as
it is actually spoken and written in everyday life. In the early stages
of putting one's 'book knowledge' into practice (no matter how
good the book and how diligent the study of it), it is a common

experience to find that most of one's productions are, to the native ear, unidiomatic. Each sentence may be strictly grammatical. The trouble is that native speakers just do not say things that way. The nature of the problem will be less obvious to those who have learned their language(s) by immersion in the speech community more or less from the start. A member of this fortunate group somehow learns how to speak idiomatically at the same time as he acquires the ability to speak grammatically.

It is tempting for the grammarian to dismiss nativelike selection as 'merely a matter of style, not grammar', as though this relieved him of the responsibility of trying to understand it. But that does no more than give a name to the problem, without accurately characterizing it or explaining it. Conversely, it may be suggested that we are actually dealing here with discourse that is ungrammatical, breaking grammatical conventions of a subtle kind which as yet have not been made explicit in grammatical analysis. While this suggestion deserves careful consideration, one must again take care to avoid a solution by naming. It is easy but unenlightening to stretch the notion 'rule of grammar' to refer to phenomena which are rather different in character from those normally treated under this heading. An unfamiliar thing is not elucidated simply by subsuming it under a familiar label, in the hope that it will turn out to be like other things so categorized. It is as well to recognize that the nature of the problem is not well understood at present. Our discussion so far may, indeed, have given a false impression that it is possible to define the exact range of material that calls for explanation. Such is not the case because there is no sharp boundary between the classes of nativelike and non-nativelike sentences (in much the same way as there is no sharp boundary between the classes of grammatical and ungrammatical sentences in English). This may be seen in the following examples.

A hostess at an evening party spoke these words to a friend who had unexpectedly brought along a mutual friend who had been out of town for some time:

(5) I'm so glad you could bring Harry!

The rules of English sentence construction would have permitted her to use any of the following paraphrases, among others:[4]

(6) That Harry could be brought by you makes me so glad.
    That you could bring Harry gladdens me so.
    Your having been able to Harry bring makes me so glad.

I am so glad Harry's being brought by you was possible.

The fact that Harry could be brought by you causes me to be so glad.

I am in a glad state because you could bring Harry.

Because of your having been able to bring Harry I am in a very high state of gladness.

A lover may express his (or her) wishes with the familiar words:

(7) I want to marry you.

The same objective information, if conveyed in the following terms, might not achieve the desired response:

(8) (a) I wish to be wedded to you.
    (b) I desire you to become married to me.
    (c) Your marrying me is desired by me.
    (d) My becoming your spouse is what I want.
    (e) I want marriage with you.
    (f) What is desired by me is to wed you.
    (g) I, who am speaking, want to marry you, whom I am addressing.
    (h) It is my wish that I become married to you. etc. etc.

While none of the alternatives listed in (6) and (8) are likely to be accepted as ordinary, idiomatic usages by English speakers, some of the sentences are less unnatural than others. But we need not be unduly concerned to find that there are degrees of naturalness. The study of grammar proceeds by comparing the properties of clear cases of grammatical and ungrammatical strings, and succeeds in isolating regularities in spite of the fact that there is a large class of unclear cases, and in spite of the fact that informants will often give inconsistent judgments, as well as 'more or less' estimations of the grammaticality of particular sequences, influenced by such factors as ease of comprehension, frequency of use and knowledge of context. It is sufficient that there be a core of agreements.

It is possible here to give no more than a few comments on the nature and explanation of nativelike selection. What follows is intended to show that the data do not permit of a unified solution, in terms of syntactic structure alone, for example, or discourse context, familiarity, etc.

Some commentators have suggested that naturalness is largely a matter of length and grammatical simplicity. Native speakers prefer the shortest and simplest of the grammatical alternatives. The maxim goes something like this: to speak idiomatically, never use a phrase where a single word will do, and never use a complex sentence where a simple sentence will do. There may be something in this suggestion but, plainly, lexical and grammatical complexity are not the sole principles to which nativelike selection answers. For instance, in everyday speech *Do what I say!* and *Do what I tell you!* are more common than the roughly synonymous *Obey me!*, while *He won't do what he's told* is just as nativelike as *He won't obey orders*, and *That's got nothing to do with it* is as idiomatic as *That's irrelevant*.

Some of the unnatural usages in (3), (6) and (8) arguably are syntactically deviant. However, the conventions concerned in most cases belong to discourse rather than sentence-level syntax, and sometimes are statable not as categorical rules but only as a scale of preferences. For example, in the series in (8), two of the sentences, (c) and (d), have the new information placed in the initial (topic) position in the sentence, a non-preferred usage in English discourse. Even so, the sequence would still be unidiomatic if *My becoming your spouse is what I want* were changed to *What I want is my becoming your spouse*. There is a preference, if not a categorical rule, that in a nominalization such as *my becoming your spouse*, which is the predicate rather than the subject, and which contains a possessive NP co-referential with the subject NP, the possessive NP must be stressed or else omitted. (*What I want is MY becoming your spouse, not BILL* seems less odd). Again, there appears to be a preference for verbal complements, such as *to marry you* with a verb such as *want*, in contrast to nominal complements (*marriage with you*, etc.); but this is, once more, no more than a preference not an absolute rule. Sentence (c) also uses the passive in the predicate phrase, and a nominalization instead of a verbal construction in the subject phrase; these usages compound the impression of formality already given by the use of *desire* rather than *want*.

That nativelike selection is not a matter of syntactic rule alone, however, nor of length or complexity, is nicely illustrated by conventions for telling the time in English (and other languages). Instead of saying:

(9) It's twenty to six.

one might say, no less grammatically and briefly:

(10) (a) It's six less twenty.

(b) It's two thirds past five.
(c) It's forty past five.
(d) It exceeds five by forty.
(e) It's a third to six.
(f) It's ten minutes after half-past five.

There happens to be a convention in English that one tells the time in half and quarter hours but not in thirds of an hour, and (in the writers' dialect) that one uses *to H* and *past H* (where H names the hour, rather than, say, the half-hour) instead of *before H, preceding H, after H*, etc.[5] Nativelike talk about other quantitative matters, such as height or weight, or amounts of money, is subject to conventions that are, grammatically, just as arbitrary. For instance, one may say that *John is five feet nine* (*inches*) but not, ordinarily, that *John is five and three quarter feet* or *John is six feet less a quarter* (*of a foot*).

It has been suggested that the problem of nativelike selection is to be solved in terms of a theory of speech acts and discourse context. Any grammatical sentence will seem unnatural in certain contexts, but conversely, contexts can be found where it will be heard as a natural thing to say.[6] According to this approach, for example, the expression *I want to marry you* is a ritual formula, appropriate in a certain type of speech context (as a serious proposal of marriage, made to a familiar in private conversation). The more or less synonymous but less natural alternatives listed in (8), on the other hand, may be appropriate to other contexts (e.g. in a letter to a woman who is known to place great store in formal patterns of address, or in humorous or satirical speech). Again, it may be held that if the sentences in (8) are transformed into statements by one person about another, so that they are no longer to be heard as marriage proposals, their unnaturalness would disappear. However, this last argument does not seem to be correct. For example:

(11) John wants to marry Nelly.

remains more natural than (12) or (13).

(12) John's becoming Nelly's spouse is what he wants.
(13) What is desired by John is to wed Nelly.

The suggestion that every grammatical sentence will fit naturally into some context may well be true but it hardly advances our understanding of how nativelike selection works. It is possible to view the problem in terms of an opposition between (more or less) marked and unmarked contexts or usages, but in the absence of a well-developed 'grammar' of speech acts and contexts in English, the puzzle still remains: what are the *linguistic* features which distinguish utterances of different degrees of markedness in different contexts? In particular, what are the features that make certain forms of expression 99 per cent more likely to occur in a given everyday context than their paraphrases, which are equally grammatical? The comparison in (9) and (10) illustrates the difficulties to be surmounted in formulating a theory of contexts to account for nativelike selection.

The unidiomaticity of the sentences in (8), in what we may call 'normal contexts', seems to be due to a variety of things. For example sentence (g) breaks a conversational convention requiring that the speaker should avoid stating the obvious, and specifically that he should not refer to the fact that he is the speaker and that he is speaking to the addressee. On the other hand, some of the sentences are unusual in employing an uncommon or formal lexical item or combination, in contrast to the ordinary or informal equivalent, e.g. *wed* for *marry*, *desire* for *want* and the circumlocutions *become married to* and *become (your) spouse* instead of *marry*. We have already referred to certain respects in which the sentences in (8) are syntactically unusual, and have noted that a sequence such as (c) *Your marrying me is desired by me* compounds a number of different marked usages.

It seems likely that familiarity will play some role in determining the native speaker's judgements about the naturalness of a sentence or utterance. Something more will be said on this matter in later sections. However, it hardly needs saying that nativelike sentences are not confined to those which the language user has heard before. The syntactic patterns, and certain other details may be familiar but in many cases the lexical combinations will be novel. One does not need to have heard the sequence *I want to marry you* before to know that it is nativelike.

3 The puzzle of nativelike fluency

It is no mean feat to keep talking more or less continuously for even ten or twenty seconds. Fluency in spontaneous connected speech may take the adult learner of a foreign language years to achieve. As a rule, the native speaker performs such feats easily in conversational talk, and may become aware of how much skill and work is needed to sustain fluency of speech only when he is required to express his thoughts on an unfamiliar subject, or to deliver an unrehearsed monologue to a silent audience, as when tape-recording a letter or radio talk, or when called upon to speak in a public address or formal interview. The intense mental activity that goes on at such times, the struggle to 'think of what to say', to 'find the right words' or to 'express oneself clearly', is reflected in the excerpts of spoken discourse which follow by the fluctuating tempo, the frequent pauses and the changes of direction in mid-construction.

In (14), F, a draughtsman in his mid-20s, is discussing evangelical Christianity with several hostel-mates. (The transcriber marked pauses with a dash but did not provide more exact details of pause length or tempo.)

(14) Yeah – I think
　　 y' know –
　　 Ah – I've found – in um –
　　 y' know – um
　　 not in religion at the beginning of this year
　　 y' know –
　　 ah – ah – the experiences I had – ah – on Queen's
　　 Birthday weekend
　　 y' know –
　　 the peace that I found –
　　 simply being able to throw my –
　　 or – not – not to throw myself just to –
　　 sort of – just to – y' know – ah
　　 just hold on to another person –
　　 y' know –
　　 let –
　　 just – just – y' know ah –
(At this point another speaker took over from F.)

Although one's first impression of F's speech is that it is disjointed and extremely hesitant, in fact there are rather few hesitations within the simple clauses that he produces. As has been shown in some detail elsewhere,[7] and as examples (3), (15) and (16) show, pause or slow down at or near clause boundary is the normal pattern in lengthy connected discourses, even among speakers who are heard as very fluent. In F's speech structural breaks as well as pauses are characteristic. What contributes most to the impression of disjointedness and nonfluency in F's monologue is his habit of changing syntactic and semantic course in mid-clause or between clauses. It is apparent that before he begins to utter a construction, F has not planned its syntactic and lexical content more than a phrase or – at most – a single clause ahead.

Speakers more able than F may show a similar pattern of hesitations and a considerable number of structural reformulations in their connected discourse. Speaker Q is a confident and experienced public speaker, recorded here during his Ph.D. oral defence, answering a question about the phonological integration of borrowed words into the phonemic system of a certain New Guinea language. Q shows no signs of examination stress during this and other replies; his relatively nonfluent speech here seems to reflect the novelty of the subject matter and a careful choosing of words in a speech situation where exactness rather than fluency is most valued.

(15) and it /seems to ˌbe – –
      [accel]
      if a /word is /fairly – – /high on the ˌfrequency /list/ –
      [slow]   [accel]
      I /haven't /made /any ˌcount –
      [accel]
      but – /just – – im/pression ˌistically – – um
                          [slow]
      um – – the /chances ˌare –
      that you get a – ˌcom/pound –
      [slow]
      or – a/nother – – phono/logically ˌdeviant – – ˌform –
                          [slow]
      with ah /which is al/ready in ˌother /words
              [accel]   [slows]
      /which is /fairly ˌfrequent – ly the /same – /phono/logical
      [accel]   [slows]
      ˌshape – –

Unlike F, Q seems to have a rough general plan of his total exposition already formulated before he begins to speak. This is indicated partly by the syntactic structure of his answer, which begins with two clauses that state a qualification and a condition, respectively, on a following assertion, and partly by the fact that he is able, eventually, to state this assertion (itself a pretty complex proposition ('the chances are … shape')) in spite of introducing a couple of hedging qualifier clauses en route. Nevertheless, the written transcript brings out clearly the difficulties of the encoding task for Q. His hesitations are as frequent as F's. His reformulations are almost as frequent though more consistently at clause boundaries rather than clause internal. It is evident that, whatever his general plan of semantic and/or syntactic content Q has not planned the actual word content of his discourse very far ahead. The pattern of his dysfluencies indicate that he does this planning a few words at a time.

There is in fact a sizeable collection of evidence of several different kinds that the largest unit of novel discourse that can be fully encoded in one encoding operation is a single clause of eight to ten words.[8] One kind of evidence pointing to this 'one clause at a time constraint' on the planning of novel speech is the distribution of dysfluencies in spontaneous connected discourse. We find that even the most skilled and consistently fluent talkers regularly pause or slow down at the end of each clause of four to ten words, during a sustained piece of discourse, though they rarely do so in mid-clause. Their 'fluent units' correlate highly with single clauses, ('Fluent unit' is used here as a technical term to refer to a stretch of pause-free speech uttered at or faster than normal rate of articulation – about five syllables per second in English.) Examples demonstrating this correlation appear in excerpt (2) cited earlier, which is much more typical of conversational speech in this respect than (14) and (15). Observation and experimental work has shown that in conversational speech English speakers typically (a) maintain a rate of articulation during fluent units which averages 270–300 syllables a minute; this rate does not increase significantly in rehearsed speech, (b) show a high proportion of fluent units (more than 50 per cent) that are complete, grammatical clauses, (c) rarely pause for longer than 0.5 seconds in mid-clause hesitations or for longer than 2.0 seconds at clause boundaries in mid-construction.[9]

In the narrative speech of George Davies, the correlation of fluent unit with clause can be seen, together with the syntactic 'strategy' which most speakers favour in formulating spontaneous connected discourse. This strategy contrasts markedly with that adopted by Q in the previous excerpt. Whereas Q used a complex 'clause-integrating' strategy, committing himself to grammatical constructions which require him to take account of the structure of an earlier or later clause when formulating a current one, George Davies prefers a 'clause-chaining' style. He strings together a sequence of relatively independent clauses, clauses which show little structural integration with earlier or later constructions.

(16) /we /had a /fan |tastic /time – – –
       [slows]   (1.1)
/there /were /all |kinds of re/lations /there/
[accel]   [slows   ]
/I dun/no |where /they /all |come /from/
[accel]   [slows   ]
I didn't |know /'alf o' them – –
[accel]   (0.9)
and' ah – the |kids /sat on the |floor – – –
    (0.2)   (1.5)
and ol' /Uncle |Bert /he /ah/
o' /course /he was the |life and soul of the |party
[accel]   [slows   ]
/Uncle /Bert 'ad a /black |bottle – – –
[accel]   [slows   ] (1.5)
an ah – 'e'd t/ tell a /few |stories
     (0.2)   [accel]   [slows]
an 'e'd /take a /sip out of the /black |bottle/
  [accel]   [slows   ]
n' the /more /sips he /took /outa /that |bottle – – –
  [accel]   (1.0)
the |worse the /stories |got – – –
          (1.6)

Davies keeps to a mainly clause-chaining style even when talking about static relationships as opposed to temporally ordered events, and in this he is typical of working class speakers – indeed of most speakers – in our sample. This style is more effective than the integrating style, as measured by fluency and grammaticality. The more frequent mid-clause pauses and structural breakdowns associated with use of a highly integrating syntactic style can be explained in terms of the one clause at a time constraint. When the spontaneous speaker embarks on a stretch of novel discourse extending over several clauses, he does not (as a rule) know in advance exactly what he is going to say beyond the first few words. He must gamble on being able to finish what he has started. The risks of syntactic breakdown are greater when using the integrating style. With the chaining style, a speaker can maintain grammatical and semantic continuity because his clauses can be planned more or less independently, and each major semantic unit, being only a single clause, can be encoded and uttered without internal breaks. To achieve the same degree of coherence using the integrating style the speaker generally must reduce his articulation rate and/or make more frequent clause-internal pauses. This choice is not much favoured either by speakers or listeners. It is a facility in the chaining style that is characteristic of all groups of English native speakers. We may speak, then, of a 'one clause at a time *facility*' as an essential constituent of communicative competence in English: the speaker must be able regularly to encode whole clauses, in their full lexical detail, in a single encoding operation and so avoid the need for mid-clause hesitations.[10]

Part of the puzzle of nativelike fluency is how the language learner achieves the one clause at a time facility. It is not just a matter of composing grammatical clauses under severe limitations imposed (a) by the time-bonding in normal speech exchange, and (b) by his restricted ability to plan novel speech. As a participant in talk exchange it is also necessary that he attend to other requirements besides grammaticality. A speaker is expected to make contributions to conversation that are coherent, sensitive to what has gone on before and what might happen later, and sensitive to audience knowledge and other features of the social situation; his talk should be nativelike and in an appropriate register and meet other general and specific requirements (e.g. of accuracy or vagueness, as the situation demands, of logic, wit, modesty and the like). He is by no means free to concentrate on the grammatical content of his productions.

There is one especially problematic feature of nativelike fluency that has not as yet been discussed. It is common for multi-clause fluent units to occur in spontaneous speech – stretches of pause-free, promptly delivered speech extending over two or more clauses. For example:

(17) I /don't /need / |anyone to /tell /|me /what to /do!

Such utterances are problematic because they appear to conflict with the one clause at a time constraint, or at any rate, with the hypothesis that there should be a pause or other dysfluency coinciding with the planning of each clause. When multi-clause fluent units follow a long silence on the speaker's part, it is possible to explain the absence of internal dysfluencies on the grounds that the speaker had time to combine several encoding stages before beginning to speak. But there is a residue of discourse-medial fluent units which still remain to be explained. We shall return to these in later sections.

4 Memorized sequences

So far the burden of our argument has been simply that nativelike selection and fluency present certain features that are not easily described or explained. The conclusion that control of a language must entail knowledge of something more than a generative grammar, as this is usually defined, is unlikely to be controversial. The question is, what additional knowledge underlies these abilities? In this section and the next we turn to the concepts of 'memorized sentence' and 'lexicalized sentence stem' as elements of linguistic knowledge. The terms refer to two distinct but interrelated classes of units, and it will be suggested that a store of these two unit types is among the additional ingredients required for native control. The present section will deal, fairly briefly, with memorized sentences. In Section 5 the idea of lexicalized sentence stems will be discussed at more length. In the final section we will consider some possible implications of what appears, at first, to be a fairly innocuous addition to the usual apparatus of linguistic description.

Observations of conversational talk indicate that there is a 'novelty scale' in the spontaneous speaker's production of clauses. A minority of spoken clauses are entirely novel creations, in the sense that the combination of lexical items used is new to the speaker; the combination will of course be put together according to familiar grammatical patterns. Some clauses are entirely familiar, memorized sequences. These are strings which the speaker or hearer is capable of conciously assembling or analysing, but which on most occasions of use are recalled as wholes or as automatically chained strings. Still other clauses fall at various points along a cline between these two extremes, consisting partly of new collocations of lexical items and partly of memorized lexical and structural material.[11]

The number of memorized complete clauses and sentences known to the mature English speaker is probably many thousands. Much more numerous still, however, is a class of phraseological expressions each of which is something less than a completely specified clause. We refer to sequences which contain a nucleus of fixed lexical items standing in construction with one or more variable elements (often a grammatical inflection), the specification of the variables being necessary to complete the clause. Such 'phraseological' units will be discussed more fully in Section 5.

206 Andrew Pawley and Frances Hodgetts Syder

A few minutes' reflection produced the following sample of clauses that are familiar to the writers as habitually spoken sequences in Australian and New Zealand English.

(18) Can I come in?
Can I help?
Need any help?
Need a hand?
Are you all right?
Is everything OK?
Are you ready?
What did you say?
What's for dinner?
Where are my keys?
Look in the drawer.
It's a matter of priorities.
It's on the tip of my
    tongue.
You would ask that
    question.
There's no pleasing some
    people.
Some people are hard to
    please.
Some people are never
    satisfied.
You can't be all things to
    all men.
You can't please everyone.
I've never noticed that
    before.
That's new.
You can't be too careful.
Where did you find it?
I looked everywhere for it.
What would I do without
    you?
Call me after work.
I'll be home all weekend.
What's your home
    number?
We're in the book.

Did you have a good trip?
How is everyone at home?
How long are you staying?
He's not in. Would you
    like to leave a message?
Can I take a message?
He's busy right now.
Would you like to wait?
I can't wait any longer.
Take one three times a day
    after meals.
Would you like some
    more?
Have some more.
I enjoyed that.
I enjoyed every minute of
    it.
I'd do it all over again.
I don't regret a single
    moment.
Have you heard the news?
Who would have thought
    it?
I'm simply amazed.
I was just trying to help.
It's none of your business.
You keep out of this.
Speak for yourself.
That's only my opinion.
Watch your step.
That was a close call.
Eight eights are sixty four.
Maths never was my strong
    point.
I'll have half a dozen.

Habitually-spoken sequences longer than a single, simple clause are also numerous. The items listed below exemplify this class:

(19) How are you going to do that?
　　Once you've done that the rest is easy.
　　I see what you mean.
　　It's as easy as falling off a log.
　　I'll believe it when I see it.
　　You don't want to believe everything you hear.
　　I knew you wouldn't believe me.
　　You can't believe a word he says.
　　If you believe that you'll believe anything.
　　There's a sucker born every minute.
　　It just goes to show, you can't be too careful.
　　There's nothing you can do about it now.
　　That's easier said than done.
　　You're not allowed to do that.
　　It's a free country isn't it?
　　Don't interrupt when someone's talking.
　　Children should be seen and not heard.
　　You shouldn't have said that, you've hurt his feelings.
　　Tell me what happened.
　　I thought you'd never ask.
　　I'm terribly sorry to hear that.
　　I'm just dying to hear all the gossip.
　　I'm surprised to hear that.
　　You just never know what they'll do next.
　　I don't know where he's gone.
　　I don't know and I don't care!
　　Call me as soon as you get home.
　　Do you know when she's coming?
　　There's something I forgot to tell you.
　　You forgot to give me my allowance.
　　Shut up and listen!
　　Do what you're told!
　　Eat your vegetables or you won't get any pudding!
　　Don't answer back or you'll get a clip over the ear.
　　It's easy to talk.
　　He never has a bad word to say about anyone.
　　Be careful what you're doing with that.
　　If I'd known then what I know now, . . .
　　He's not the man he used to be.

I told him but he wouldn't listen.
You can lead a horse to water but you can't make it drink.

Memorized clauses and clause-sequences form a high proportion of the fluent stretches of speech heard in everyday conversation. In particular, we find that multi-clause fluent units – apparent exceptions to the one clause at a time constraint – generally consist partly or wholly of a familiar collocation. Speakers
show a high degree of fluency when describing familiar experiences or activities in familiar phrases.[12] It is notorious that speakers are at their most hesitant when describing the unfamiliar.[13] The
attempt to find a novel turn of phrase to describe the familiar is
also likely to produce dysfluencies: it is easier to be commonplace.
Recognizing the difficulty of talking about unusual things, or in
talking about ordinary things in an unusual way, listeners are tolerant, up to a point, of mid-construction dysfluencies in such discourse. But they do not care for more than a little of this at a time.

It should not be thought that a reliance on ready-made expressions necessarily detracts from the creativity of spoken discourse.
Novelty of clause or sentence is only one element in the creative
use of language in talk exchange. As already noted, the conversationalist has many matters to attend to besides the syntactic form
and lexical content of his discourse. Possession of a large stock of
memorized sentences and phrases simplifies his task in the following way. Coming ready-made, the memorized sequences need
little encoding work. Freed from the task of composing such
sequences word-by-word, so to speak, the speaker can channel his
energies into other activities. He can, for example, attend to
matching the timing, tone and rhythm of his utterance to his conversational purpose; he can produce a slightly novel, unexpected
variation on the familiar usage; and he can do the work of constructing a larger piece of discourse by expanding on, or combining
ready-made constructions. Indeed, we believe that memorized
sentences and phrases are the normal building blocks of fluent
spoken discourse, and at the same time, that they provide models
for the creation of many (partly) new sequences which are memorable and in their turn enter the stock of familiar usages.

5 Lexicalized sentence stems

A distinction must be made between a morpheme sequence that
is memorized and one that is lexicalized. Memorization belongs

to the domain of 'performance' and lexicalization to 'competence', in the Chomskyan sense. In speaking of a word, phrase, etc. as being retrieved as a whole, or by an automatic chaining response, we are speaking of a particular action, performed by an individual, rather than of a piece of timeless knowledge shared by the members of a language community. Not all sequences memorized by individual speakers are lexicalized. What makes an expression a lexical item, what makes it part of the speech community's common dictionary, is, firstly, that the meaning of the expression is not (totally) predictable from its form, secondly, that it behaves as a minimal unit for certain syntactic purposes, and third, that it is a *social institution*. This last characteristic is sometimes overlooked, but is basic to the distinction between lexicalized and non-lexicalized sequence.

In saying that a lexical item is a social institution we mean that the expression is a conventional label for a conventional concept, a culturally standardized designation (term) for a socially recognized conceptual category. Rather than being a 'nonce form', a spontaneous creation of the individual speaker, the usage bears the authority of regular and accepted use by members of the speech community. Both the meaning and its formal expression are familiar; it is their conjuction which forms the social institution. Thus, the expression *lóng hòuse* is lexicalized when it refers to the kind of communal dwelling traditionally built by the Land Dayaks of Borneo. When the same sequence simply describes a house in London as being long, however, it is not the token of a lexical item. Native English society does not recognize a traditional architectural type, 'long house', and as a description of a particular English dwelling the expression hardly has special claims to the status of normal description above those, say, of *elongated house, house that is long, house of elongated shape, longish sort of house*, etc. Similarly, the terms *backache* and *headache* refer to culturally recognized types of physical disability in our society and are the standard labels for these conditions, whereas *footache, thighache*, and *toeache* do not have this status. The latter conditions may be common enough, in fact, but they do not enjoy the same degree of social recognition as the former group,[14] and in any case are more likely to be referred to by such expressions as *I have an ache in my thigh, I have an aching toe, my toe hurts*, etc. Whereas the sentence *I have an ache in the head* would be an unusual way of paraphrasing *I have a headache*.

By now it will have occurred to the reader that if we pursue this line of argument we will be led to recognize degrees of lexicalization. The difference between standard label and nonce form, between official designation and casual description, is not in all cases a clear-cut thing. An expression-meaning pairing may be more or less arbitrary, more or less standardized, more or less of an institution; we end up dealing with a cline rather than discrete classes. But it should be recognized that this situation reflects the facts of language, i.e. of the native speaker's knowledge, not a weakness in the definition of lexical item.[15]

The number of single morpheme lexical items known to the average mature English speaker is relatively small; a few thousand. The number of morphologically complex lexical items is much greater, running – it will be argued below – into the hundreds of thousands. A very considerable proportion of the total body of (relatively) well-defined complex lexical items consists of what we will term here 'lexicalized sentence stems'.

A sentence stem consists either of a complete sentence, or, more commonly, an expression which is something less than a complete sentence. In the latter case, the sentence structure is fully specified along with a nucleus of lexical and grammatical morphemes which normally include the verb and certain of its arguments; however, one or more structural elements is a class, represented by a category symbol such as TENSE, NP or PRO. For example, in the conventional expressions of apology:

(20) I'm sorry to keep you waiting.
     I'm so sorry to have kept you waiting.
     Mr X is sorry to keep you waiting all this time.

a recurrent collocation can be isolated together with a grammatical frame:[16]

(21) NP be-TENSE sorry to keep-TENSE you waiting

Such a collocation, with the obligatory elements in its associated sentence structure, is a sentence *stem*. The realizations of the variable constituents in the stem are termed its *inflections*. If there are additional constituents of an optional kind these are its *expansions*. In the above examples, *I'm* and *Mr X* are inflections, the subject NP being an integral (though deletable) part of the unit, while *so* and *all this time* are expansions.

In the sentences

(22) Tell the truth!
Jo seldom tells the truth.
I wish you had told me the truth.

the recurrent sentence stem is:

(23) NP tell – TENSE the truth

the subject NP being variable in content, as is the tense.

A sentence or sentence stem is lexicalized if it
 (i) denotes a meaning which is culturally authorized, i.e. is a standard concept in the speech community.
(ii) is recognized to be a standard expression for the meaning in question,
(iii) is an arbitrary choice (or somewhat arbitrary choice), in terms of linguistic structure, for the role of standard expression. That is, there is nothing in its structure which would uniquely select it as the standard from among the larger class of synonymous expressions. For example, *I want to marry you* has this status as an arbitrary standard usage, in contrast to some of its paraphrases listed in Section 2.

Idioms, epithets and many other types of sentential expressions fall into the class of lexicalized sentence stems. *A stitch in time saves nine* for example, is an institutionalized sentence – but not *a stitch in time saves twenty-six*, nor *By taking the trouble to repair a small defect now you may save yourself from having to do a much bigger repair job later.* But most lexicalized sentence stems are not true idioms, in the sense of having a meaning not predictable from the internal structure. Rather they are literal expressions, in most cases. They may, however, have conversational uses (implicatures, speech act functions, etc.) in addition to their literal sense, and these additional uses may also be conventionalized and to some extent arbitrary, for example:

(24) Why do-TENSE n't NP_i pick on someone PRO_i-gen own size!
(Why doesn't that bully pick on someone his own size.
Why don't you pick on . . ., etc.)

(25) Who (the EXPLET) do-PRES NP_i think PRO_i be-PRES!
(Who the hell do you think you are. Who does that woman think she is, etc.)

(26) That be-TENSE the last time I'll (ever) ask NP to V (NP) for
me!
(That'll be the last time I'll ever ask Harry to do a job for
me, etc.)

Each is used to express a particular reaction of indignation by the
speaker, and as such has a conventional conversational force quite
distinct from its literal meaning.

Similarly, the expression

(27) If it be-TENSE good enough for NP_i it be-TENSE good enough
for me_j

has a specific conversational force which is not fully predictable
from its literal meaning. We use this expression, for instance, to
explain or justify conduct that is queried by reference to a distinguished precedent for our action, e.g. *If it's good enough for the
Queen of England to wear jeans to work it's good enough for me.*

There are many problems in the treatment of lexicalized sentence stems that cannot be given extended discussion here. The
reader will, for instance, wish for an answer to this question: How
is a lexicalized sentence stem defined? How do you tell it apart
from non-lexicalized sequences? There is no simple operation for
doing this. The problem is essentially the same as in distinguishing
any morphologically complex lexical item from other sequences;
the question is what is 'lexicalization'? What makes something a
lexeme? A number of defining features were listed earlier in this
section, and there are various tests relevant to these criteria which
may be applied. However, particular cases are not always capable
of a clearcut classification, because lexicalization is a matter of
degree, as we have had occasion to mention. An expression may
be more or less a standard designation for a concept, more or less
clearly analysable into morphemes, more or less fixed in form,
more or less capable of being transformed without change of
meaning or status as a standard usage, and the concept denoted
by the expression may be familiar and culturally recognized to
varying degrees. Nor is there a sharp boundary between the units
termed here 'sentence stems' and other phraseological units of a
lower order.[17] A collocation may be more or less a complete sentence (clause, phrase, etc.). Again we would assert that this feature of gradation is a fact of language, and in seeking discrete
classes we are in danger of misrepresenting the nature of the native
speaker's knowledge.

The number of sentence-length expressions familiar to the ordinary, mature English speaker probably amounts, at least, to several hundreds of thousands. The extent of this familiar material can be gauged roughly by noting the number of frequently-used morphemes or words and listing the sentential expressions in which a sample of these elements participates in. The following is a partial list of habitually-used expressions in which the verb *think* occurs. (We have not attempted in all cases to distinguish the fixed elements from the variable elements in these collocations.)

(28) Come to think of it, . . .
 What do you think?
 I thought better of it.
 Think nothing of it.
 Think it over.
 I hardly dare think about it.
 It doesn't bear thinking about.
 (Just) think about it for a (moment, second, minute, while).
 I'd think none the worse of you . . .
 I think I'd have done the same thing in his (shoes, etc.).
 Do you think I came down in the last shower?
 Do you think I was born yesterday?
 Who do you think you are?
 I don't think much of that (suggestion, idea, etc.).
 Can you think of a better one?
 I (just) can't think straight.
 I'll need a few days to think it over.
 I haven't stopped to think about it.
 Think twice before you VP.
 Who (ever) would have thought it!
 I don't think NP will like that.
 I think a *lot* of P.
 P_i thinks the *world* of P_j.
 P_i thinks the sun shines out of P_j's (bottom, arse, etc.).
 P_i thinks PRO_i is really somebody.
 P_i thinks PRO_i shit doesn't stink.
 P_i think's he's the cat's pyjamas.
 P_i thinks nothing of P_j.
 P thinks nothing of v-ing NP (e.g. walking 50 miles).
 Think what that could mean to P.
 I thought you'd never ask!

[s, NP, ADJ], I don't think. (ironic tone)
I was (just, only) thinking aloud.
Think before you open your mouth!
I couldn't think of (a single thing, anything) to say.
I don't know *what* to think!
I thought you knew better (than that, than to s).
I thought you knew!
I think so.
I thought I told you not to do that!
What I think is, . . .
Do you really think so?
He only thinks of himself.
He thinks highly of you.
Think again!
Think nothing *of* it!

A similarly extensive list may be compiled for many other reasonably common words.

The relevance of this repertoire of familiar sentence-length expressions to nativelike fluency in English was discussed in the preceding section. There it was suggested that lexicalized sentence stems and other memorized strings form the main building blocks of fluent connected speech. This claim can of course be tested only by examining spoken discourse: written text should not be taken as representative of the spoken language, either in regard to syntactic structure or in regard to the frequency of standard collocations as opposed to nonce forms.[18] Space does not permit analysis here, but the reader is invited to examine the transcribed material in (3), (14), (15) and (16), noting the relationship between fluent units and standard or formulaic expressions.

It seems likely that lexicalized sentence stems also play a role in nativelike selection. The role may be a limited one, in that the set of lexicalized sequences is only a small subset of the total class of nativelike sentences (leaving aside the probability that neither set is sharply delimited). It has been pointed out that lexicalized sentence stems may be 'inflected' or 'expanded', except for a minority of expressions that are completely rigid in their form. In order for a speaker to derive (partly) novel forms using a given lexicalized sentence stem, it is necessary for him to know the grammar of that stem. A novel sequence will be nativelike at least to the extent that it consists of an institutionalized sentence stem plus permissible variations. It appears, however, that each such sentence stem has a more or less unique grammar; each one is subject to a somewhat different range of phrase structure and transformational restrictions. It is a characteristic error of the language learner to assume that an element in the expression may be varied according to a phrase structure or transformational rule of some generality, when in fact the variation (if any) allowed in nativelike usage is much more restricted. The result, very often, is an utterance that is grammatical but unidiomatic e.g. *You are pulling my legs* (in the sense of deceiving me). *John has a thigh-ache*, and *I intend to teach that rascal some good lessons he will never forget!*[19]

6 Theoretical implications

Let us assume for the present that the hypothesis put forward in the previous section is true. What might the implications be, then, for the theory of grammar? While a full consideration of this question would require lengthy study, the observations that follow, though necessarily sketchy, suggest that such study may be worthwhile.

The hypothesis holds that by far the largest part of the English speaker's lexicon consists of complex lexical items including several hundred thousand lexicalized sentence stems.

One possible reaction to this claim might be that it requires no basic change in existing models of English grammar – that it can be accommodated within the framework of any theory of grammar which distinguishes a dictionary from a set of productive syntactic rules – phrase structure, transformational, or whatever. While recognition of a vast number of new complex lexical items may alter the quantitative balance among the major components of the grammar, it might be argued that no important *qualitative* change is entailed. True, the dictionary will be bigger than before and probably more complex in respect of the grammatical information it contains (see below). But the basic components of the description will remain constant, with certain information about possible (or nativelike) sentences being provided by a set of syntactic rules that are productive or have general application, and with other information (about each lexical form and its syntactic properties) being provided by the dictionary.

It is possible, however, to see in the theory of lexicalized sentence stems more serious consequences. One possible consequence has to do with procedures for evaluating a description or theory of grammar, a matter discussed at length by Chomsky (especially 1964, 1965). In normal descriptive practice, choice among rival treatments of a particular body of syntactic data is made, for the most part, in terms of economy and generality – we prefer that account which specifies all and only the grammatical sentences, and their internal structure, in the most parsimonious manner. It will be recalled, however, that 'descriptive adequacy' in the sense of Chomsky is achieved when a (partial) description corresponds to our evidence about the form of the native speaker's internalized knowledge of his grammar, i.e. when the units and rules are those tacitly recognized by the native speaker. The question arises as to what parsimony has to do with the organization of the speaker's linguistic knowledge.

In the hypothesis under consideration, the internal structure of many complex items must be specified at least twice in the description. This duplication applies to lexicalized sentence stems of regular formation, for example, as well to idiomatic sequences other than those of irregular structure. There is a difference between a lexicalized sentence stem such as *Will you marry me?* and an idiom such as *beat around the bush*, however, in that the meaning of the former is regular ('literal') while the meaning of the idiom is by definition irregular ('non-literal'). Form-meaning pairings of literal sequences will be specified twice insofar as these sequences are picked out by the language as institutionalized usages (standard terms). This duplication is necessary in order to account for the fact that such a sequence has a dual status in the language. On the one hand, its potential occurrence and meaning is predicted by the productive rules of syntax and semantics. These account for its status as a grammatical string and specify its internal structure and structural relationship to other sequences; they do not, however, mark the sequence as having a special status among the set of grammatically possible strings. On the other hand, the dictionary entry for the same sequence (say, for *Will you marry me?*) should note its status as a lexical item, a (somewhat) arbitrary selection as a standard expression or name for a culturally authorized concept; that is, it should record the fact that the sequence is an actually occurring, nativelike form, a 'common usage' having an institutionalized function, in contrast to other sequences which do not have this status.

Each dictionary entry for a complex lexical form of literal meaning will, presumably, be a mini-grammar. The entry will give the morphological structure of the sequence, and state the ways in which the lexicalized sequence may be 'inflected' and 'expanded' (in the sense described in Section 5) and transformed, without changing its status as a nativelike and lexicalized unit. Complex lexical forms are usually transformationally 'defective' in that certain transformations, when applied to these forms (or their underlying structures) result in strings that are grammatically acceptable but are non-nativelike or non-lexical usages, e.g. § *Nine stitches are saved by a stitch in time*, § *Pleasing (John, some people) is hard*, § *Who is it thought by you that you are*? But many forms are capable of some transformations without losing their nativelike usages or as lexical items. For instance, one can *lead someone up the garden path* or *be led up the garden path by someone*, and besides *Some people are hard to please* we find *It is hard to please some people*.

It is possible to achieve a more economical description of the sequences in question by specifying them only once. Each sequence can be treated as an unanalysable lexical item, i.e. as a morpheme, or it can be left out of the lexicon altogether, i.e. specified only as a potential well-formed string by the rules of syntax. The shortcomings of these two alternatives as treatments of *idioms* have been well described by Weinreich (1969) and a number of other writers who are troubled by the difficulty of choosing between a 'lexical' and a 'syntactic' description of idioms.[20]

The 'problem' of choice between a lexical and a syntactic treatment of derived words, idioms and other complex lexical items is, however, surely not a genuine difficulty if we accept Chomsky's definition of descriptive adequacy. For what really matters is not the economy of the description but its fit with what the native speaker knows of his language. If the native speaker knows certain linguistic forms in two ways, both as lexical units and as products of syntactic rules, then the grammarian is obliged to describe *both* kinds of knowledge; anything less would be incomplete.

If we ask why there should often be two modes of knowing we come to the question of 'explanatory adequacy' as defined by Chomsky. Is there something in the language learner's natural capacities, in the structure of the human brain, that makes such dual knowledge advantageous, or inevitable? It is not difficult to see why this might be so. On the one hand, people are good at generalizing, at perceiving patterns, and there is no doubting the importance of general rules in language learning. On the other hand, people are not good (compared, say, with man-made computers) at performing a number of different mental acts simultaneously or in rapid succession; however, they do possess an enormous memory capacity.[21]

The generalizing capacity is essential to the acquisition of linguistic competence in Chomsky's sense, knowledge-in-principle, separated from limitations of time, processing ability, and other external matters. The processing capacity is vital to the language user in his normal situation, when he is required to compose and decode spoken discourse, often under a tight time-bonding. What may be an economical or efficient way of organizing knowledge-in-principle may not be efficient for the demands of ordinary language use. Holistically stored sequences have the advantages of being quickly retrievable and of being familiar to the hearer as well as to the speaker. And they have certain advantages in the use of language as a cultural instrument. They provide convenient ways of referring to those concepts that happen to be salient in a particular culture and which are not provided for by the stock of unitary lexical items. Furthermore, the class of morphemes in a language is virtually closed and it is often not convenient to extend the use of existing morphemes to new concepts. But the class of standard concepts in a language is not closed; new names are constantly required for new ideas. It is always possible to draw on the fully-productive and semi-productive syntactic and semantic rules to provide morphologically complex *descriptions*, however, and in due course one or more of the descriptive expressions for a new concept may become its conventional *designation*, i.e. it may be lexicalized.

Once again, it may be argued that this discussion of evaluation procedures and the problem of duplication of information in the description need have no bearing on the structure of the grammar. The grammar still consists of the same *types* of rules as before, and one might hold that there is still a fundamental division between the lexicon and the productive syntactic rules which apply to classes of lexemes, phrases, etc. It appears that this last position is not compatible with the theory of lexicalized sentence stems adumbrated above. The locus of the conflict is among those patterns that are semi-productive and those sequences that are semi-lexicalized.

In the final sections of *Aspects*, Chomsky refers to derivational processes as a particularly problematic feature of language for the generative grammarian. The difficulty posed by derivational processes stems from the fact that they are 'typically sporadic and only quasi-productive' (184). Compare, for example, the gaps in the realization of derivational possibilities exhibited by groups of forms like *horror, horrid, horrify; terror, *terrid, terrify*; and *candor, candid* and **candify*. As there are 'no rules of any generality that produce the derived items . . . it seems that these items must be entered in the lexicon directly' (186).[22] However, Chomsky considers this a very unfortunate conclusion, 'since it is clear that from the point of view of both the semantic and the phonological interpretation it is important to have internal structure represented in these words' (186). This dilemma is noted to be 'typical of a wide class of examples with varying degrees of productivity, and it is not at all clear how it is to be resolved, or in fact, whether there is any non-*ad hoc* solution that can be achieved at all' (187). Elsewhere he remarks that, possibly, 'we are approaching here the fringe of marginal cases, to be expected in a system as complex as a natural language, where significant generalization is just not possible' (192).

In speaking of 'marginal cases' Chomsky is, of course, referring to marginality in the sense of not being amenable to systematic analysis, to the methods which linguists have successfully applied to regular processes. He does not say that material which is hard to systematize is of only marginal interest in the study of language, or that it makes up only a small part of any language. However, it is only a short step to this last position. Indeed, it is possible to detect in many works in modern linguistics the assumption that a language consists essentially of its productive elements – the rules of grammar – and that material which is not part of this system of rules plays a relatively small and unimportant part in the ordinary use of language.

We must be careful not to take this step. While it is a legitimate research strategy to exclude certain recalcitrant data from one's domain of study, for a time, on the grounds that although the present theory cannot accommodate these data it is otherwise successful, the problematic data are not to be permanently excluded nor downgraded in importance. It has been suggested here that complex lexical items are much more numerous than has generally been conceded and that semi-productive grammatical patterns play an important part in the creation of new linguistic forms.

It may be convenient to posit a separate component in the description to handle the large body of institutionalized complex lexical forms, and the semi-productive rules for generating new, nativelike sequences by inflecting, expanding or transforming these forms. This 'phrase book with grammatical notes' would occupy an intermediate position between the general grammatical patterns (described in terms of productive rules applying to category symbols) and the list of unitary lexical items (described in terms of their phonological form and meaning and their privileges of occurrence in basic structures defined by the general, productive rules). But any strict compartmentalization would not truly reflect the native speaker's grammatical knowledge if the facts are (as we believe) that lexicalization and productivity are each matters of degree.

Notes

1. We would like to thank the many people who have discussed with us the problems treated in this paper, earlier versions of which were presented in Pawley's lectures at the 1977 Institute of the Linguistic Society of America and to the Linguistic Society of Hawaii in March 1978. In particular, we are indebted to Peter Crisp and George Grace for observations which helped to set us thinking about nativelike fluency and selection, and to Laurie Bauer, Chris Corne, Talmy Givon, George Grace, Jeannette Gundel, John Herbert, Greg Lee and Ricky Jacobs for critical commentary on a draft. Funds supporting the collection of conversational data were provided by a 1972 grant from the New Zealand Council for Educational Research.
2. In transcribing spoken discourse we have followed the notational conventions used by Crystal (1969, 1975) with some modifications. Pauses are marked by dashes: – for a silence of less than 0.5 of a second, – – for one of 0.5 to 0.9, – – – for one of 1.0 to 2.0, and – – – – for silences of more than 2 seconds. A double bar ⁼ over a letter indicates a phoneme which is perceptibly longer than normal for its position; ⌐marks the tonic or nuclear stress in an intonation contour; other stressed syllables are preceded by a slash /; a half-raised dot · indicates a break between two different intonation contours which is not accompanied by pause as when a speaker suddenly reformulates in mid-construction. CAPITALS mark sustained very loud volume or an unusually prominent tonic stress. In the transcripts given here these and other details are omitted when not relevant to the problem under discussion.
3. But for Charles Darwin the term 'natural selection' might have done just as well here. 'Idiomatic selection' would also do, though 'idiomatic' has two distinct senses only one of which we intend. George Grace (1981, p. 40) describes this sense of idiomaticity as follows, in the course of an account of translation types:

> The other [type] is 'pragmatic' or 'free' translation or 'paraphrase', which retains the substance of the content of the original but expresses it in a form which is 'idiomatic' in the language being translated into. . . . We say, for example, that something is not

'idiomatic' English when it (perhaps) is said in English, but not in the way a native speaker would say it. The Oxford English Dictionary defines this sense of 'idiomatic' as follows:

1. Peculiar to or characteristic of a particular language; pertaining to or exhibiting the expressions, constructions, or phraseology approved by the peculiar usage of a language, esp. as differing from a strictly grammatical or logical use of words; vernacular; colloquial.

There seems to be no place for this concept of idiomaticity in the current grammar-lexicon models of languages.

4. We are not concerned here with exactly synonymous alternatives (arguably these do not exist) but with the kind of pragmatic synonymity or functional equivalence that is recognized to be a feature of ordinary language use; for example, with utterances that are regarded as 'saying the same thing' in translation between languages, in legal judgments, in newspaper reporting of speeches, and in conversationalists' recounting of their own utterances.
5. We are informed that Danes speak of the time as being ten minutes past half past an hour and that Egyptians conventionally divide the hour into thirds.
6. Highly marked paraphrases of normal usages are sometimes used to make a conversational implicature in the sense of Grice (1975). If a concert reviewer says, instead of *Miss X sang 'Home Sweet Home'*, that *Miss X produced a series of sounds that corresponded closely with the score of 'Home Sweet Home'* he may be presumed to have flouted the brevity and clarity maxims in order to imply that Miss X's singing was bad (Grice 1975, p. 55–6). Searle has, however, noted (e.g. 1975, p. 76) that it is difficult to use an unidiomatic sentence as an indirect speech act, because the normal conversational assumptions which underly indirect speech acts are largely suspended by hearers of an odd-sounding expression.
7. The extensive literature reporting experimental studies on the pattern and significance of pauses in spontaneous speech is partly summarized in Goldman-Eisler (1968) and Rochester (1973). While observers have consistently found that pauses occur at most clause boundaries, some experimenters have found that fluent stretches are normally shorter than a clause in spontaneous speech, as opposed to reading or well-practised speech, nearly half of all pauses occur in non-grammatical places (Goldman-Eisler 1958; Henderson *et al.* 1966). Following a study (Goldman-Eisler 1961b) which found that in speech describing and interpreting cartoons, 75 per cent of fluent chunks were four words or fewer, Goldman-Eisler (1968, p. 31) concludes that 'Spontaneous speech was shown to be a highly fragmented and discontinuous activity. . . . [The] attribute of flow and fluency in spontaneous speech must be judged an illusion.' Other studies, however, show that in some types of spontaneous connected discourse, a high proportion of clauses are uttered as fluent units (Pawley and Syder 1975, 1976) or single

intonation contour units (Crystal 1969, p. 256). As Goldman-Eisler's own experiments demonstrate, clause-internal pauses are most frequent when the cognitive task is most difficult, as in a first formulation of ideas about a newly observed set of relationships (e.g. in stating the point of a cartoon), and that when the task is easier, hesitations at places other than major grammatical boundaries diminish markedly. Some subjects are much easier to talk about than others, and practice enables us to become more fluent in talking about a subject matter that was found difficult at first (Goldman-Eisler 1961b; Goldman-Eisler 1968 pp. 17, 51–8). Stating the moral of a cartoon is a much harder subject than the average one attempted in everyday conversation. See also Note 12.

8. The one clause at a time hypothesis is discussed in detail in Pawley and Syder (1975, 1976). See also Chafe (1979).

9. Goldman-Eisler (1968) describes several of her own studies of rate of articulation (esp. 1954, 1961a), noting the average rate of articulation to vary between speakers from 4.4 to 5.9 syllables per second. She found that frequency and duration of pauses varies considerably according to difficulty of cognitive task (see Note 8), but that pauses in 'discussions' were never longer than 3 seconds and 99 per cent were less than 2 seconds (1961b, 1968, p. 15). See also Note 12.

10. We are not claiming here that it is impossible to fill in the lexical details of a clause, without hesitation, while one is actually uttering that clause. Experiments have repeatedly shown, however, that decision-making in speech normally requires a pause and that it is difficult to combine the tasks of speech planning and speech production (articulation) (Goldman-Eisler 1968; Miller 1951). Memorized clauses are a partial exception. Here the speaker can attend to planning tasks while leaving the production of the current clause 'on automatic pilot', as it were. Besides the one clause at a time facility, nativelike fluency also demands an ability to plan the approximate content and form of sequences longer than a clause. But it is necessary to distinguish between semantic and syntactic planning (Keenan 1977; Kroll 1977; Stratton 1971) and full lexical planning of an utterance. It is one thing to plan a syntactic frame such as *If* s *then* s, *While you* vp *I'll* v *that* s, and it is another thing to produce the complete sentence without hesitation or change of course. It appears that by adopting the 'chaining strategy' a speaker reduces the risk of mid-clause as well as between-clause dysfluencies.

11. Examples illustrating this cline appear in Section 5. Evidence for two types of speech production or 'language' has been reported by neurologists and linguists concerned with localization of function in the brain, e.g. the opposition between 'propositional' or creative speech associated with the left hemisphere, and 'automatic' or memorized speech associated with the right hemisphere. See van Lancker (1973, 1975).

12. Experiments show that speakers do not talk any faster after much practice in, say, a particular task of description, but the *length* of

fluent (pause-free) units increases significantly. Thus, Goldman-Eisler (1961b) found that when a group of subjects had to describe and interpret cartoons, only 25 per cent of their fluent units were five words or more on the first trial, but on their sixth attempt the percentage rose to 50. Observers have often pointed out that public speakers depend heavily on prefabricated sequences to maintain the flow of their oratory, and we find close parallels in studies of the 'impromptu' composition of epic verse in Homer's Greece and in certain contemporary European traditions. Porter (1962, p. 2) observes that 'If the poet . . . is to tell long stories in a highly metrical form, he must not only know the stories well but he must also have at hand a very large store of lines, half-lines, or whole passages, ready fashioned, on which to draw as he recites.' A very insightful analysis of the strategies of narrative composition used by contemporary American English speakers of diverse backgrounds is given by Labov and Waletzky (1967) and Labov (1972a). Labov notes that the most effective narrators are able to speak with great fluency and rhythm, using an extremely simple syntax in relating the 'narrative action' of familiar events.

13. Compare, for example, the transcripts in (14) and (15), where the speakers are trying to say something quite new, with those in (2) and (16), where the speaker is reminiscing. See also Notes 8 and 12.
14. In our society, the statement *I have a headache* is, for instance, sufficient and immediately understood grounds for a person to retire from a social gathering. By contrast, *I have an ache in the knee* is not such an immediately acceptable excuse.
15. In view of the evidence for gradations in grammaticality, productivity of rules, markedness and idiomaticity, the suggestion that there are degrees of lexicalization should occasion little surprise. Work on complex nominals, from Lees (1960) to Downing (1977) and Levi (1978), although not directly concerned with the question of degrees of lexicalization, provides much evidence bearing on this matter. See also Weinreich (1969).
16. In writing lexicalized sentence stems here, the following abbreviations and other notational conventions are used:

lower case	part of the expression in which the individual morphemes are fixed (fully specified)
CAPS	part of the expression in which there is some variability of morphemic (lexical) content
i, j	referential indices
N	noun
NP	noun phrase
P	personal name
PAST	past tense
poss	possessive ending on noun or pronoun, e.g. *boy's, his*
PRES	simple (habitual) present tense
PRO	personal pronoun
TENSE	tense

sÿllable	ʹmarks tonic (contour peak) stress
$	non-nativelike but grammatical string
v	verb
VP	verb phrase
(X)	X is an optional constituent.
[x, y, . . . n]	a choice of one among the bracketed elements is allowed in this constituent

17. Cf. Weinreich's (1969) discussion of the treatment of idioms in a grammatical description, where he notes that 'familiar phrases' other than true idioms have a claim to be represented in the dictionary of complex lexical items.

18. Modern grammatical descriptions are to a remarkable degree still based on the study of written texts and/or self-consciously composed, 'citation form' utterances whose form tends to resemble the written standard. Although the tape recorder has been available for more than 30 years, learning methods for recording natural conversation is still not a standard part of a training in linguistics and linguists are only now beginning to develop conventions for representing many features of spoken discourse. Habits of data collection that go back over 2000 years are not easily broken. What is not yet widely appreciated, perhaps, is how far this bias in the sample of data has narrowed our view of (a) what is normal or typical in spoken discourse, (b) what the important research problems are in linguistics. A similar point is made by Givon (1979, p. 228). The nature of fluency in a language, and the psychological basis of fluency, for instance, have not been important topics of descriptive and theoretical research.

19. On the other hand, native speakers sometimes deliberately make an unusual substitution, expansion or transformation to a lexicalized phrase in order to add an element of freshness, humour, surprise, etc. to their talk. Oscar Wilde is one wit who exploited this procedure to considerable effect.

20. Besides Weinreich, who presents perhaps the most detailed discussion of this problem, writers such as Chafe (1968); Fraser (1970); Bolinger (1975, 1976) and Makkai (1972) deal with various aspects of it.

21. The distinction between holistic and analytic knowledge is considered by Grace (1978–79) and noted to present certain problems for the theory of grammar. In particular, Grace comments on the uncritical acceptance of Occam's Razor as providing a satisfactory way of choosing between competing theories, not only in linguistics but in Western science generally since Newton. Ann Peters (1977, and especially 1980) has recently discussed the consequences for children's language acquisition of their limited processing capacity vs. their excellent long term memory. See also Wong-Fillmore (1976).

22. Bauer (personal communication) suggests that the generality of the rules in this case, and in derivational processes generally, has been underestimated. In word-derivation we find many instances of the contrast between grammatical forms that are nativelike and non-

nativelike, as well as of gradations between familiar, less familiar and strange usages. Compare, for example, the forms in each of the following groups: *see*, $*seeable*, *visible*, *foreseeable*; *marry*, $*marriable*, *marriageable*; *steal*, *stealable*, *thief*, ?*stealer*; *type*, *typist*, $*typer*.

Questions for discussion, study and further research

1. English time-telling conventions do not allow expressions like 'It's four and a third', though that would be the idiomatic Egyptian Arabic expression for 4.20. In Tunisian Arabic, which counts minutes by five minute intervals, the same time would be labelled 'four and four'. Compare nativelike talk about time or some other quantitative matter (height, weight, age, cost, etc.) in English with the way those concepts are idiomatically expressed in some other language you are familiar with. Pay attention to the selection of modifiers such as *only*, *nearly*, *more or less*, *about*, *around*, *over*, *under*, *at least*, etc., which may be associated with quantitative measurement. To what extent is a theory of contexts sufficient and/or necessary to explain nativelike selection in your examples?

2. Even when standard labels are equivalent across languages, the culturally recognized concepts with which they are matched may vary. The expression 'next year' may mean various things in English: some point in time approximately 12 months hence, or some time between January 1 and December 31 of the following calendar year, or the entire duration of the coming calendar year, or some point in an academic or fiscal or other specially defined year. Collect examples of utterances containing the expression 'next year' which have different meanings and compare their meanings to speakers of various English dialects.

One thing 'next year' is not likely to mean in sentences like 'I'm going to buy a new car next year', said on December 20, is January 1, 2 or 3. This least likely interpretation in English is the most likely interpretation in Japanese. Compare the concepts behind such expressions in English with those of equivalent expressions in a language you know. To what extent might differences in interpretation be attributable to extralinguistic cultural factors, such as the importance of the New Year festival as a landmark in Japanese life and culture?

3. Collect some tape-recorded data of your own and analyse it to see whether the correlation reported here of fluency with clause-chaining style (and of nonfluent speech with clause-integrating

style) hold for data from other sources. In your data is it possible to identify novel sentences? If these can be identified, are there more of them in your samples of nonfluent speech?

4. Compare the lexicalized sentence stems reported in this chapter for apologies with those indicated for compliments by Wolfson in Chapter 3. Can you identify lexicalized sentence stems for other speech acts, such as: praise, blame, promise, threaten, etc.?

5. It is suggested here that the grammar of a language contains, in addition to productive rules, a 'phrase book with grammatical notes'. Does this argue that phrase books such as those widely available as quick introductions to a language for the tourist should become part of a modern teaching programme? How can memorized sentences and lexicalized sentence stems be taught? Consider at least the possible roles of dialogues, vocabulary lessons, class discussion and cross-language comparisons.

6. Language learners are said to build up their grammatical competence in a language through the use of innate principles of language learning (inferencing, generalization, etc.) rather than through imitation. How do you think they acquire the ability to produce sentences that are both grammatical *and* likely or natural, that is, to speak idiomatically?

7. In what ways does Pawley and Syder's description of the components of nativelike speech compare with that given by Canale?

8. Try translating some of the clauses given on page 206 into another language you know. Is a similar 'memorized' clause available or are you required to generate a non-memorized utterance?

Introduction to Chapter 8

In this chapter, Donald Morrison and Graham Low examine the concept of *monitoring*, which is familiar to those in the fields of applied linguistics and second language acquisition primarily through the work of Krashen. Morrison and Low suggest that the theory be expanded from Krashen's specialized sense of *the Monitor*, which refers to the conscious application of rules of grammar which have been formally *learned* to edit the output of the learner's *acquired* (not consciously learned) system, to a much broader sense in which monitoring is seen as a deep seated ability on which *all* language use depends, the critical and corrective faculty which balances the creative faculty of language. Evidence is produced in support of this broader concept of monitoring and a plausible model of the interaction of linguistic monitoring and creativity is developed.

Viewed as a basic psycholinguistic (ultimately neurolinguistic) process and as a general principle of communication, monitoring becomes relevant to reception as well as production, planning as well as repair, and relates to all four of the basic components of communicative competence identified by Canale: grammatical, sociolinguistic, discourse and strategic. By broadening the focus from monitoring as something the individual learner does to improve the quality of his grammar to monitoring as a complex and subtle social activity which is an essential part of the struggle to communicate meaning, Morrison and Low's version of the theory is not only in harmony with all of the other chapters of this book, which have attempted to characterize how language functions in use, but further suggests ways in which interactive models may be used to characterize and perhaps ultimately explain language learning as well.

8 Monitoring and the second language learner[1]

Donald M. Morrison and Graham Low

Introduction

Human language use depends on both creative and critical faculties. A creative faculty, dipping down into the internal reservoir of stored rules and patterns, assembles strings of language for private consumption or for articulation as utterances. At the same time, a critical faculty, here called *monitoring* (Laver 1970, pp. 72–75),[2] gives awareness of what has been created, making it possible to check, either before or after articulation, for the frequent slips of the tongue, grammatical errors, social infelicities and other deviations from intention that characterize normal speech.

The same two faculties are also brought into play in our attempts to understand language strings generated by other users. Recent processing models (e.g. Massaro 1975; Goodman and Goodman 1977) view comprehension (in respect to both reading and speech perception) as partly or largely a process of creative guesswork, involving attempts both to match reconstructed perceptions of incoming strings against strings generated internally, and to monitor the accuracy of these reconstructions using clues such as the context of situation, knowledge about the interlocuter (or writer) and reconstructions of preceding strings.

When these two faculties act in harmony, we may find ourselves saying what we wish to say, and our interpretations of what others have said become relatively accurate. When one faculty is in some way weakened or assumes undue dominance, the system tends to break down. We become tongue-tied with fear of saying something wrong, or we speak too loosely; we hear what we *wish* others to say rather than what they intended us to hear. In short, monitoring, in this general (and traditional) sense, is the faculty that gives critical awareness of our creativity and hence allows us to control it.

In recent years, however, the term 'monitoring' has come to be used in a quite specialized and restricted sense in respect to the performance of the second language user. Largely as a result of the work of Stephen Krashen and his associates at the University of Southern California (e.g. Krashen 1977, 1978a, 1978b, 1979a; Krashen, Butler, Birnbaum and Robertson 1978; Stafford and Covitt 1978), the term is now often taken to refer to the conscious application of pedagogical rules on the part of the formally instructed adult learner. A hypothetical device, 'the Monitor',[3] is postulated, and learners who successfully employ this device (apply formal rules) are said to be 'optimal users'. Others may be either 'over-users' or 'under-users' (Krashen 1979a, p. 44).

To the extent that this restricted view of the monitoring function has taken hold in recent models and studies of L2 acquisition (e.g. see Bialystock 1978; Palmer 1979) monitoring now tends to be seen as a superficial artifact of classroom instruction rather than as a deep-seated ability on which all language use depends. For example, it seems typical that Palmer (1979, p. 175) employs the term in reference to an instructed skill picked up in 'grammar translation courses', while Bialystock (1978, p. 78) defines it as essentially 'a formal strategy' that operates by 'exploiting formal information about the language'. And although D. R. Richards (1979) rejects certain aspects of Krashen's model, he seems to accept the underlying dichotomy that equates monitoring with the conscious application of formal rules.

Although Krashen himself has frequently acknowledged that all of us monitor in the more general sense (monitoring by 'feel'; Krashen *et al.* 1978, p. 79), the interest generated by Monitor Theory has gone far to obscure the role that this more basic type of monitoring might have to play in the acquisition and use of second languages. In the present paper we therefore argue for a *return* to a more comprehensive view of the monitoring function in respect to the situation of the L2 learner. More specifically, we want to show that monitoring takes place on many levels and under circumstances that would, according to Monitor Theory, tend to discourage it. We also wish to show that it is open to varying degrees of awareness and manipulation, and that it is closely tied in with other key learning strategies such as risk-taking and inferencing (Carton 1971). Perhaps most importantly, we attempt to illustrate how monitoring can become a social activity, thus pointing the way toward an interactive model of the learning process (see Hatch 1976, 1978; Snow and Ferguson 1977; the references in Bruner 1978). It is at this level, we feel, that the pedagogical implications become most profound.

1 Krashen's 'Monitor model'

As most readers will be aware, Monitor Theory is based on a distinction between language *acquisition* and language *learning*, processes viewed as 'two ways of internalizing linguistic generalizations' (Krashen 1979a, p. 39). Whereas acquisition refers to the natural process children use to internalize representations of a language, learning involves what Krashen calls the '*conscious internalization of rules*' (p. 42, italics supplied). In the adult learner with a history of formal instruction in a second language, these processes result in two distinct internal systems, an acquired system and a learned one. As illustrated in Figure 1, the driving force behind any adult's second language performance is assumed to be the acquired system (Krashen *et al.* 1978, p. 73); however, some adults are able to modify output through application of the learned rule system, on condition that (a) there is sufficient time to apply rules, and (b) the emphasis is on 'form' rather than communication.

Figure 1 Krashen's 'Monitor model'[4]

output from the
'acquired system'

```
        |←─────────  mediation by the
        |                'learned system'
        ↓
monitored output
```

Now, certain features of this model will be intuitively satisfying, at least to those of us who resort to devices such as the rule '*i* before *e* except after *c*' to fill in the gaps in our 'acquired system'. However, while accepting a valid distinction between internalized linguistic knowledge and metalinguistic knowledge, one may question whether the hodgepodge of quasi-linguistic description of the sort that a learner is likely to pick up over the years in various language classrooms can be said to constitute a separate 'system' in any interesting sense of the word. In fact, as Seliger (1979) has pointed out, the number of pedagogical rules that might conceivably be employed in mediating output becomes insignificant in comparison to the large amount of sophisticated information (phonological and lexical, as well as syntactic) that learners must and do acquire. And even in the case of relatively 'simple' rules (such as that governing the choice between allomorphs of the indefinite article *a/an*), there seems to be little relationship between the learner's ability to verbalize a workable rule and his ability to put that rule to work. As Seliger has shown, some learners make the right choice of a form on the basis of 'bad rules' (rules that could not actually account for their choices), while others may have 'good rules' but can't make them work (Seliger 1979, p. 364). Other writers have reported similar findings (e.g. Stafford and Covitt 1978).

Apart from being unnecessarily elaborate, in the sense of being based on a distinction which can be shown to have very little practical relevance, Monitor Theory also seems in a number of ways too *narrow* in scope. It fails to account for reception, it operates only at the level of syntax, it deals primarily with the isolated learner (but see Bennett 1978), and it fails to come to terms with the precise nature of the relationship between application of the Monitor (monitoring by formal rule) and monitoring in the traditional sense (monitoring by 'feel' – Krashen and Scaracella 1978, p. 79). Also, as D. R. Richards (1979) has noted, there are problems in viewing any kind of monitoring as an all-or-nothing process, responsive only to gross dichotomies such as formal/informal, speaking/writing and user/non-user because this makes it impossible to account for the apparent fluctuations that may be observed in a single user in a single situation. Finally, in failing to adequately link the operations of the Monitor with other basic operations such as planning and repair (both external and internal), Krashen is unable to give due attention to the various pathways that an utterance may follow from its initial assembly at a pre-conscious level through to articulation.

In short, while the monitoring function is clearly an interesting and important aspect of language learning and language use, one feels it deserves to be represented as a complex and subtle activity, responsive to a variety of social and psychological pressures.

2 A look at some data

In his insightful discussion of slips of the tongue, Hockett (1967) makes a strong case for the need to study the way an actual utterance is built. 'It is possible,' he suggests, 'to think of a language as a system whose design is reflected not only by the utterances produced by its speakers but also by the process of production itself' (p. 911). In smooth speech, in printed texts (such as this), and in the idealized sentences that form the basis of formal grammars, the production process is largely obscured by an editing process that removes false starts, tongue slips, typing and spelling errors, grammatical errors, and other important evidence. To get a clearer view of the building process as it takes place in real time, one needs to look at utterances just as they are produced, distortions and all.

The following texts have been transcribed from recordings made of adult second language users engaged in relatively informal group discussions. The topic, 'A Close Brush with Death' was chosen in the hope of arousing a degree of emotional involvement which would tend to relax the attentions of the Monitor, as described by Monitor Theory (see Labov 1970, p. 182; Tarone 1979).[5] As is the case with all the subjects quoted in the paper, Aouda is a native speaker of Cantonese. At the time the recording was made she was a first-year student at the (English-speaking) University of Hong Kong, having already been subjected to approximately fourteen years of formal English-language instruction:

> Uh ... I ... I am nearly ... I am ... I was ... I was nearly
> drowned once ... in ... uh ... in a campsite in Sai Kung
> ... um ... we were ... we were driving some ... were ...
> were ... driving canoe ... we were ... we were canoeing
> ... we were canoeing on the sea ... and somehow ... I ...
> I am on the same canoe ... with some little ... little kids
> ... they're very naughty ... and they ... and they jumped
> ... and they jumped down ... eh ... into the sea ... from
> the canoe ... and somehow the canoe capsized and I ...
> and I fell into the sea ... and I ... I cannot swim (*laughter*)
> ... I can't swim ... I ... I ... I ... I feeled ... I felt that I
> am just sinking ... sinking ... (*laughs*) ... and ... but ...
> uh ... the feeling is very short ... the duration.

Several points are worth noting. First, in spite of conditions that would presumably tend to inhibit use of the Monitor (in Krashen's sense), monitoring in the more general sense is very much in evidence. In the absence of a teacher, in the company of peers (fellow second language users), and caught up in the story of a frightening adventure, Aouda is clearly making full use of an internal feedback system that allows her to keep track of output on a number of different levels more or less at the same time. For example, she changes *I am* to *I was,* *driving canoe* to *canoeing* and *feeled* to *felt.* At the end of the text, she also appears to reject the adjective *short* as a modifier of *feeling,* and tacks on the noun *duration,* apparently to make it clear that it was not the feeling itself that was 'short', but the length of time it was experienced.

Importantly, Aouda makes these changes on her own initiative, without benefit of audience feedback (cf. Vigil and Oller 1976). Furthermore, the internal feedback system that triggers the changes frequently appears to involve something less straightforward than a statable pedagogical rule. It seems difficult (and certainly unnecessary) to believe that Aouda's qualms about the idea of a 'short feeling', or her substitution of the standard phrase *canoeing* for nonstandard *driving canoe* bears very much relationship to something a teacher may once have written on a blackboard. Also, although Aouda's efforts to produce an appropriate form for an intended meaning often produce happy results, it should be noted that the monitoring function sometimes fails her. For example, whereas surface present tense forms are detected and marked for past tense in some cases (e.g. *I am nearly drowned – I was nearly drowned.*), at other times an inappropriate form escapes detection, or is perhaps detected and then not bothered with. As D. R. Richards (1979) has noted, an adequate Monitor Theory needs to account for apparent lapses as well as successful repairs.

The breadth of scope that the monitoring function can encompass over even a short stretch of discourse is even more evident in the following text produced by Winnie, a learner with a background similar to Aouda's:

> Well I myself . . . um . . . have not experienced such things
> before and I'm . . . I do not have uh . . . great incident . . .
> uh . . . accidents . . . uh . . . or hurt . . . um . . . but I have an
> experience . . . this is . . . um . . . I think it's funny . . . uh
> . . . when I am now talking . . . but I think it's . . . well . . .
> it's something about my . . . um . . . my birth . . . um . . .
> when I was . . . um . . . uh . . . well let me start again . . . my
> mother told me this . . . uh . . . told me this experience . . .
> uh . . . I was born in . . . uh . . . summer . . . and at that time
> . . . the . . . the typhoon number hoisted

(*inaudible*) it was a typhoon called . . . Wendy . . . uh . . . and
that . . . then is number ten and when . . . at that time I was
living in um . . . Diamond Hill, and stone houses in Diamond
Hill and that time . . . we were not very . . . uh . . . very
rich . . . well . . . well can . . . can consider as poor . . . and my
father at that time was . . . um . . . a worker in a (*inaudible*)
factory. And the day when I was born was . . . um . . . uh
. . . was . . . uh . . . pouring rain . . . and the rain(?) was very
heavy . . . and there was no . . . there was no cars on . . . on
the street . . . and . . . and . . . there was floods . . . um . . .
the . . . the water I think is about . . . uh . . . to the knees
/m'haih/ (*Cantonese negative*) to the waist . . . and my father
had to rush to Wong Tai Sin to cross the harbour . . .
because I . . . um . . . um . . . but . . . um . . . he can . . . he
can't . . . he couldn't get . . . um . . . get private doctors or
. . . other . . . uh . . . hospitals and he . . . uh . . . at last . . .
um . . . call for help from the St. John's . . . um . . . yes . . .
and . . . and . . . they . . . they . . . uh drove . . . uh . . . an
ambulance to the . . . to Diamond Hill and . . . and . . . bring
my moth . . . brought my mother to the hospital . . . and
then . . . after I was born . . . uh . . . they typhoon
was gone.

Here we see evidence of monitoring at four different levels: at
the level of lexis (*incident → accident*); syntax and morphology
(*can't → couldn't, bring → brought*); discourse (*let me start
again*); and simple truth (*knees → waist; not very rich → poor*).
And again, conscious application of formal rules of grammar
could at best account for only a few of the repairs, perhaps the
two past forms. Finally, we may again note that although Winnie's output is subjected to a great deal of checking, the editing
process is far from perfect, with a rather large number of errors
seeming to escape detection.

Up to this point we have been looking at what Hockett (1967,
p. 917) calls 'overt editing', in the sense that perceived errors are
repaired *after* articulation and are therefore apparent to the
listener. The other side of the coin is 'covert editing' (Hockett
1967, p. 936), which we take to be linked with a process we will
here call *pre-articulatory* monitoring, meaning an attempt is made
to inspect strings internally, prior to uttering them. Although this
kind of monitoring is less apparent to us as hearers, as speakers

we know what it means to 'weigh' our words, and may suspect others of doing so when we hear long, unfilled pauses before a low-frequency lexical item or after a particularly difficult or touchy question. Pre-articulatory monitoring could account for the long pauses in the following text produced by another learner, Phoebe. The topic is the same:

> Well I remember that when I was ... uh ... (*unfilled pause, then articulated slowly and evenly*) five-years-old ... um ... my ... (*long unfilled pause*) ... neighbour ... uh ... took me ... uh ... to ... to ... uh ... the Kindergarten ... and while I was crossing the road ... eh ... she ... uh ... she take ... she took care of her own child ... and she just neglect (*short pause*) -ted me. And so I cross the road and a car come ... and it nearly (*long unfilled pause*) ... and then ... and now I ... I ... (*unfilled pause*) ... fell down ... and at that moment I feel very fr ... I felt very frightened and I cried loudly ... calling my mama (*laughter from listeners*) ... and luckily ... uh ... because the driver can stop the car ... uh ... quickly and so I ... (*unfilled pause*) ... I was not killed.

Although here again we find evidence of post-articulatory monitoring (*I feel frightened* → *I felt frightened, take* → *took*), and even one case in which an error is corrected almost *during* the act of articulation (*neglect...ted*), for Phoebe the struggle to communicate tends to be waged internally, and thus the general impression of hesitance. Note also that in some cases the attempt to summon a string that will pass internal inspection can be abandoned completely, as appears to be the case with the sequence '... *and it nearly* ... (knocked me down?)'

We round off our presentation of data for the time being with a text produced by another learner (name not available) whose performance is interesting largely because of the relative absence of repairs.

> First of all ... um ... I would like to talk ... um ... um ... once I have all ... almost died. It was in ... last year ... um ... u ... summa ... and I went to ... I went to camp ... in Peng Chau ... and er ... er ... (we were ... we were ... ?) and on that day I can't catch the train and so ... um ... we five person ... um ... went by taxi. When

we ... when we went to ... um ... Chinese University ...
um ... the car before ... before ours had suddenly stop ...
and .:. the driver of the (*sic*) tax ... um ... um ... also
can stop and at the ... at the very minute ... but the car
after can't see what happen ... he just rush to our car so ...
um ... the ... the force is very ... um ... very large and
push our car towards the first car ... I sit in the ... in the
front chair ... and suddenly I feel very shock-ted ... and
... and then ... but no hurt ... only the ... uh ... the car
on ... the right side of the car um ... had dam ... had ...
damage ... and then we run out the car and ... even cannot
stand by ourself.

This learner speaks haltingly, with many filled pauses, and
therefore gives some evidence of pre-articulatory monitoring.
However, the relatively large number of non-standard forms suggests that either: (a) she is relatively less capable of detecting
errors than, say, Aouda or Phoebe, (b) she is less interested in
doing so, or (c) she can detect errors but is less interested in
attempting to repair them, being content to have communicated
something close to her intended meaning.

Data such as this (and it is easily gathered) clearly demonstrates the complexity and subtlety of the monitoring function.
Even under circumstances that would assumedly discourage application of the Monitor (in Krashen's sense), the adult second
language users we have been dealing with pay active attention to
the form of their utterances on a number of different levels, and
are capable of making edits for lexis, discourse, and truth value,
as well as syntax, without benefit of audience feedback, all in the
same stretch of discourse. Secondly, although there appear to be
interesting individual differences with respect to the relative
proportions of pre- and post-articulatory monitoring, the level of
focus, and the degree to which a learner is successful in detecting
and repairing deviations from intention and other types of error,
these differences are themselves a matter of degree. We cannot
say, for example, that learner A monitors and learner B does not,
or that learner A monitors internally while learner B waits until
after articulation. Finally, while we may expect to find differences
in the type, degree and level of monitoring observed in the same
learner in different situations (e.g. 'formal' versus 'informal'),
what is perhaps more interesting is that even in the same situation, and over a relatively short stretch of discourse, we find evi-

dence of the Monitor (in the broader traditional sense) busily responding in a number of different and subtle ways to constantly changing internal and external circumstances.

3 Inside the black box

Surface phenomena related to the production process naturally lead to speculation about the nature of the underlying mechanisms. An obvious source of information for this purpose, and one that has often been ignored, is simply introspection. Recently McLaughlin (1978) has criticized Krashen's model partly on the grounds of his use of intuitive data. However, one feels inclined to agree with Krashen's response that while intuitions and feelings cannot legitimately be seen as appropriate tests of hypotheses about language use, this kind of data can clearly provide useful input to the construction of such hypotheses (Krashen 1979b, p. 160).

In fact, our own feeling is that Krashen himself may not have gone as far as he might have in tapping the evidence of internal experience in the area of interest; after all, the ability to monitor language output (especially at the pre-articulatory level) is an important component of our general awareness of what goes on in the conscious sector of the mind, and it therefore seems only logical that one should make use of this faculty (internal awareness) in a study of internal language use (see Chafe 1974, p. 122).

Although the model depicted in Figure 2 is based on our own shared internal experience, we make no stronger claim for it than the reader's own investigations can support.[6] We begin with the assumption that a potential utterance first takes on its broad semantic content during a pre-linguistic 'ideation' phase, and then undergoes a highly complicated process of linguistic encoding, resulting in the assembly of an 'articulatory programme' (Laver 1970, p. 62; see also Fromkin 1971; Hill 1972).[7] In the case of sudden exclamations, phatic greetings, warning shouts and the like, the assembled programme may be articulated immediately without prior inspection; however, as the articulated utterance immediately provides input to the system for speech processing, with a sound image of the utterance immediately becoming available for internal display, it is subject to post-articulatory monitoring. This sequence, which might be termed *spontaneous articulation*, is represented by the vertical route A-B-E-F on the chart.

Alternatively, as indicated by the route A-B-C, a string of lan-

Figure 2 A partial model of linguistic monitoring and creativity

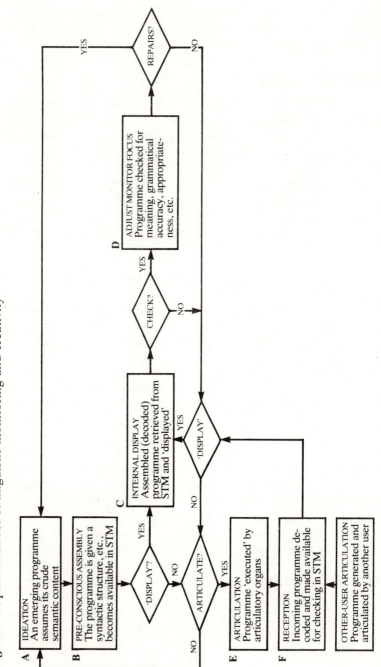

guage that has risen to consciousness can be monitored prior to articulation, and need not in fact be uttered at all. Furthermore, it can be repeatedly recalled to mind for short periods of time. As a working hypothesis, we therefore suggest that after pre-conscious assembly, the rising string emerges into some form of short-term working memory where it becomes temporarily available for retrieval whether or not articulation follows.[8] In either case monitoring can take place on a number of different levels with checks being made for social appropriateness, grammaticality, simple truth value, etc. If difficulties are encountered on any of these levels, a repair can be made in the sense that a new programme may be assembled, possibly drawing on fragments of the faulty string still held in a working memory store. Finally, strings of language bubbling up from the pre-conscious assembly area can simply be allowed to fade from memory without thought of articulation (although we may be caught muttering). This internally-experienced language is a form of daydreaming (Hill 1972, p. 206).

Although at any given point in time a particular string of language may be following one or another of these routes, and although the tendency of strings over a given stretch of time to follow a particular route may help us to characterize the user's orientation (e.g. giving a speech, daydreaming, speaking spontaneously to friends), a typical situation will probably involve successive strings following various different routes in a complex pattern. For example, at the same moment one string may be rising into consciousness, another fading from memory, another on the point of articulation, and yet another, generated by another user, attempting to penetrate the system.

4 Linked systems

This latter possibility brings us to an important juncture in the discussion. Up to this point we have been considering only the movement of strings generated internally, by the user himself. We must now account for the fact (also illustrated in Figure 2) that the same system deals with incoming strings generated by other users as well.

Following Massaro (1975) we assume that the decoding of these incoming strings (whether in the form of an acoustic signal or written text) involves an active reconstruction process. First of all, the incoming signal is transformed through a process of feature detection into an abstract pattern and dumped to some form or area of working (short-term) memory.[8] Next, with recourse to a variety of information sources including recollections of material contained in preceding strings, abstract syntactic, semantic and pragmatic rules, lexical knowledge, knowledge of the real world, and expectations based on knowledge of the interlocuter, the user attempts to reconstruct (guess at) a possible rendition of the string under scrutiny.

Under certain conditions, as when the interlocuters are of one language and one mind, the match between the speaker's intended meaning and the hearer's reconstruction of the meaning may be so perfect that one has only to begin to speak before the other understands the complete message (Vygotsky 1962, pp. 199–200). In other situations, as with a foreigner attempting to process a completely unfamiliar language, the input may be perceived as little more than noise.

Of the many possibilities existing between these two extremes, we may single out two that have particular interest in the context of the present discussion. First, it may be that the hearer's initial reconstruction of an incoming string in some way seriously distorts the speaker's intended meaning, as when 'This food tastes like crab' comes across as 'This food tastes like crap'.[9] Alternatively, it may be that on the basis of contextual information and internalized linguistic knowledge, the hearer is able to find a way to process most of the string, leaving a residue of unfamiliar material partially unprocessed. For example, a learner might hear 'Have you heard the rumour about the new teacher?' as something like 'Have you heard the /ruma(?)/ about the new teacher?'.

In the first instance, the hearer may monitor the initial reconstruction ('This food tastes like crap.'), reject it as inappropriate in view of the context (a semi-formal dinner) and knowledge of the speaker (a normally polite person), and then summon a new reconstruction to match against the original sound image now fading rapidly from working memory. Alternatively, the hearer could question the speaker directly ('What do you mean, 'crap'?').

In the second instance, the hearer would also have different options available. These might include ignoring the unfamiliar element altogether, making a direct appeal to the interlocuter for assistance ('Roomer?'), or working out some hypothesis about the meaning of the unfamiliar element on the basis of context, i.e. *inferencing* (Carton 1971; Bialystock and Fröhlich 1977; Bialystock 1978).

In either case, the similarity between monitoring internally-generated strings and monitoring incoming strings generated by other users is striking. In both situations, an abstract image held in the working memory store is analysed on the basis of stored information with the object of achieving a match between what was perceived and what was intended. In the event of an apparent discrepancy, this matching process may result in some form of editing (either overt or covert), inferencing, or some direct appeal for involvement on the part of the interlocuter, as when we ask for assistance in a word search ('Hey, I saw... uh... what's his name the other day.') or invite the attentions of the interlocuter's monitoring capabilities ('Correct me if I'm wrong...').

As these latter examples show, monitoring can become a social activity, and not simply in the sense that the amount of attention paid to output is conditioned by social factors. Where two or more speakers are monitoring each other's output, as will often be the case in face-to-face interaction, the struggle to communicate can be a kind of a team effort. We have a good example of this from our own data, gathered under the same conditions described above. The topic is 'What are you afraid of?' and the first speaker is talking about her fear of heights:

FIRST SPEAKER: Well ... uh ... uh ... I don't know what ... what would ... what I would feel if I was standing on the ... the ... the mansion(?) ... the Im ... Imperial ...

SECOND SPEAKER: (*softly*) Skyscraper.

THIRD SPEAKER: Skyscrape ...

FIRST SPEAKER: ... Imperial skyline ... skylark ... skylighter ... sky what?

SECOND SPEAKER: Skyscraper.

FOURTH SPEAKER: Skyscraper.

FIRST SPEAKER: Skyscraper.

Here we see an interesting interplay of strategies at both the individual and social level. While the exchange took place rapidly and was difficult to transcribe, we gather that the first speaker (Aouda again) is attempting to communicate the idea of a very high building. She first comes up with something like the word *mansion*, rejects it as not conveying the feature of 'height' in sufficient degree, and then (this is a guess) seems to be trying to assemble *Empire State Building*.

In the meantime another learner in the group has guessed at Aouda's intended meaning on the basis of context and offers the term *skyscraper*, which another learner attempts to repeat. Probably because she is so absorbed in monitoring her own internally generated strings, Aouda does not at first realize she has been given assistance. However, either entirely on her own or stimulated in part by partial awareness of the supplied answer, she starts to have a 'tip-of-the-tongue' experience (Brown and McNeil 1966), generating and rejecting in rapid order *skyline, skylark* and **skylighter*. Giving up, she finally appeals for help and hence the happy ending.

Unfortunately, as can be seen from the following exchange, our learning groups do not always manage to achieve this degree of cooperation. The topic is something like 'Reading habits':

FIRST SPEAKER: We don't need one hour to read the Chinese newspaper . . .

SECOND SPEAKER: Who?

FIRST SPEAKER: Huh?

THIRD SPEAKER: Me too.

FIRST SPEAKER: No no no . . . I just read one news . . . uh . . . Chinese newspaper. But . . . just . . . uh . . . I think . . . half an hour I can finish it.

THIRD SPEAKER: You just skim through it?

FIRST SPEAKER: Yeah . . . scream through it . . .

SECOND SPEAKER: Are they . . .

FIRST SPEAKER: Yes yes . . .

THIRD SPEAKER: I took much time in finish reading . . . uh . . . a newspaper . . . one newspaper.

SECOND SPEAKER: Yes . . . because I don't think it's very satisfaction . . . you . . . you just skim through the newspaper.

FIRST SPEAKER: I screamed it once . . . and after I have found out which topic I like to read . . . I would . . . jump into the . . . the topic.

SECOND SPEAKER: Yes, but I don't really like the . . . uh . . . what? /fou hon/ (*Cantonese for 'entertainment section'*) /dim gong/? (*Cantonese for "How can I say this?"*) I think the Hong Kong newspaper are very weak at . . . what? . . . that kind of things.

In clear contrast to the situation in the preceding extract, the speakers here combine self-absorption in their own meanings with a seemingly superficial interest in the intended meanings of others. This is especially true of the first speaker. Her vague use of *we* (probably in the sense of 'we Chinese' – even though all participants in the discussion share this trait) is justly questioned, but she fails to understand the source of the confusion. Ignoring this difficulty, the third speaker jumps in and agrees with the first speaker's opening statement, but this leads to further confusion when the first speaker internally reconstructs *me too* as *two* and wrongly concludes that she has been contradicted. Unfortunately, no one troubles to clear up the misunderstanding here either, nor is any assistance forthcoming when the first speaker hears *skim* as *scream*. Later, when the second speaker tries to find a suitable expression meaning 'entertainment section' she is again left to struggle on her own.

A comparison of these two extracts shows how individual variation in the amount of attention paid to the form of utterances can be reflected at the social level. Just as we find differences in the extent to which individuals monitor their own output, so too are there differences in the extent to which a group monitors the output of its members.

5 Toward an expanded version of Monitor Theory

As we stated at the outset, our chief problem with Krashen's 'Monitor Theory' is that in equating the term 'monitoring' with the conscious application of pedagogical rules, his model has a tendency to distract attention away from the more basic psycholinguistic processes with which the term has traditionally been associated. Although Krashen has repeatedly acknowledged that the 'acquired system' can play a role in self-correction (e.g. Krashen 1979b, p. 161), and although to his credit he has tended to downplay the role of the 'Monitor' and stress the importance of acquisition in the classroom as well as in the street, the end result is that Monitor Theory has not had much to offer those concerned with the problem of formal language instruction other than to cast further doubt on the already-discredited grammar-translation method.

If, on the other hand, we begin to develop a monitor theory which takes as its starting point the observation that learners are

244   *Donald M. Morrison and Graham Low*

capable of monitoring output, both their own and that of others, using their *acquired system*, the potential explanatory power of the theory may be enhanced. The focus would no longer be on those few situations (e.g. discrete point tests) in which a few learners (ideal Monitor users) are said to be able to improve their performance to some degree. Rather, it would be on the part that monitoring as a basic psycholinguistic process might play in language acquisition and language use (including both production and reception) on the part of *all* learners, in a wide variety of situations.

While we do not feel in a position at this point to make formal hypotheses concerning the role of this more general monitoring function, it seems clear that an adequate theory would have to come to grips with the following basic issues:

(a) The Monitor as an acquisition device

In Krashen's theory it is stated that the acquired system is available for self-correction (Krashen 1979b, p. 161), but it is not clear what the role of self-correction might play in the acquisition process itself. A weak version of an expanded monitor theory might state that monitoring is simply a kind of quality control mechanism with which the user is able to edit out 'silly mistakes' resulting from inadvertent errors in the articulatory programme. A stronger version, however, might give monitoring a more central role in the acquisition process, especially if it could be shown that the Monitor, in mediating between conflicting internal rules coinciding with different stages in the evolution of the learner's internal grammar, might eventually help to settle these differences. If, for example, Aouda is in the future more likely to produce the phrase *canoeing* than *driving canoe*, then we might have reason to suspect that for her at least the monitoring function is something more than a quality control device, and that the act of detecting and subsequently repairing certain mistakes may have longitudinal repercussions.

If inferencing, like editing, is seen as fundamentally linked to monitoring, and if we accept that inferencing is an important way of developing new linguistic competence, then one might see these three functions as constituting some important part of the elusive 'Language Acquisition Device' (Chomsky 1961). Also, if the Monitor is viewed as a component of the LAD then it would follow that individual differences in both the intensity and focus of the monitoring function might help to account for differences in learning. This seems to be the view taken in profiles of the 'good language learner' (Rubin 1975; Naiman, Fröhlich, Stern and Todesco 1975) which include monitoring, risk-taking, inferencing and attention to form as characteristics of the successful learner. We might also expect to find that differences in customary level of attention correlate with characteristic differences in the learner's acquired system. For example, some learners may tend to monitor more at the level of phonology, others for lexis, and others for syntax, depending partly on individual preferences, and partly on the attained degree of proficiency (see Snow and Hoefnagel-Hohle 1979).

(b) Variability

As stated earlier, an adequate monitor theory would have to come to terms with the fact of variable performance within even a relatively short stretch of discourse, as when a learner successfully supplies appropriate markers for past tense at one point and omits them at others. One way of dealing with such inconsistencies is to assume a fairly high degree of control and then explain particular variations as rule-governed (Dickerson 1975) or as consequences of a more or less conscious decision-making process. This seems to be the kind of solution that D. R. Richards (1979) is opting for with his principle of 'communicative efficiency', according to which the L2 learner is seen as continually striving to balance the demands of grammatical accuracy with a desire to communicate as simply and as efficiently as possible. Where alternative forms are observed in the same stretch of discourse, one conforming to the TL norm and one not, Richards would appear to assume that in the latter case the learner has *deliberately* chosen a degree of communicative efficiency at the cost of violating a TL norm because communication was viewed as a priority at that particular point in time.

An alternative approach to the problem of variability might start from an assumption of fluctuating degrees of control, with variability being handled as an offshoot of the economics of attention. Apparent differences in the level and degree of monitoring over a given stretch of discourse would be seen as indications of an interplay between limited resources (e.g. the limited storage capacity of working memory, limited acquisition of relevant rules and lexical information, limited breadth of focus) and competing demands, measured in terms of factors such as the complexity of the processing or production task relative to the user's competence, demands of time, and the presence or absence of various social constraints.

Under optimum conditions, i.e. where demands on the system do not exceed the ability to cope, we may assume that the user has fairly good control over output. Under less than optimum conditions however (and this is probably the normal situation) demands on the system may constantly threaten to exceed capacity, and thus the user will be at best only barely in control. A simple example would be the case where, in the middle of a conversation, something that our interlocuter has said brings forth such a sudden rush of internal speech that the system is flooded and attention distracted away from the interlocuter's subsequent remarks, with the result that we must either pretend to have been listening or apologize and call for a repetition. It would not be appropriate to label this deliberate inattention. In fact it might be argued that we had found the conversation *too* intriguing.

Perhaps a useful analogy here would be the case of a juggler with too many objects in the air. To try to construct a theory of juggling errors on the basis of whether it is the plate, the cane, or the pitcher of water that hits the floor first may be to place too much faith in the juggler's command of the situation. It may be that the cane was deliberately sacrificed to save the water, or it may be that the juggler was trying to save both and failed. Similarly, if we find an L2 learner using an appropriate form one minute and 'backsliding' the next (Selinker 1972, p. 215), it may be best to assume that the attentions of the monitor have been diverted to some more pressing task rather than to think that the learner has momentarily rebelled against target language norms.

6 Summary and implications

To return to a point made at the start of this paper, the struggle to communicate meaning, as well as to understand the meanings of others (whether in a first or second language), brings into play both creative and critical faculties. The creative faculty operates beyond the back edge of consciousness and is therefore essentially unruly. Although it dutifully generates strings as mundane as 'Good morning' and may sometimes surprise us with a particularly apt expression, it often happens that the rising programme is in some way not quite what was wanted. The name might not fit the face, the sounds in words are reversed, or the expressed thought may seem suddenly foolish. Similarly, our reconstructions of what others say to us (or of sentences written on a page) may be *too* creative, in the sense that they distort the original meaning.

The critical faculty, which we have been calling monitoring, and which is essentially our awareness of language, gives leash to the creative faculty, keeps it in check and possibly learns from it. Either before or after articulation, rising programmes can be inspected and judgements made as to whether they 'feel right' in terms of phonological shape, syntax, choice of words, truth value, or social propriety. Where errors or other discrepancies from intention are detected, repairs may be made, i.e. new programmes may be summoned. Where incoming strings contain elements that are unfamiliar, the creative faculty can generate a hypothetical reconstruction and the monitoring function can pass judgement on the accuracy of the reconstruction, a process known as inferencing.

When things are going well, the two faculties can work together like Jack Sprat and his wife, each making up for the other's deficiencies. At other times the relationship may be more awkward. The Monitor may become so suspicious of the creative faculty that it hardly allows anything to pass without the most rigorous inspection, and the creative faculty may not be up to these demands. Alternatively, we may 'speak without thinking' or listen without bothering to understand. In short, humans are not automatons, smoothly and automatically encoding and decoding whatever messages they wish. The system is full of bugs and its capabilities frequently fall short of the demands placed upon it.

This is especially the case when the task is to communicate in a weaker second language. As the texts produced by Aouda and her classmates clearly show, the language learner must wage an almost constant battle to make the best of limited resources. Not surprisingly, there are defeats (*a car come and it nearly...*) as well as successes (*we were canoeing on the sea*) but, to us, perhaps the most important things are that first, the battle is waged at all, and secondly, that it does not need to be waged alone. This is most evident in the 'skyscraper' sequence, where a strong desire to communicate, a willingness to take risks and a careful attention to form provided the ingredients for the eventual victory. If Aouda had not been daring enough to stretch out slightly beyond the edge of her own ability to communicate a particular meaning, and if her interlocuters had not been willing to participate in the struggle to find an appropriate form for that meaning, then the potential learning event might not have been triggered. When it is triggered, the mechanism is not just a single psycholinguistic system acting in isolation, but four linked systems acting in concert. The Monitor has in a sense risen above the level of the individual and become an attribute of the group.

This, in our view, provides an important clue to the direction that future research ought to take. In its expanded version, a monitor theory designed to account for language behaviour in the classroom should ultimately be able to deal with monitoring phenomena associated with group interaction.

Notes

1. The authors would like to acknowledge helpful comments on earlier versions of this paper from Geoff Blowers, Robert Keith Johnson, Jonathan Lee, Lee Yick-Pang and Jack Richards. We would also like to thank Phinney Morrison for her help with the flow chart in Figure 2.
2. For Laver, the term 'monitoring' refers to the 'neural function of detecting and correcting errors in the neurolinguistic program' (p. 137), and is essentially a post-articulatory phenomenon. While we share Laver's view of monitoring as a basic psycholinguistic process, we would like to distinguish between inspection (or simple awareness) and 'editing', which we see as a possible, though not necessary consequence of an inspection procedure. We would also depart from Laver's definition to the extent we see monitoring as taking place either before or after articulation. However, like Laver, we are interested primarily in monitoring as a relatively high-level phenomena, to be distinguished from sensory feed-back mechanisms involved in the direct control of articulatory movements such as discussed by Lashley (1951), and more recently Dalton and Hardcastle (1977, pp. 15–24). We would also like to distinguish between purely linguistic monitoring and 'monitoring for extraneous signals' such as flashes of light or non-speech noises.
3. It should be noted that Laver (1969, pp. 140–141) also speaks of a 'monitor', referring to a basic neurolinguistic mechanism employed regularly by all language users. It is in this sense that we will use the term, unless referring specifically to Krashen's special meaning.
4. The configuration here is slightly different from that in Krashen's customary presentation (e.g. Krashen 1977, p. 154) in that whereas Krashen shows output moving from left to right, ours is 'gravity-driven', with output spilling from top to bottom (see MacNeilage 1971). The purpose of this alteration is simply to bring the presentation into line with our own model, depicted in Figure 2.
5. The recordings were made with a boom microphone suspended well above the speakers' line of vision, but not out of sight. Although the speakers may have been marginally aware that they were being recorded and would therefore have produced something less than completely unguarded speech, this factor should have been at least partially offset by the nature of the topic, the fact that participants in

the discussion were all L2 learners at about the same level, and the fact that group members were familiar with each other, having been speaking together in the same group for several weeks.

6. While sharing Baddeley's (1978) misgivings about linear models of human information processing, we feel that the model represented in Figure 2 at least allows a rough description of the gross mental states and decisions involved in linguistic monitoring.

7. Although this sequence of steps is often treated *en bloc* as the 'planning stage' (e.g. Clark and Clark 1977) we feel that this is something of a misnomer. Whereas 'planning' (at least to us) implies a degree of conscious awareness, we note that the initial assembly process is blocked to introspection. We cannot directly witness, let alone manipulate, the neural magic that first gives rise to a potential utterance. It is only after a word, phrase or some longer string has emerged to conscious awareness that the user can begin to play an active role in rejecting, articulating or simply experiencing the piece of language that has arrived over the threshold of consciousness.

   The passive nature of our relationship with the pre-conscious assembly process is, as one of our colleagues has pointed out (R. Keith Johnson 1981, personal communication), well-illustrated in our inability to actually 'search for a word'; all we can do is clear our mind and wait to accept or reject the candidates that rise to consciousness.

8. We mean to stay well clear of the argument over how memory processes operate; positing short-term memory as a separate entity simply allows us to achieve some degree of compatibility with the speech perception models proposed by Massaro (1975) and Oden and Massaro (1978).

9. This example of what might be called a 'slip of the ear' is taken from personal experience. Other examples include 'Have you replaced the gas yet?' for 'Shall we use the new plates for the guests tonight?' and (taken from a local newspaper) 'Priest Dan queer after dolls' for 'Please stand clear of the doors!'.

Questions for discussion, study and further research

1. How would you characterize the various relationships between linguistic monitoring, editing, inferencing, assembly, and general awareness of language processing? To what extent do these functions overlap and depend on each other? In what ways are they separate?

2. Look carefully at the various routings depicted in the flow chart in Figure 2, page 238. Does this model accord with your own internal experience? What modifications would you suggest making? Do you note any routes of interest not discussed in the article?

3. Toward the end of the article the authors speak of the possibility of psycholinguistic systems 'acting in concert' such that the

monitoring function becomes a social activity. Does the tradition-al, teacher-centred approach to classroom language learning en-courage or discourage this phenomenon? What methods of learn-ing management might help to promote an optimum degree of cooperative risk-taking, inferencing and monitoring?

4. What, if any, are the *essential* differences between linguistic monitoring in a first language and linguistic monitoring in a second language? Are there any other differences?

5. Try to replicate the authors' findings by making recordings of second language learners engaged in discussions among them-selves on topics chosen to arouse emotions. Do you find evidence of monitoring? Do you notice any apparent differences in the degree, level or type of monitoring (pre-articulatory vs. post-articulatory)?

6. If possible, quantify your data from question 5. Try to corre-late this data with other information you may have (or obtain) from these learners, such as attitudinal data. For example, do learners who combine risk-taking with fairly active post-articulatory monitoring tend to reveal more positive attitudes to-ward the second language than those who show little evidence of monitoring? Also try to correlate your data with information about the longitudinal development of the learning groups you study. Do mature groups tend to show more evidence of risk-taking and monitoring than newly formed groups? Also, what about the group structure? Do group leaders tend to reveal charac-teristic monitoring styles?

7. If possible, observe small children at the onset of language. Do you find evidence of a monitoring function, or do you find only spontaneous articulation? From this, can you construct any hypotheses about the role of the monitoring function in language development? Does monitoring serve simply as a quality control device, or is it more deeply implicated in language acquisition?

8. On page 241, the authors cite the familiar phrase 'Correct me if I'm wrong' as an example of an invitation to the interlocuter to engage in social monitoring. Collect other examples of language associated with risk-taking, inferencing, monitoring, and other strategies. Can you use the resulting data to suggest how a moni-tor theory might eventually overlap with speech act theory? What would be the implications for the classroom teacher?

Bibliography

Allen, J. P. B. (1980). 'A three-level curriculum model for second language education'. Keynote address presented at the annual meeting of the Ontario Modern Language Teachers' Association, Toronto, April. Mimeo.

Allen, J. P. B. and Widdowson, H. G. (1975). 'Grammar and Language teaching', in Allen, J. P. B. and Corder, S. Pit (eds.), *The Edinburgh Course in Applied Linguistics*, Vol. 2, Oxford University Press.

Allen, J. P. B., Burnaby, B., Marshall, W. E. and Scott J. (1980). *Teaching English as a Second Language: An Introduction*, Module 1 of the ESL Professional Development Modules Project, Toronto: OISE.

Atkinson, M. A., Cuff, E. C. and Lee, J. R. E. (1978). 'The recommencement of a meeting as a member's accomplishment', in Schenkein J. (ed.), (1978a) 133–154.

Austin, J. L. (1962). *How to Do Things with Words*, Oxford: Clarendon Press.

Bach, K. and Harnish, R. M. (1979). *Linguistic Communication and Speech Acts*, Cambridge, Massachusetts: MIT Press.

Bachman, L. and Palmer, A. S. (1981). 'The construct validation of tests of communicative competence'. Paper read at the Colloquium on the Validation of Oral Proficiency Tests, University of Michigan, March. To appear in the proceedings.

Bachman, L. and Palmer, A. S. (in press). 'The construct validation of the FSI oral interview', *Language Learning*.

Baddeley, A. D. (1978). 'The trouble with levels: a re-examination of Craik and Lockhart's framework for memory research', *Psychological Review*, **85/3**, 139–152.

Bales, F. (1950). 'A set of categories for the analysis of small group interaction', *American Sociological Review*, **15**, 257–263.

Basso, K. (1970). 'To give up on words: silence in the Western Apache culture', *Southwestern Journal of Anthropology*, **26/3**, 213–230.

Bateson, G. (1972). *Steps to an Ecology of Mind*, New York: Ballantine Books.

Bateson, G. (1979). *Mind and Nature: A Necessary Unity*, New York: E. P. Dutton.

Bateson, G. and Ruesch. J. (1951). *Communication: The Social Matrix of Psychiatry*, New York: Norton.

Bauer, L. (1978). 'On lexicalization (neither a lexicalist nor a transformationalist be)', *Archivum Linguisticum*, **9/1**, 3–14.

Bauman, R. (1974). 'Speaking in the light: the role of the Quaker minister', in Bauman, R. and Sherzer, J. (eds), *Explorations in the Ethnography of Speaking*, Cambridge University Press.

Bauman, R. and Sherzer, J. (eds.) (1974). *Explorations in the Ethnography of Speaking*, Cambridge University Press.

Bennett, A. and Slaughter, H. (1981). 'A sociolinguistic/discourse approach to the description of communicative competence of linguistic minority children'. Paper presented at the Language Proficiency Assessment Symposium, Airlie House, Virginia, March. To appear in the proceedings.

Bennett, T. L. (1978). 'The speaker-hearer dichotomy in linguistic variation and the linguistic attitudes of second language learners', *ITL*, **39/40**, 5–22.

Bereiter, C. and Scardamalia, M. (1981). 'From conversation to composition: the role of instruction in a developmental process', in R. Glaser (ed.), *Advances in Instructional Psychology*, Vol. 2, Hillside, New Jersey: Lawrence Erlbaum.

Bialystok, E. (1978). 'A theoretical model of second language learning', *Language Learning*, **28/1**, 69–83.

Bialystock, E. (1980a). 'The Role of Linguistic Knowledge in Second Language Use', Toronto: OISE. Mimeo.

Bialystok, E. (1980b). *Form-function Relationships in Second Language Learning*, Toronto: OISE.

Bialystok, E. and Fröhlich, M. (1977). 'Aspects of second language learning in classroom settings', *Working Papers on Bilingualism*, **13**, 1–26.

Bialystok, E., Fröhlich, M. and Howard, J. (1979). *Studies on Second Language Learning and Teaching in Classroom Settings: Strategies, Processes and Functions*, Toronto: OISE.

Blom, J. P. and Gumperz, J. J. (1972). 'Social meaning in linguistic structures: code-switching in Norway', in Gumperz, J. J. and Hymes, D. H. (eds.), *Directions in Sociolinguistics*, 407–434.

Blum-Kulka, S. (1980). 'Learning to say what you mean in a second language'. Paper presented at the University of Wisconsin-Milwaukee Symposium on Discourse, Milwaukee, February. To appear in the proceedings.

Bobrow, D. G. and Collins, A. (1975). *Representation and Understanding: Studies in Cognitive Science*, New York: Academic Press.

Bobrow, D. G. and Norman, D. A. (1975). 'Some principles of memory schemata', in Bobrow, D. G. and Collins, A. (eds.), *Representation and Understanding: Studies in Cognitive Science*.

Bolinger, D. (1975). *Aspects of Language* (2nd ed.), New York: Harcourt Brace Jovanovich.

Bolinger, D. (1976). 'Meaning and memory', *Forum Linguisticum*, **1/1**, 1–14.

Bode, S., Whitley, C. G. and James, G. (1980). *Listening In and Speaking Out*, New York: Longman.

Bode, S., Whitley, C. G. and James, G. (1981). *Listening In and Speaking Out: Advanced*, New York: Longman.

Borkin, N. and Reinhart, S. M. (1978). "Excuse me" and "I'm sorry", *TESOL Quarterly*, **12/1**, 57–70.

Boydell, D. (1974). 'Teacher-pupil contact in junior classrooms', *British Journal of Educational Psychology*, **44**, 313–318.

Breen, M, and Candlin, C. N. (1980). 'The essentials of a communicative curriculum in language teaching', *Applied Linguistics*, **1/2**, 89–112.

Brown, P. and Levinson, S. (1978). 'Universals in language usage: politeness phenomena', in Goody E. (ed.), *Questions and Politeness: Strategies in Social Interaction*, Cambridge University Press.

Brown, R. and Ford, M. (1961). 'Address in American English', *Journal of Abnormal and Social Psychology*, **62**, 375–385. Reprinted in D. H. Hymes (ed.) (1964) *Language in Culture and Society*.

Brown, R. and McNeil, D. (1966). 'The tip of the tongue phenomenon', *Journal of Verbal Behavior*, **5**, 325–337.

Bruner, J. S. (1978). 'Berlyne memorial lecture: acquiring the uses of language', *Canadian Journal of Psychology*, **32/4**, 204–218.

Canale, M. (1980a). 'A communicative approach to second language teaching and testing'. Paper presented at the RELC Regional Seminar on Evaluation and Measurement of Language Competence and Performance, Singapore, April. To appear in the proceedings.

Canale, M. (1980b). *Introduction to the Ontario Assessment Pool for French as a Second Language*, Toronto: Research and Evaluation Branch, Ontario Ministry of Education.

Canale, M. (1981a). 'A communicative approach to language proficiency assessment in a minority setting'. Paper presented at the Language Proficiency Assessment Symposium, Airlie House, Virginia, March. To appear in the proceedings.

Canale, M. (1981b). 'On some dimensions of language proficiency', in Oller, J. W. Jr. (ed.), *Current Issues in Language Testing Research,* Rowley Massachusetts: Newbury House (in press).

Canale, M. and Swain, M. (1979). 'A domain description for core ESL: communication skills',Toronto: Research and Evaluation Branch, Ontario Ministry of Education. Mimeo.

Canale, M. and Swain, M. (1980). 'Theoretical bases of communicative approaches to second language teaching and testing', *Applied Linguistics*, **1/1**, 1–47. (Revised version of *Communicative approaches to second language teaching and testing*, Toronto: Ontario Ministry of Education, 1979.)

Candlin, C. N. (1980). 'Discoursal patterning and the equalizing of interpretive opportunity', in Smith, L. (ed.), *English for Cross-Cultural Communication*, New York: Macmillan.

Carroll, B. J. (1980). *Testing Communicative Performance*, Oxford: Pergamon Press.

Carton, A. S. (1971). 'Inferencing: a process in using and learning language', in Pimsleur, P. and Quinn, T: (eds.), *The Psychology of Second Language Learning*, Cambridge University Press, 45–58.

Cazden, C. (1972). 'The situation: A neglected source of social class differences in language use', in Pride, J. B. and Holmes, J. (eds.), *Sociolinguistics*, Harmondsworth: Penguin.

Chafe, W. L. (1968). 'Idiomaticity as an anomaly in the Chomskyan paradigm', *Foundations of Language*, **4**, 109–127.

Chafe, W. L. (1974). 'Language and consciousness', *Language*, **50/1**, 111–133.

Chafe, W. L. (1976). 'Givenness, contrastiveness, definiteness, subjects, topics and point of view', in Li, Charles N. (ed.), *Subject and Topic*, New York: Academic Press.

Chafe W. L. (1979). 'The flow of thought and the flow of language', in Givon, T. (ed.), *Syntax and Semantics*, Vol. 12, *Discourse and Syntax*, New York: Academic Press.

Charolles, M. (1978). Introduction aux problèmes de la cohérence des textes. *Langue française,* **38**, 7–41.

Chomsky, N. (1957). *Syntactic Structures*, The Hague: Mouton.

Chomsky, N. (1961). 'Some methodological remarks on generative grammar', *Word*, **17**, 219–239.

Chomsky, N. (1964). *Current Issues in Linguistic Theory*, The Hague: Mouton.

Chomsky, N. (1965). *Aspects of the Theory of Syntax*, Cambridge, Massachusetts: MIT Press.

Chomsky, N. (1968). *Language and Mind*, New York: Harcourt, Brace and World.

Chomsky, N. (1975). *Reflections on Language*, New York: Pantheon Books.

Chomsky, N. (1980). *Rules and Representations*, New York: Columbia University Press.

Clark, J. L. D. (1972). *Foreign Language Testing: Theory and Practice*, Philadelphia: The Center for Curriculum Development.

Clark H. E. and Clark, E. V. (1977). *Psychology and Language: an introduction to psycholinguistics*, New York: Harcourt, Brace, Jovanovich.

Clements, P. (1979). 'The effects of staging on recall from prose', in Freedle, R. O. (ed.), *New Directions in Discourse Process*, Norwood, New Jersey: Ablex.

Clifford, R. (1980). 'Oral language proficiency testing: a dynamic model'. Paper presented at the Second International Language Testing Symposium, Darmstadt, West Germany, June. To appear in the proceedings.

Clifford, R. (1981). 'Oral proficiency performance profiles and global rating'. Paper presented at the Pre-Conference on Oral Proficiency Assessment, Georgetown University Round Table, Washington, D.C., March. To appear in the proceedings.

Clyne, M. (1975). 'Intercultural communication breakdown and communication conflict: towards a linguistic model and its exemplification' (ms).

Cole, P. and Morgan, J. (eds.), (1975). *Syntax and Semantics*, Vol. 3: *Speech Acts*, New York: Academic Press.

Cook-Gumperz, J. and Gumperz, J. J. (1980). 'From oral to written culture: the transition to literacy', in Whiteman, M. F. (ed.), *Variation in Writing*, New York: Lawrence Erlbaum.

Corder, S. Pit (1973). *Introducing Applied Linguistics*, Harmondsworth: Penguin.

Corder, S. Pit 'Some problems in the design of a functional syllabus'. *Proceedings and Papers of the Eighteenth Congress of the Australian Universities Language and Literature Association*, Wellington (in press).

Coulmas, F. (ed.) (1981). *Conversational Routine: Explorations in Standardized Communication Situations and Prepatterned Speech*, The Hague: Mouton.

Coulthard, M. (1977). *An Introduction to Discourse Analysis*, London: Longman.

Crystal, D. (1969). *Prosodic Systems and Intonation in English*, Cambridge University Press.

Crystal, D. (1975). *Intonation*, Cambridge University Press.

Cummins, J. (1980). 'Cognitive/academic language proficiency, linguistic interdependence, the optimum age question and some other matters', *Working Papers on Bilingualism*, **19**, 197–205.

Cummins, J. (1981a). 'Language proficiency and academic achievement among minority students'. Paper presented at the Language Proficiency Assessment Symposium, Airlie House, Virginia, March. To appear in the proceedings.

Cummins, J. (1981b). 'Is academic achievement distinguishable from language proficiency?' in Oller, J. W. Jr., (ed.), *Current Issues in Language Testing Research*, Rowley, Massachusetts: Newbury House.

Dalton, P. and Hardcastle, W. (1977). *Disorders of Fluency*, London: Edward Arnold.

Darnell, R. (1979). 'Reflections on Cree international etiquette education implications', *Working Papers in Sociolinguistics*, **57**, Austin, Texas: Southwest Educational Development Laboratory.

Delamont, S. (1976). *Interaction in the Classroom*, London: Methuen.

Dickerson, L. (1975). 'The learner's language as a system of variable rules', *TESOL Quarterly*, **9/4**, 401–7.

Dobson, J. M. (1979). 'The Notional Syllabus: Theory and Practice', *English Teaching Forum*, **17/2**, 2–10.

Downing, P. A. (1977). 'On the creation and use of English compound nouns', *Language*, **53**, 810–42.

Edmondson, W. J. (n.d.) 'Some problems concerning the evaluation of foreign language classroom discourse'. Ms.

Edmondson, W. J. (1981). 'On saying you're sorry', in Coulmas, F. 273–288.

Edwards, A. D. (1976). *Language in Culture and Class*, London: Heinemann.

Eichler, L. (1928). *The Book of Conversation*, New York: Doubleday, Doran and Co.

Erickson, F. (1976). 'Gatekeeping encounters: a social selection process', in Sanday, P. R. (ed.), *Anthropology and the Public Interest: Fieldwork and Theory*, New York: Academic Press.

Ervin-Tripp, S. (1964). 'Interaction of language, topic and listener', *American Anthropologist*, **66**, 86–102.

Ervin-Tripp, S. M. (1969). 'Sociolinguistics', in L. Berkowitz, (ed.), *Advances in Experimental Social Psychology*, Vol. 4, New York: Academic Press, 91–165. Reprinted in Fishman, J. A. (1971), Vol. 1.

Ervin-Tripp, S. M. (1972). 'On sociolinguistic rules: alternation and co-occurrence', in Gumperz, J. J. and Hymes, D. H. (eds.) (1972).

Ervin-Tripp, S. (1976). 'Is Sybil there? The structure of American English directives', *Language in Society*, **5**, 25–66.

Ervin-Tripp, S. (1977). 'Wait for me roller-skate', in Ervin-Tripp, S. and Mitchell-Kernan, C. (1977).

Ervin-Tripp, S. and Mitchell-Kernan, C. (eds.) (1977). *Child Discourse*, New York: Academic Press.

Farhady, H. (1979). 'New directions for ESL proficiency testing', Los Angeles: UCLA. Mimeo.

Farhady, H. (1980). 'Justification, development and validation of functional language tests'. Unpublished Ph.D. dissertation, UCLA.

Ferguson, C. A. (1976). 'The structure and use of politeness formulas', *Language in Society*, **5**, 135–51. Reprinted in Coulmas, F. (ed.) (1981). 21–35.

Fillmore, C. J. (1981). 'Ideal readers and real readers'. Paper presented at the Georgetown University Round Table, Washington, D.C., March. To appear in the proceedings.

Fishman, J. A. (ed.) (1968). *Readings in the Sociology of Language*, The Hague: Mouton.

Fishman, J. A., (ed.) (1971). *Advances in the Sociology of Language*, The Hague: Mouton.

Flanders, N. (1970). *Analysing Teaching Behaviour*, London: Addison-Wesley.

Foucault, M. (1977). *Language, Counter-memory, Practice*, Ithaca: Cornell University Press.

Fraser, B. (1970). 'Idioms within transformational grammar', *Foundations of Language*, **6**, 22–42.

Fraser, B. (1981a). 'On requesting: an essay on pragmatics', Boston University. Mimeo.

Fraser, B. (1981b). 'Some insulting problems in second language acquisition', *TESOL Quarterly*, **15/4**, 435–441.

Fraser, B. and Nolen, W. (1980). 'The relationship of deference to linguistic form', *International Journal of the Sociology of Language*, **27**, 93–109.

Freedle, R., Fine, J. and Felbaum, C. (1981). 'Selected discourse devices and their power for discriminating good and bad writing'. Paper presented at the Georgetown University Round Table, Washington, D.C., March. To appear in the proceedings.

Fromkin, V. A. (1971). 'The non-anomalous nature of anomalous utterances', *Language*, **47/1**, 27–52. Reprinted in Fromkin, V. A. (ed.) (1973). *Speech Errors as Linguistic Evidence*, The Hague; Mouton, 213–242.

Gardner, P. (1966). 'Symmetric respect and memorate knowledge: the structure and ecology of individualistic culture', *Southwestern Journal of Anthropology*, **22**, 389–415.

Garfinkel, H. (1971). *Studies in Ethnomethodology*, Englewood Cliffs, New Jersey: Prentice-Hall.

Garvey, C. (1975). 'Requests and responses in children's speech', *Journal of Child Language*, **2**, 41–63.

Givon, T. (1979). *On Understanding Grammar*, New York: Academic Press.

Godard, D. (1977). 'Same settings, different norms: phone call beginning in France and the United States', *Language in Society*, **6**, 209–19.

Goffman, E. (1971). *Relations in Public: Microstudies of the Public Order*, Harmondsworth: Penguin.

Goffman, E. (1974). *Frame Analysis: An Essay on the Organization of Experience*, Cambridge, Massachusetts: Harvard University Press.

Goffman, E. (1976). 'Replies and responses', *Language in Society*, **5/3**, 257–313.

Goldman-Eisler, F. (1954). 'On the variability of speed of talking and on its relation to the length of utterance in conversation', *British Journal of Psychology*, **45**, 94–107.

Goldman-Eisler, F. (1958). 'Speech production and the predictability of words in context', *Quarterly Journal of Experimental Psychology*, **10**, 96–106.

Goldman-Eisler, F. (1961a). 'The continuity of speech utterance, its determinants and its significance', *Language and Speech*, **4**, 220–31.

Goldman-Eisler, F. (1961b). 'The distribution of pause durations in speech', *Language and Speech*, **4**, 232–37.

Goldman-Eisler, F. (1968). *Psycholinguistics: Experiments in Spontaneous Speech*, New York: Academic Press.

Goodman, K. S. and Goodman, Y. M. (1977). 'Learning about psycholinguistic processes by analyzing oral reading', *Harvard Educational Review*, **47/3**.

Grace, G. W. (1981). *An Essay on Language*, South Carolina: Hornbeam Press.

Grace, G. W. (1978–9). Ethnolinguistic notes. New series. Mimeo. University of Hawaii. (Ref. is especially to Note 7; where does 'the economy of linguistic description' come from?)

Grice, H. P. (1975). 'Logic and conversation', in Cole, P. and Morgan, J. (eds.), *Syntax and Semantics*, Vol. 3, 41–58.

Groot, P. J. M. (1975). 'Testing communicative competence in listening comprehension', in Jones, R. L. and Spolsky, B. (eds.), *Testing Language Proficiency*, Arlington, Virginia: Centre for Applied Linguistics.

Gumperz, J. J. and Hymes, D. H. (eds.) (1972). *Directions in Sociolinguistics*, New York: Holt, Rinehart, and Winston.

Gumperz, J. J. (1977a). 'Sociocultural knowledge in conversational inference', *28th Annual Round Table Monograph Series on Languages and Linguistics*, Georgetown University, Washington, D.C.

Gumperz, J. J. (1977b). 'The conversational analysis of interethnic communication', in Ross, E. Lamar (ed.), *Interethnic Communication*. Proceedings of the Southern Anthropological Society, University of Georgia: University of Georgia Press.

Gumperz, J. J. (1978). 'The retrieval of sociocultural knowledge in conversation'. Paper presented at the American Anthropology Association, Nov. To be published in Boyd, J. and Searle, J. (eds.), *Speech Acts Ten Years Later*.

Gumperz, J. J. and Hymes, D. H. (eds.) (1972). *Directions in Sociolinguistics: the Ethnography of Communication*, New York: Holt, Rinehart and Winston.

Gumperz, J. J. and Roberts, C. (1978). *Developing Awareness Skills for Interethnic Communication*, Middlesex, England: National Centre for Industrial Language Training.

Hakuta, K. (1974). 'Prefabricated patterns and the emergence of structure in second language acquisition', *Language Learning*, **24/2**, 287–298.

Haley, J. (1963). *Strategies of Psychotherapy*, New York: Grune and Stratton.

Halliday, M. A. K. (1973). *Explorations in the Functions of Language*, London: Edward Arnold.

Halliday, M. A. K. (1975). *Learning How to Mean: Explorations in the Development of Language*, London: Edward Arnold.

Halliday, M. A. K. (1978). *Language As Social Semiotic*, London: Edward Arnold.

Halliday, M. A. K. and Hasan, R. (1976). *Cohesion in English*, London: Longman.

Harley, B. and Swain, M. (1978). 'An analysis of the verb system used by young learners of French', *Interlanguage Studies Bulletin*, **3/1**, 35–79.

Hatch, E. M. (1976). 'Discourse analysis, speech acts and second language acquisition', *Workpapers in TESL*, University of California, Los Angeles, **10**, 51–64.

Hatch, E. M (1978). 'Discourse analysis, and second language acquisition', in Hatch, E. M. (ed.), *Second Language Acquisition*, Rowley, Massachusetts: Newbury House.

Hatch, E. M. (1979). 'Simplified input and second language acquisition'. Paper presented at the 54th Annual Meeting of the Linguistic Society of America.

Hatch, E. M. and Long, M. H. (1980). 'Discourse analysis, what's that?' in Larsen-Freeman, D. (ed.), *Discourse Analysis in Second Language Acquisition*, Rowley, Massachusetts: Newbury House.

Henderson, A., Goldsman-Eisler, F. and Skarbek, A. (1966). Sequential temporal patterns in spontaneous speech, *Language and Speech*, **9**, 207–16.

Herdan, G. (1964). *Quantitative Linguistics*, London: Butterworths.

Hill, A. A. (1972). 'A theory of speech errors', in Firchow, E. S. *et al.* (eds.), *Studies Offered to Einar Haugen*, Mouton. Reprinted in Fromkin, V. A. (ed.), *Speech Errors as Linguistic Evidence*, The Hague; Mouton (1973) 205–214.

Hinofotis, F. E. (1980). 'Communicative competence in an educational environment? Paper presented at the RELC Regional Seminar on Evaluation and Measurement of Language Competence and Performance. Singapore, April. To appear in the proceedings.

Hinofotis, F. E. (1981a). 'Communicative competence in an educational environment: the relationship of quantifiable components', in Read, J. (ed.), *Proceedings of the 15th RELC Seminar on Evaluation and Measurement of Language Competence and Performance*, Singapore: RELC.

Hinofotis, F. E. (1981b). 'The structure of oral communication in an educational environment: a comparison of factor analytic rotational procedures', in Oller, J. W. Jr. (ed.), *Current Issues in Language Testing Research*, Rowley, Massachusetts: Newbury House.

Hippler, A. E. and Conn, S. (1972). 'Traditional Athabascan law ways and their relationship to contemporary problems of "bush justice" ', Fairbanks: Institute of Social, Economic, and Government Research Occasional Papers, No. **7**, August.

Hippler, A. E. (1973). 'Northern Eskimo law ways and their relationships to contemporary problems of "bush justice"', Fairbanks: Institute of Social, Economic and Government Research Occasional Papers, No. **10**, July.

Hockett, C. F. (1967). 'Where the tongue slips, there slip I', in Fromkin, V. A. (ed.), *Speech Errors as Linguistic Evidence*, The Hague: Mouton, 93–119.

Holmes, J. (1978). 'Sociolinguistic competence in the classroom', in Richards, J. C. (ed.), *Understanding Second and Foreign Language Learning*, Rowley, Massachusetts: Newbury House.

Holmes, J. and Brown, D. F. (1976). 'Developing sociolinguistic competence in a second language', *TESOL Quarterly*, **10/4**, 423–431.

Hopper, P. and Thompson, S. 'Transitivity in grammar and discourse', *Language* (to appear).

Hymes, D. H. (1964a). 'Introduction: towards ethnographies of communication', *American Anthropologist*, **66/6**, part 2, 1–34.

Hymes, D. H. (1964b). *Language in Culture and Society*, New York: Harper and Row.

Hymes, D. H. (1967). 'Models of the interaction of language and social setting', in Macnamara, J. (ed.), *Problems of Bilingualism, Journal of Social Issues*, **23**, 8–28.

Hymes, D. H. (1972a). 'Models of the interaction of language and social life', in Gumperz, J. J. and Hymes, D. H. (eds.) (1972) 35–71.

Hymes, D. H. (1972b). 'On communicative competence', in Pride, J. B. and Holmes, J. (eds.), *Sociolinguistics*, Harmondsworth: Penguin.

Hymes, D. H. (1974). *Foundations in Sociolinguistics*, University of Pennsylvania Press.

Jackson. P. W. (1968). *Life in Classrooms*, New York: Holt, Rinehart and Winston.

Jacob, E. and Sanday, P. R. (1976). 'Dropping out: a strategy for coping with cultural pluralism', in Sandy, P. G. (ed.), *Anthropology and the Public Interest: Fieldwork and Theory*, New York: Academic Press.

Jacobovits, L. and Gordon, B. (1974). *The Context of Foreign Language Learning*, Rowley, Massachusetts: Newbury House.

Jacobovits, L. and Gordon, B. (1975). *Community Cataloguing Practices*, Department of Psychology, University of Hawaii.

Jakobovits, L. and Gordon, B. (1980). 'Language teaching vs. the teaching of talk', *International Journal of Psycholinguistics*, **6/4**, 5–22.

Jakobson, R. (1960). 'Concluding statement: linguistics and poetics', in Sebeok, T. A. (ed.), *Style and Language*. Cambridge, Massachusetts: MIT Press.

Jefferson, G. (1972). 'Side sequence', in Sudnow, D. (1972), 294–338.
Jesperson, O. (1951). *The Philosophy of Language*, London: Allen and Unwin.
Johnson, K. and Morrow, K. (1979). *Communicate: the English of Social Interaction*, Cambridge University Press.
Jones, R. L. (1977). 'Testing: a vital connection', in Phillips, J. K. (ed.), *The Language Connection: from the Classroom to the World*, Skokie, Illinois: National Textbook Co.
Jones, R. L. (1978). 'Interview techniques and scoring criteria at the higher proficiency levels', in Clark, J. L. D. (ed.), *Direct Testing of Speaking Proficiency: Theory and Application*, Princeton: Educational Testing Service.
Jones, R. L. (1981). 'Scoring procedures in oral language proficiency testing', in Read, J. (ed.), *Proceedings of the 15th RELC Seminar on Evaluation and Measurement of Language Competence and Performance*, Singapore: RELC.
Joyce, B. and Weil, M. (1972). *Models of Teaching*, Englewood Cliffs: Prentice-Hall.
Just, M. A. and Carpenter, P. A. (1977). *Cognitive Processes in Comprehension*, Hillsdale, New Jersey: Lawrence Erlbaum.
Keenan, E. O. (1976). 'On the universality of conversational postulates', *Language in Society*, **5**, 67–80.
Keenan, E. O. (1977). 'Why look at unplanned and planned discourse?', in Keenan, E. O. and Bennett, T. E. (eds.).
Keenan, E. O. and Bennett, T. E. (eds.), (1977). *Discourse Across Time and Space*, Los Angeles: University of Southern California, Occasional Papers in Linguistics No. 5.
Keller, E. (1976). 'Gambits', *TESL Talk*, **7/2**, 18–21.
Keller, E. and Taba-Warner, S. (1976). *Gambits I, Openers*, Ottawa: Supply and Services Canada.
Keller, E. and Taba-Warner, S. (1976). *Gambits 2, Links*, Ottawa: Supply and Services Canada.
Keller, E. and Taba-Warner, S. (1979). *Gambits 3, Responders, Closers and Inventory*, Hull, Quebec: Canadian Government Publishing Centre, Supply and Services.
Kempson, R. M. (1977). *Semantic Theory*, Cambridge University Press.
Kennedy, G. D. (1978). 'Conceptual aspects of language learning', in Richards, J. C. (ed.), *Understanding Second and Foreign Language Learning*, Rowley, Massachusetts: Newbury House.
Kennedy, G. D. (1979). 'Semantic Priorities in English Language Teaching', *RELC Journal*, **10/2**, 14–35.
Kintsch, W. (1977). 'On comprehending stories', in Just, M. A. and Carpenter, P. A. (eds.), *Cognitive Processes in Comprehension*, Hillsdale, New Jersey: Lawrence Erlbaum.
Kintsch, W. and Greene, E. (1978). 'The role of culture-specific schemata in the comprehension and recall of stories', *Discourse Processes*, **1/1**, 1–13.
Kochman, T. (1979). 'Boasting and bragging: 'Black' and 'White'', *Working Papers in Sociolinguistics*, **58**, Austin: Southwest Educational Development Laboratory.

Krashen, S. D. (1977). 'The monitor model for adult second language performance', in Burt, M., Dulay, H. and Finocchiaro, M. (eds.), *Viewpoints on English as a Second Language*, New York: Regents.

Krashen, S. D. (1978a). 'Second language acquisition', in Dingwall, W. O. (ed.), *A Survey of Linguistic Science*, Connecticut: Greylock, 317–338.

Krashen, S. D. (1978b). 'Individual variation in the use of the Monitor', in Ritchie, W. (ed.), *Principles of Second Language Learning*, New York: Academic Press.

Krashen, S. D. (1979a). 'Adult second language acquisition as post-critical period learning', *ITL*, **43**, 39–52.

Krashen, S. D. (1979b). 'A response to McLaughlin, "The monitor model: some methodological considerations"', *Language Learning*, **29/1**, 151–167.

Krashen, S. D. (1979c). 'The monitor model for second language acquisition', in Gingras, R. (ed.), *Second Language Acquisition and Foreign Language Teaching*, Arlington: Centre for Applied Linguistics.

Krashen, S. D., Butler J., Birnbaum R., Robertson, J. (1978). 'Two studies in language acquisition and language learning', *ITL*, **39–40**, 73–92.

Krashen, S. D. and Scaracella, R. (1978). 'On routines and patterns in language acquisition and performance', *Language Learning*, **28**, 283–300.

Krashen, S. D. and Terrell, T. D. 'The natural approach: language acquisition in the classroom'. Mimeo, (forthcoming).

Kroll, B. (1977). 'Combining ideas in written and spoken English: a look at subordination and coordination', in Keenan, E. O. and Bennett, T. E. (eds.).

Labov, W. (1969). 'The logic of nonstandard English', *Georgetown Monographs on Language and Linguistics*, Vol. 22, Georgetown University, Washington, D.C.

Labov, W. (1970). 'The study of language in its social context', in Pride, J. and Holmes, J. (eds.), *Sociolinguistics*, Harmondsworth: Penguin, 180–282.

Labov, W. (1972a). *Language in the Inner City: Studies in the Black English Vernacular*, Philadelphia: University of Pennsylvania Press.

Labov, W. (1972b). 'Rules for ritual insults', in Sudnow, D. (ed.), (1972).

Labov, W. (1972c). 'The transformation of experience in narrative syntax', in Labov, W. *Language in the Inner City*.

Labov, W. and Fanshel, D. (1977). *Therapeutic Discourse: Psychotherapy as Conversation*, New York: Academic Press.

Labov, W. and Waletzky, J. (1967). 'Narrative analysis', in *Essays on the Verbal and Visual Arts*, Seattle: University of Washington Press, 12–44.

Lado, R. (1978). 'Scope and limitations of interview-based language testing: are we asking too much of the interview?', in Clark, J. L. D. (ed.), *Direct Testing of Speaking Proficiency Theory and Application*, Princeton: Educational Testing Service.

Lane, Christopher. (1978). 'Analysing English conversation: on moves and sequencing rules', M. A. Thesis. University of Auckland.

Larsen-Freeman, D. (1981). 'The WHAT of second language acquisition'. Plenary paper presented at the TESOL 1981 Meeting, Detroit. March.

Lashley, K. S. (1951). 'Serial order in behavior', in Jeffress, L. A. (ed.), *Cerebral Mechanisms in Behavior*, New York: John Wiley.

Laver, J. D. M. (1969). 'The detection and correction of slips of the tongue', *Work in Progress* 3, Department of Phonetics and Linguistics, University of Edinburgh. Reprinted in Fromkin, V. A. (ed.) *Speech Errors as Linguistic Evidence*, The Hague: Mouton 1973, 132–143.

Laver, J. (1970). 'The production of speech', in Lyons, J. (ed.), *New Horizons in Linguistics*, Harmondsworth: Penguin, 53–75.

Leech, G. N. (1977). 'Language and tact', LAUT University of Trier, Series A, Paper 46.

Leech, G. N. and Svartvik, J. (1978). *A Communicative Grammar of English*, London: Longman.

Lees, R. B. (1960). *The Grammar of English Nominalizations*, The Hague: Mouton.

Lein, L. and Brenneis, D. (1978). 'Children's disputes in three speech communities', *Language in Society*, **7/3**, 299–323.

Lepicq, D. (1980). 'Aspects théoriques et empiriques de l'acceptabilité linguistique: le cas du français des élèves des classes dimmersion'. Unpublished doctoral thesis, University of Toronto.

Levi, J. N. (1978). *The Syntax and Semantics of Complex Nominals*, New York: Academic Press.

Levinson, S. C. (1979). 'Activity types and language', *Linguistics*, **17**, 365–99.

Linde, C. and Labov, W. (1975). 'Spatial networks as a site for the study of language and thought', *Language*, **51**, 924–39.

Low, G. D. (1981). 'The direct testing of academic writing in a second language', University of Hong Kong. Mimeo.

Lowe, P. (1981). 'Components of oral examiner/interviewer training'. Paper presented at the Pre-Conference on Oral Proficiency Assessment, Georgetown University Round Table, Washington, D.C., March. To appear in the proceedings.

MacNeilage, P. F. (1971). 'Some observations on the metatheory of speech perception', *Language and Speech*, **14/1**, 12–17.

Makkai, A. (1972). *Idiom Structure in English*, The Hague: Mouton.

Manes, J. and Wolfson, N. (1981). 'The compliment formula', in F. Coulmas, (ed.), 115–132.

Massaro, D. (ed.) (1975). *Understanding Language: An Information-Processing Analysis of Speech Perception, Reading, and Psycholinguistics*, New York: Academic Press, 3–27.

McLaughlin, B. (1978). 'The monitor model: some methodological considerations', *Language Learning*, **28/2**, 309–332.

Mead, M. (1977). 'End linkage: a tool for cross-cultural analysis', in Brockman, J. (ed.), *About Bateson*, New York: E. P. Dutton.

Meehan, H. and Wood, H. (1975). *The Reality of Ethnomethodology*, New York and London: John Wiley.

Merritt, M. (1976). 'On questions following questions in service encounters', *Language in Society*, **5**/**3**, 315–357.

Miller, G. A. (1951). *Language and Communication*, New York: McGraw Hill.

Mitchell-Kernan, C. (1972), 'Signifying and marking: two Afro-American speech acts', in Gumperz, J. J. and Hymes, D. H. (eds.).

Mitchell-Kernan, C. and Kernan, K. T. (1977). 'Pragmatics of Directive Choice among children', in Ervin-Tripp, S. and Mitchell-Kernan, C. (eds.), *Child Discourse*, New York: Academic Press.

Morgan, J. (1981). 'Discourse grammar and linguistic theory'. Paper presented at the Georgetown University Round Table, Washington, D.C., March. To appear in the proceedings.

Morrow, K. E. (1977). *Techniques of Evaluation for a Notional Syllabus*, London: The Royal Society of Arts.

Munby, J. (1978). *Communicative Syllabus Design*, Cambridge University Press.

Naiman, N, Fröhlich, M., Stern, H. H. and Todesco, A. (1975). *The Good Language Learner*, Toronto: OISE.

Nattinger, J. R. (1980). 'A lexical phrase grammar for ESL', *TESOL Quarterly*, **14**/**3**, 337–344.

Oden, G. and Massaro, D. (1978). 'Integration of featural information in speech perception', *Psychological Review*, **85**/**3**, 172–191.

Ogbu, J. (1974). *The Next Generation: an Ethnography of Education in an Urban Neighbourhood*, New York: Academic Press.

Oller, J. W. Jr. (1978). 'The language factor in the evaluation of bilingual education', in Alatis, J. E. (ed.), *Georgetown University Round Table on Languages and Linguistics*, Washington, D.C.: Georgetown University Press.

Oller, J. W. Jr. (1979). *Language Tests at School*, London: Longman.

Olson, D. R. (1973). 'What is worth knowing and what can be taught', *School Review*, **82**/**1**, 27–43.

O'Neill, R. and Scott, R. (1974). *Viewpoints*, London: Longman.

Ong, W. (1977). *Interfaces of the Word*, Ithaca: Cornell University Press.

Ortony, A., (ed.) (1979). *Metaphor and Thought*, Cambridge University Press.

Palmer, A. S. (1977). *Getting Help with Your Thai*, Bangkok: American University Alumni Association Language Centre.

Palmer, A. S. (1978). 'Measures of achievement, communication, incorporation and integration for two classes of formal EFL learners'. Paper read at the 5th AILA Congress, Montreal, August. Mimeo.

Palmer, A. S. (1979). 'Compartmentalized and integrated control; an assessment of some evidence for two kinds of competence and implications for the classroom'. *Language Learning*, **29**/**1**, 169–179.

Palmer, A. S. and Bachman, L F. (1980a). 'The construct validation of the constructs "communicative competence in speaking" and "communicative competence in reading": a pilot study'. Paper presented at the Annual Meeting of TESOL, San Francisco. March. Mimeo.

Palmer, A. S. and Bachman, L F. (1980b). 'Basic concerns in test validation'. Paper presented at the RELC Regional Seminar on Evaluation and Measurement of Language Competence and Performance, Singapore, April. To appear in the proceedings.

Palmer, A. S. and Bachman, L. F. (1981). 'Basic concerns in test validation', in Read, J. (ed.), *Proceedings of the RELC Seminar on Evaluation and Measurement of Language Competence and Performance*, Singapore: RELC.

Paulston, C. B., (1974). 'Linguistic and communicative competence', *TESOL Quarterly*, **8**/**4**, 347–367.

Paulston, C. B. and Bruder, M. N. (1976). *Teaching English as a Second Language: Techniques and Procedures*, Cambridge: Winthrop Publishers.

Pawley, A. K. and Syder, F. H. (n.d.) Lectures notes on conversational analysis.

Pawley, A. K. and Syder, F. H. (1975). 'Sentence formation in spontaneous speech', *New Zealand Speech Therapists' Journal*, **30**/**2**, 2–11.

Pawley, A. K. and Syder, F. H. (1976).'The one clause at a time hypotheses'. Paper read to first Congress of N. Z. Linguistic Society, Auckland, August.

Peters, A. M. (1977). 'Language learning strategies: does the whole equal the sum of the parts?' *Language*, **53**, 560–73.

Peters, A. M. (1980). 'The units of language acquisition', *University of Hawaii Working Papers in Linguistics*, **12**/**1**, 1–72.

Pomerantz, A. (1978). 'Compliment responses: notes on the cooperation of multiple constraints', in Schenkein, J. (1978a), 79–112.

Porter, H. (ed.) (1962). *The Odyssey*, Bantam Books.

Post, E. L. (1975). *The New Emily Post's Etiquette*, New York: Funk and Wagnalls.

Psathas, G. (1979). *Everyday Language: Studies in Ethnomethodology*, New York: Irvington Publishers.

Reisner, L. D. (forthcoming). 'Expressions of disapproval'. To appear in Wolfson, N. and Judd, E. L. (eds), *TESOL and Sociolinguistic Research*, Rowley, Massachusetts: Newbury House.

Richards, D. R. (1979). 'On the contributions of formal and informal environments to adult second language learning'. Paper given at Seameo Regional Language Centre, Fourteenth Regional Seminar, April 19, 1979.

Richards, J. C. (1977). 'Answers to yes-no questions', *English Language Teaching Journal*, **31**/**2**, 136–141.

Richards, J. C. (1981). 'Talking across cultures', *The Canadian Modern Language Review*, **37**/**3**, 572–582.

Rivers, W. M. (1975). *A Practical Guide to the Teaching of French*, New York: Oxford University Press.

Rivers, W. M. (1980). 'Foreign language acquisition: where the real problems lie', *Applied Linguistics*, **1**/**1**, 48–59.

Roberts, S. and Sloan. L. (1978). *The World's Worst Riddles*, Los Angeles: Price, Stern, Sloan.

Rochester, S. R. (1973). 'The significance of pauses in spontaneous speech', *Journal of Psycholinguistic Research*, **2**, 51–81.

Rubin, J. (1975). 'What the "good language learner" can teach us', *TESOL Quarterly*, **9**, 41–51.

Rutherford, W. (1980). 'Aspects of pedagogical grammar', *Applied Linguistics*, **1/1**, 60–73.

Ryave, A. L. (1978). 'On the achievement of a series of stories', in Schenkein, J. (1978a), 113–132.

Ryle, G. (1949). *The Concept of Mind*, London: Hutchinson.

Sacks, H. (1972a). 'On the analysability of stories by children', in Gumperz, J. J. and Hymes, D. H. (eds.), 329–45.

Sacks, H. (1972b). 'An initial investigation of the usability of conversational data for doing sociology', in Sudnow, D. (1972), 31–74.

Sacks, H., Schegloff, E. A. and Jefferson, G. (1974). 'A simplest systematics for the organization of turn taking for conversation', *Language*, **50/4**, 696–735.

Sadock, J. (1974). *Toward a Linguistic Theory of Speech Acts*, New York: Academic Press.

Sampson, G. P. (1979). *New Routes to English*, Toronto: Collier Macmillan.

Savignon, S. J. (1972). *Communicative Competence: an Experiment in Foreign Language Teaching*, Philadelphia: Centre for Curriculum Development.

Savignon, S. J. (1981). 'The use of dictation for the assessment of integrative second language skills'. Paper presented at the Colloquium on the Validation of Oral Proficiency Test, University of Michigan, March. To appear in the proceedings.

Schank, R. C. and Abelson, R. P. (1977). *Scripts, Plans, Goals and Understanding: An Inquiry into Human Knowledge Structures*, Hillsdale, New Jersey: Lawrence Erlbaum.

Schegloff, E. A. (1968). 'Sequencing in conversational openings', *American Anthropologist*, **70**, 1075–95. Reprinted in Gumperz, J. J. and Hymes, D. H. (1972).

Schegloff, E. A. (1971). 'Lecture notes and conversational transcripts'. Linguistic Society of American Summer Linguistic Institute. SUNY, Buffalo, New York.

Schegloff, E. A. (1972). 'Notes on a conversational practice: formulating place', in Sudnow, D. (1972), 75–119.

Schegloff, E. A. (1979). 'The relevance of repair to syntax for conversation', in Givon, T. (ed.), *Syntax and Semantics*, Vol. 12: *Discourse and Syntax*, New York: Academic Press, 261–86.

Schegloff, E. A., Jefferson, G. and Sacks, H. (1977). 'The preference for self-correction in the organization of repair in conversation', *Language*, **53**, 361–82.

Schegloff, E. A. and Sacks, H. (1973). 'Opening up closings', *Semiotica*, **8**, 289–327.

Schenkein, J. (ed.) (1978a). *Studies in the Organization of Conversational Interaction*, New York: Academic Press.

Schenkein, J. (1978b). 'Identity negotiations in conversation', in Schenkein (1978a), 57–58.

Schmidt, R. W. (1975). 'Sociolinguistic rules and foreign language teaching'. Paper presented at the Symposium on Sociolinguistics and Applied Anthropology. Annual meeting of the Society for Applied Anthropology, Amsterdam.

Schmidt, R. W. and Richards, J. C. (1980). 'Speech acts and second language learning', *Applied Linguistics*, 1/2, 129–157.

Schwartz, J. (1977). 'Extralinguistic features in conversational repairs of adult second language learners', in Henning, C. (ed.), *Proceedings of the Los Angeles Second Language Research Forum*, Los Angeles:UCLA.

Scollon, R. 'The role of audience in the structure of Athabaskan oral performance'. Proceedings of the XLIII International Congress of Americanists, August 1979, (to appear).

Scollon, R. and Scollon, S. B. K. (1981). *Narrative, literacy and face in interethnic communication*, Norwood, New Jersey: Ablex.

Scollon, R. and Scollon, S. B. K. (1979). 'Athabascan English interethnic communication'. Mimeo. (cited in Richards, 1981).

Searle, J. R. (1965). 'What is a speech act?', in Black, M. (ed.), *Philosophy in America*, Ithaca: Cornell University Press.

Searle, J. R. (1969). *Speech Acts*, Cambridge University Press.

Searle, J. R. (1975). 'Indirect speech acts', in Cole, P. and Morgan, J. (eds.), 59–82.

Searle, J. R. (1976). 'A classification of illocutionary acts', *Language in Society*, 5/1, 1–23.

Seliger, H. W. (1979). 'On the nature and function of language rules in language teaching', *TESOL Quarterly*, 13/3, 359–369.

Selinker, L. (1972). 'Interlanguage', *IRAL*, 10/2, 209–231.

Shohamy, E. (1980). 'Students' attitudes towards tests: affective considerations in language testing'. Paper presented at the TESOL 1980 Meeting, San Francisco, March.

Shohamy, E. and Jorstod, H. L. (1980). 'Students' attitudes towards testing: a consideration in test development and use'. Paper presented at the Northeast Conference on the Teaching of Foreign Languages, New York, April.

Sinclair, J. M. and Coulthard, R. M. (1975). *Towards an Analysis of Discourse*, Oxford University Press.

Snow, C. E. and Ferguson, C. A. (eds.) (1977). *Talking to Children: Language Input and Acquisition*, Cambridge University Press.

Snow, C. E. and Hoefnagel-Höhle, E. (1979). 'Individual differences in second-language ability', *Language and Speech*, 22/2, 151–162.

Speier, M. (1972). 'Some conversational problems for interactional analysis', in Sudnow, D. (1972), 397–427.

Stafford, C. and Covitt, G. (1978). 'Monitor use in adult second language production', *ITL*, 39/40, 103–125.

Stern, H. H. (1978). 'The formal-functional distinction in language pedagogy: a conceptual clarification'. Paper read at the 5th International Congress of Applied Linguistics, Montreal, August. Mimeo.

Stratton, C. (1971). 'Linguistics, rhetoric and discourse structure'. Doctoral dissertation, University of Wisconsin.

Stubbs, M. (1976a). *Language, Schools & Classrooms*, London: Methuen.

Stubbs, M. (1976b). 'Keeping in touch: some functions of teacher-talk', in Stubbs, M. and Delamont, S. (eds.), *Explorations in Classroom Observation*, London: John Wiley.

Sudnow, D. (1967). *Passing On*, Englewood Cliffs: Prentice-Hall.

Sudnow, D. (1972). *Studies in Social Interaction*, New York: The Free Press.

Swain, M. (1977). 'Future directions in second language research', in Henning, C. (ed.), *Proceedings of the Los Angeles Second Language Research Forum*, Los Angeles: UCLA.

Swain, M. (1980). 'Immersion education: applicability for non-vernacular teaching to vernacular speakers'. Paper presented at the Symposium on Standard Language/Vernacular Relations and Bilingual Education. Racine, Wisconsin, November.

Swain, M. and Canale, M. (1979). 'The grammatical component in a communicative approach to second language teaching'. Plenary paper presented at the 1st TESOL Summer Institute, UCLA, July. Mimeo.

Swain, M. and Canale, M. (1980). 'The grammatical component in a communicative approach to second language teaching', in Campbell, R. *et al.* (eds.), *Plenary papers from the 1st TESOL Summer Institute*, Rowley, Massachusetts: Newbury House.

Tannen, D. (1977). 'Well what did you expect?' in *Proceedings of the Third Annual Meeting of the Berkeley Linguistics Society*, Berkeley, California.

Tannen, D. (1979a). 'Ethnicity as conversational style'. *Working Papers in Sociolinguistics*, **55**, Austin, Texas: Southwest Educational Development Laboratory.

Tannen, D. (1979b). 'What's in a frame: surface evidence for under-lying expectations', in Freedle, Roy O. (ed.), *New Directions in Discourse Processing*, Norwood, New Jersey: Ablex.

Tannen, D. (1980). 'Implications of the oral/literate continuum for cross-culture communication, in Alatis, J. E. (ed.), *Georgetown University Round Table on Languages and Linguistics 1980*, Washington, D.C.: Georgetown University Press.

Tarone, E. (1977). 'Conscious communication strategies: a progress report', in Brown, H. D., Yorio, C. and Crymes, R. (eds.), *On TESOL 1977*, Washington: TESOL.

Tarone, E. (1979). 'Interlanguage as Chameleon', *Language Learning*, **29/1**, 181–191.

Tarone, E. (1980). 'Some thoughts on the notion of "communicative strategy"', in Campbell, R. *et al*, (eds.), *Plenary papers from the first TESOL Summer Institute*, Rowley, Massachusetts: Newbury House.

Terrell, T. D. (1977). 'A natural approach to second language acquisition and learning', *The Modern Language Journal*, **61/7**, 325–37.

Terrell, T. D. (1980). 'The natural approach to language in language teaching: an update', University of California, Irvine. Mimeo.

Turner, J. H. (1974). *The Structure of Sociological Theory*, Homewood, Illinois: The Dorsey Press.

Turner, R. (1970). 'Words, utterances and activities', in Douglas, J. (ed.), *Understanding Everyday Life*, 165–187, Aldine.

Turner, R. (1972). 'Some formal properties of therapy talk', in
Sudnow, D. (1972), 367–396.

Turner, R. (ed.) (1974). *Ethnomethodology*, Harmondsworth: Penguin.

Upshur, J. A. and Palmer, A. (1974). 'Measures of accuracy,
communicativity, and social judgements for two classes of foreign
language speakers', in Verdoot, A. (ed.), *AILA Proceedings,
Copenhagen 1972*, Vol. II: *Applied Sociolinguistics*, Heidelberg: Julius
Gross Verlag.

van Lancker, D. (1973). 'Language Lateralization and grammars', in
Kimball, J. P. (ed.), *Syntax and Semantics*, Vol. 2.

van Lancker, D. (1975). 'Heterogeneity in language and speech',
UCLA Working Papers in Phonetics, **29**.

Vigil, N. and Oller, J. (1976). 'Rule fossilization: a tentative model',
Language Learning, **26/2**, 291–295.

Vygotsky, L. S. (1962). 'Thought and Word', in Vygotsky, L. S.,
Thought and Language, Cambridge, Massachusetts: MIT Press,
114–153.

Wallat, C. (1981). 'An overview of communicative competence'. Paper
presented at the Language Proficiency Assessment Symposium, Airlie
House, Virginia, March. To appear in the proceedings.

Waller, W. (1965). (Reprint of 1932 edition). *The Sociology of Talking*,
London: John Wiley.

Weinreich, U. (1969). 'Problems in the analysis of idioms', in Puhvel,
J. (ed.). *Substance and Structure of Language*, Berkeley and Los
Angeles: University of California Press.

Wells, G. (1981). *Learning through Interaction: The Study of Language
Development*, Cambridge University Press.

Wetzel, P. J. and Ladd, R. (1979). 'Between spoken and written style:
a practical exercise in "syntax beyond the sentence" ', in the
Proceedings of NELS 9 (*CUNY Forum* Vols. 5 & 6), New York: City
University of New York.

Whorf, B. L. (1956). In Carroll, J. B. (ed.), *Language. Thought and
Reality: Selected Writings on Benjamin Lee Whorf*, Cambridge,
Massachusetts: MIT Press.

Widdowson, H. G. (1978). *Teaching Language as Communication*,
Oxford University Press.

Wiemann, J. M. and Backlund, P. (1980). Current theory and research
in communicative competence, *Review of Educational Research*, **50/1**,
185–199.

Wilkins, D. A. (1973). 'The linguistic and situational content of the
common core in a unit/credit system', in *Systems Development in Adult
Language Learning*, Strasbourg: Council for Cultural Co-operation,
Council of Europe.

Willes, M. (1975). 'Early lessons learned too well?' Birmingham:
University of Birmingham, Department of English. Mimeo.

Williams, E. S. (1977). 'Discourse and logical form', *Linguistic Inquiry*,
8/1, 101–140.

Winskowski, C. (1977). 'Topicalization work in telephone
conversations', *International Journal of Psycholinguistics*, **4/1**, 77–93.

Winskowski, C. (1978). 'A study of the development of topical behaviour within an experimental relationship frame'. Unpublished doctoral dissertation. University of Hawaii.

Wolfson, N. (1976a). 'Speech events and natural speech: some implications for sociolinguistic methodology', *Language in Society*, **5/2**, 189–209.

Wolfson, N. (1976b). 'The conversational historical present in American English narrative'. Ph.D. dissertation. University of Pennsylvania.

Wolfson, N. (1978). 'A feature of performed narrative: the conversational historical present', *Language in Society*, **7/2**, 215–237.

Wolfson, N. (1979a). 'The conversational historical present alternation', *Language*, **55/1**.

Wolfson, N. (1979b). 'Let's have lunch together sometime: perceptions of insincerity'. Paper presented at the TESOL Convention, Boston, March.

Wolfson, N. and Manes, J. (1979). 'Don't dear me', *Working Papers in Sociolinguistics,* **53**. To appear in Borker, R., Furman, N. and McConellginet, S. (eds.), *Language in Women's Lives*, Cornell University Press.

Wolfson, N. and Manes, J. (1981). 'The compliment formula', in Coulmas, F. (ed.)

Wolfson, N. and Taylor, B. (1978). 'Breaking down the free conversation myth', *TESOL Quarterly*, **12/1**.

Wong-Fillmore, L. (1976). 'The second time around'. Doctoral dissertation, Stanford University.

Wong-Fillmore, L. (1979). 'Individual differences in second language acquisition', in Fillmore, C. J., Kempler, D. and Wong, W. S. Y. (eds.), *Individual Differences in Language Ability and Language Behaviour*, New York: Academic Press.

Yorio, C. A. (1980). 'Conventionalized language forms and the development of communicative competence', *TESOL Quarterly*, **14/4**, 433–442.

Index